THOUGHTS ON RELIGION
BY

Archibald Alexander

FOREWORD

Archibald Alexander was an American theologist and a professor at the Princeton Theological Seminary. Archibald was also a popular writer.

Thoughts on Religious Experience

PREFACE

There are two kinds of religious knowledge which, though intimately connected as cause and effect, may nevertheless be distinguished. These are the knowledge of the truth as it is revealed in the Holy Scriptures; and the impression which that truth makes on the human mind when rightly apprehended. The first may be compared to the inscription or image on a seal, the other to the impression made by the seal on the wax. When that impression is clearly and distinctly made, we can understand, by contemplating it, the true inscription on the seal more satisfactorily, than by a direct view of the seal itself. Thus it is found that nothing tends more to confirm and elucidate the truths contained in the Word, than an inward experience of their efficacy on the heart. It cannot, therefore, be uninteresting to the Christian to have these effects, as they consist in the various views and affections of the mind, traced out and exhibited in their connection with the truth, and in their relation to each other.

There is, however, one manifest disadvantage under which we must labor in acquiring this kind of knowledge, whether by our own experience or that of others; which is, that we are obliged to follow a fallible guide; and the pathway to this knowledge is very intricate, and the light which shines upon it often obscure. All investigations of the exercises of the human mind are attended with difficulty, and never more so, than when we attempt to ascertain the religious or spiritual state of our hearts. If indeed the impression of the truth were perfect, there would exist little or no difficulty; but when it is a mere outline and the lineaments obscure, it becomes extremely difficult to determine whether it be the genuine impress of the truth: especially as in this case, there will be much darkness and confusion in the mind, and much that is of a nature directly opposite to the effects of the engrafted word. There is, moreover, so great a variety in the constitution of human minds, so much diversity in the strength of the natural passions, so wide a difference in the temperament of Christians, and so many different degrees of piety—that the study of this department of religious truth is exceedingly difficult. In many cases the most experienced and skillful theologian will feel himself at a loss, or may utterly mistake, in regard to the true nature of a case submitted to his consideration.

The complete and perfect knowledge of the deceitful heart of man is a prerogative of the omniscient God. "I the Lord search the hearts and try the reins of the children of men." (Psalm 7:9; Rev 2:23) But we are not on this account forbidden to search into this subject. So far is this from being true, that we are repeatedly exhorted to examine ourselves in relation to this very point, and Paul expresses astonishment that the Corinthian Christians should have made so little progress in self-knowledge. "Examine yourselves, to see whether you are in the faith. Test yourselves. Or do you not realize this about yourselves, that Jesus Christ is in you?—unless indeed you fail to meet the test!" (2 Cor 13:5)

In judging of religious experience it is all-important to keep steadily in view the system of divine truth contained in the Holy Scriptures; otherwise, our experience, as is too often the case, will degenerate into wild enthusiasm. Many ardent professors seem too readily to take it for granted that all religious feelings must be good. They therefore take no care to discriminate between the genuine and the spurious, the pure gold and the tinsel. Their only concern is about the ardor of their feelings; not considering that if they are spurious, the more intense they are, the further will they lead them astray. In our day there is nothing more necessary than to distinguish carefully between true and false experiences in religion; to "test the spirits—whether they are from God." (1 John 4:1) And in making this discrimination, there is no other test but the infallible Word of God; let every thought, motive, impulse and emotion be brought to this touchstone. "To the law and the testimony; if they speak not according to these, it is because there is no light in them." (Isa 8:20)

If genuine religious experience is nothing but the impression of divine truth on the mind, by the energy of the Holy Spirit, then it is evident that a knowledge of the truth is essential to genuine piety. Error never can under any circumstances produce the effects of truth. This is now generally acknowledged. But it is not so clearly understood by all, that any defect in our knowledge of the truth must, just so far as the error extends, mar the symmetry of the impression produced. The error, in this case, is of course not supposed to relate to fundamental truths, for then there can be no genuine piety; but where a true impression is made, it may be rendered very defective, for lack of a complete knowledge of the whole system of revealed truth; or its beauty marred by the existence of some errors mingled with the truth, which may be well illustrated by returning again to the seal. Suppose that some part of the image inscribed on it has been defaced, or that some of the letters have been obliterated, it is evident that when the impression is made on the wax, there will be a corresponding deficiency or deformity, although in the main the impress may be correct.

There is reason to believe, therefore, that all ignorance of revealed truth, or error respecting it, must be attended with a corresponding defect in the religious exercises of the person. This consideration teaches us the importance of truth, and the duty of increasing daily in the knowledge of our Lord and Savior Jesus Christ. This is the true and only method of growing in grace. There may be much correct theoretical knowledge, I admit, where there is no impression corresponding with it on the heart; but still, all good impressions on the heart are from the truth, and from the truth alone. Hence we find, that those denominations of Christians which receive the system of evangelical truth only in part, have a defective experience; and their Christian character, as a body, is so far defective; and even where true piety exists, we often find a sad mixture of wild enthusiasm, self-righteousness, or superstition. And even where the theory of doctrinal truth is complete, yet if there be an error respecting the terms of Christian communion, by narrowing the entrance into Christ's fold to a degree which His Word does not authorize, this single error, whatever professions may be made to the contrary with the lips, always generates a narrow spirit of bigotry, which greatly obstructs the free exercise of that brotherly love which Christ made the badge of discipleship.

If these things be so, then let all Christians use unceasing diligence in acquiring a correct knowledge of the truth as it is in Jesus; and let them pray without ceasing for the influence of the Holy Spirit to render the truth effectual in the sanctification of the whole man, soul, body, and spirit. "Sanctify them through your truth; your word is truth", (John 17:17) was a prayer offered up by Christ in behalf of all whom the Father had given Him.

Chapter 1: Early religious impressions—Different results—Classes of people least

impressed—Examples of ineffectual impressions

There is no necessity for any other proof of native depravity than the aversion which children early manifest to pious instruction and to spiritual exercises. From this cause it proceeds, that many children who have the opportunity of a good pious education learn scarcely anything of the most important truths of Christianity. If they are compelled to commit the catechism to memory, they are accustomed to do this without ever thinking of the doctrines contained in the words which they recite; so that, when the attention is at any time awakened to the subject of religion as a personal concern, they feel themselves to be completely ignorant of the system of divine truth taught in the Bible. Yet even to these the truths committed to memory are now of great utility. They are like a treasure which has been hidden, but is now discovered. Of two people under conviction of sin, one of whom has had sound religious instruction and the other none, the former will have an unspeakable advantage over the latter in many respects.

Many children, and especially those who have pious parents who speak to them of the importance of salvation, are the subjects of occasional religious impressions of different kinds. Sometimes they are alarmed by hearing an awakening sermon, or by the sudden death of a companion of their own age; or again, they are tenderly affected even to tears from a consideration of the goodness and forbearance of God, or from a representation of the love and sufferings of Christ. There are also seasons of transporting joy which some experience, especially after being tenderly affected with a sense of ingratitude to God for His wonderful goodness in sparing them, and bestowing so many blessings upon them. These transient emotions of joy cannot always be easily accounted for—but they are commonly preceded or accompanied by a hope or persuasion that God is reconciled and will receive them.

In some cases it would be thought that these juvenile exercises were indications of a change of heart, did they not pass away like the morning cloud or early dew, so as even to be obliterated from the mind which experienced them. Some undertake to account for these religious impressions merely from the susceptible principle of human nature, in connection with the external instructions of the Word and some striking dispensations of Providence; but the cause assigned is not adequate, because the same circumstances often exist when no such effects follow. Others ascribe them to the evil spirit, who is ever seeking to deceive and delude unwary souls by inspiring them with a false persuasion of their good estate, while they are in the gall of bitterness and bond of iniquity. While I would not deny that Satan may take advantage of these transient exercises to induce a false hope, I cannot be persuaded that he produces these impressions; for often the people, before experiencing them, were as careless and stupid as he could wish them to be, and because the tendency of these impressions is beneficial. The youth thus affected becomes more tender in conscience, forsakes known sin before indulged, has recourse to prayer, and feels strong desires after eternal happiness. These are not what Satan would effect, if he could, unless we could suppose that he was operating against himself, which our Savior has taught us to be impossible.

I am of opinion, therefore, that these transient impressions should be ascribed to the common operations of the Spirit of God, and may have some inexplicable connection with the future conversion and salvation of the person. There is a common practical error in the minds of many Christians in regard to this matter. They seem to think that nothing has any relation to the conversion of the sinner but that which immediately preceded this event; and the Christian is ready to say, I was awakened under such a sermon, and never had rest until I found it in Christ; making nothing of all previous instructions and impressions. So, when a revival occurs under the awakening discourses of some evangelist, people are ready to think that he only is the successful preacher whose labors God owns and blesses; whereas he does but bring forward to maturity, feelings and convictions which have been long secretly forming and growing within the soul—but so imperceptibly that the person himself was little sensible of any change.

It may be justly and scripturally compared to a growing crop: after the seed is sown it vegetates, we know not how, and then it receives daily the sun's influence, and from time to time refreshing showers; and later, after a long drought, there comes a plentiful shower, by means of which, nutriment is afforded for the formation of the full corn in the ear. No one will dispute the importance and efficacy of this last shower in maturing the grain; but had there been no cultivation and no showers long before, this had never produced any effect.

Whether those who are never converted are the subjects of these religious impressions, as well as those who are afterwards brought to faith in Christ, is a question not easily answered. That they experience dreadful alarms and pungent convictions at times, and also tender drawings, cannot be doubted; but whether those "chosen in Christ" are not, in their natural state, subject to impressions which others never experience, must remain undetermined, since we know so little of the real state of the hearts of most men; but as there is undoubtedly a special providence exercised by Christ over those sheep not yet called into the fold, I cannot but think it probable that they are often influenced by the Holy Spirit in a peculiar manner, to guard them against fatal errors and destructive habits, and to prepare them, by degrees, to receive the truth.

We know very little, however, of what is passing in the minds of thousands around us. The zealous preacher often concludes and laments that there is no impression on the minds of his hearers, when, if the covering of the human heart could be withdrawn, he would be astonished and confounded at the variety and depth of the feelings experienced. Those impressions which manifest themselves by a flow of tears are not the deepest—but often very superficial; while the most solemn distresses of the soul are entirely concealed by a kind of hypocrisy which men early learn to practice, to hide their feelings of a religious kind from their fellow creatures. A man may be so much in despair as to be meditating suicide, when his nearest friends know nothing of it.

The attempt at immediate effect, and the expectation of it, is one of the errors of the present times; indeed, it is the very watchword of a certain party. But let us not be misunderstood; we do not mean to say that all men are not under indispensable obligations immediately to obey all the commands of God. Concerning this, there can be no difference of opinion. But the people to whom we refer, seem to think that nothing is done towards the salvation of men but at the moment of their conversion, and that every good effect must be at once manifest. Perhaps some one may infer that we believe in a gradual regeneration, and that special grace differs from common only in degree; but such an inference would be utterly false, for there can be no medium between life and death; but we do profess to believe and maintain, that there is a gradual preparation, by common grace, for regeneration, which may be going on from childhood to mature age; and we believe that, as no mortal can tell the precise moment when the soul is vivified, and as the principle of spiritual life in its commencement is often very feeble, so it is an undoubted truth, that the development of the new life in the soul may be, and often is, very slow; and not infrequently that which is called conversion is nothing else but a more sensible and vigorous exercise of a principle which has long existed; just as the seed under ground may have life, and may be struggling to come forth to open day; but it may meet with various obstructions and unfavorable circumstances which retard its growth. At length, however, it makes its way through the earth, and expands its leaves to the light and air, and begins to drink in from every source that nutriment which it needs. No one supposes, however, that the moment of its appearing above ground is the commencement of its life; but this mistake is often made in the analogous case of the regeneration of the soul. The first clear and lively exercise of faith and repentance is made the date of the origin of spiritual life, whereas it existed in a feeble state, and put forth obscure acts long before. I find, however, that I am anticipating a discussion intended for another part of this work.

At present I wish only to remark further, that what has been said about early impressions and juvenile exercises of religion—is not applicable to all.

There are, alas! many who seem to remain unmoved amidst all the light and means by which most are surrounded in this land; and these too are often found in the families of the pious, and do actually pass through more than one revival without partaking of any unusual influence, or experiencing any strong religious feeling. Esau had a title to the birthright, and yet he so despised this peculiar blessing that he actually sold it for "some lentil stew". (Gen 25:34; Heb 12:16) Abraham, too, had his Ishmael, and Jacob a troop of ungodly children. Eli's sons were wicked in the extreme, and Samuel's came not up to what was expected from the children of such a father. Among all David's children we read of none who feared God, but Solomon. Those, however, who become extremely wicked have often resisted the strivings of the Spirit; and not infrequently the most impious blasphemers and atheists have once been much under the influence of religious light and feeling; but quenching the Spirit, have been given up to "believe a lie", (2 Thess 2:11) and "to work all uncleanness with greediness". (Eph 4:19)

We have said that there are some people who grow up to manhood without experiencing any religious impressions, except mere momentary thoughts of death and judgment; and these may be people of a very amiable disposition and moral deportment; and these very qualities may be, in part, the reason of their carelessness. They commit no gross sins, the remembrance of which wounds the conscience. Being of a calm and contented temper, and fond of taking their ease—they shun religious reflection, and turn away their thoughts from the truth, when it is presented to them from the pulpit. Some people of this description have been awakened and converted at mature age, and have then confessed that they lived as much without God as atheists, and seldom, if ever, extended their thoughts to futurity. Of course they utterly neglected secret prayer, and lived in the midst of gospel light without being in the least affected by it.

There is, moreover, another class who seem never to feel the force of religious truth. They are such as spend their whole waking hours in the giddy whirl of amusement or company. Full of health and spirits, and optimistic in their hopes of enjoyment from the world, they put away serious reflection as the very bane of pleasure. The very name of religion is hateful to them: and all they ask of religious people is to let them alone, that they may seize the pleasures of life while within their reach. If we may judge from appearances, this class is very large. We find them in the majority in many places of fashionable resort. The theater, the ballroom, and the very streets are full of such. They flutter gaily along, and keep company with each other—while they are strangers to all grave reflection, even in regard to the sober concerns of this life. If a pious friend ever gets the opportunity of addressing a word of serious advice to them, their politeness may prevent them from behaving rudely—but no sooner is his back turned, than they laugh him to scorn, and hate and despise him for his pains. They habituate themselves to think that religion is an awkwardly foolish thing, and wonder how any person of sense can bear to attend to it.

Very often this high reverie of pleasure is short: in such a world as this, events are apt to occur which dash the 'cup of sensual delights' while it is at the lips. Death will occasionally intrude even upon this mirthful circle and put a speedy end to their unreasonable merriment. O how sad is the spectacle, to see one of the 'votaries of fashion' suddenly cut down, and carried to the grave! When mortal sickness seizes such people, they are very apt to be delirious, if not with fever, yet with fright; and their meddlesome and cruel friends make it their chief study to bar out every idea of religion, and to flatter the poor dying creature with the hope of recovery, until death has actually seized his prey. Such an event produces a shock in the feelings of survivors of the same class—but such is the buoyancy of their feelings and their forgetfulness of mournful events—that they are soon seen dancing along the slippery path, with as much insane thoughtlessness as before!

Nothing which ever occurs tends so much to disturb the career of this multitude, as when one of their number is converted unto God. At first they are astounded, and for a moment pause—but they soon learn to ascribe the change to some natural cause, or to some strange capriciousness of temper, or disappointment in earthly hopes. Very soon you will see them as much estranged from such an one, although before an intimate friend, as if he had never been of the number of their acquaintances. Often his nearest relatives are ashamed of him, and, as much as possible, shun his company. How absurd then is it for any to pretend that men naturally love God, and only need to know His character to revere it! If there be a truth established beyond all reasonable question by uniform experience, it is, that lovers of pleasure are the enemies of God.

The class of speculating, moneymaking, business-doing men is probably as numerous, and though more sober in their thoughts, yet as far from God, and as destitute of true religion as those already described; but as we find these not commonly among the youth—but middle aged, we shall not attempt to delineate their character or describe their feelings. I must return to the consideration of early religious impressions which do not terminate in a sound conversion to God.

Some forty-five years ago, I was frequently in a family where the parents, though respecters of religion, were not professors. They had a sweet, amiable little daughter, eight or ten years of age, who had all the appearance of eminent piety. She loved the Bible, loved preaching and pious people, was uniform and constant in retiring for devotional exercises, and spoke freely, when asked, of the feelings of her own mind. I think I never had less doubt of any one's piety than of this little girl's. There was no forwardness nor pertness, nor any assumption of sanctimonious airs. All was simplicity, modesty, and consistency; she was serious but not somber, solemn and tender in her feelings, without affectation. She applied for admission to the communion—and who dare refuse entrance into the fold to such a dear lamb? Here my personal acquaintance ends.

But years afterwards, upon inquiry, I found that when she grew to womanhood, she became mirthful and careless, and entirely relinquished her religious profession. My Arminian neighbor, I know, if he had the chance to whisper in my ear, would say, "I have no difficulty in accounting for this case; she was a child of God—but fell from grace." But I have never been able to adopt this method of explaining such phenomena.

There are few truths of which I have a more unwavering conviction, than that the sheep of Christ, for whom He laid down His life, shall never perish. I do believe, however, that grace may for a season sink so low in the heart into which it has entered, and be so overborne and buried over—that none but God can perceive its existence. Now that may have been the fact in regard to this dear child, for her later history is unknown to me. She may, for anything I know, be still alive, and be now a living, consistent member of Christ's Church, and may possibly peruse these lines, though if she should, she may not recognize her own early features, taken down from memory after the lapse of so many years. But the picture is not of one person only—but of many, differing only in trivial circumstances.

I retain a distinct recollection of another case of a still earlier date, and where the history is more complete. An obscure youth, the son of pious parents, in a time of awakening seemed to have his attention drawn to the concerns of his soul, so that he seriously and diligently attended on all religious meetings. He had the appearance of deep humility, and though free to speak, when interrogated, was in no respect forward or self-sufficient. Indeed, he was scarcely known or noticed by the religious people who were in the habit of attending prayer meetings. It happened that, on an inclement evening, very few were present, and none of those who were accustomed to take a part in leading the devotional exercises. The person at whose house the meeting was held, not wishing to dismiss the few who were present with a single prayer, asked this youth if he would not attempt to make a prayer. He readily assented, and performed this service with so much fervor, fluency, and propriety of expression, that all who heard it were astonished. From this time he was called upon more frequently than any other and often in the public congregation; for some people preferred his prayers to any sermons; and I must say, that I never heard any one pray who seemed to me to have such a gift of prayer. The most appropriate passages of Scripture seemed to come to him in rapid succession, as if by inspiration. Now the common cry was, that he ought to be taken from the trade which he was learning (for he was an apprentice) and be put to theological study. The thing demanded by so many was not difficult to accomplish. He began a regular course of academical studies, and his progress, though not extraordinary, was respectable. But, alas! how weak is man! how deceitful is the heart! This young man soon began to exhibit evidence too plain, that conceit and self-confidence were taking root and growing very rapidly. He became impatient of opposition, arrogant towards his superiors, and unwilling to yield to reproof administered in the most paternal spirit. When the time came to enter upon trials for the ministry, the Presbytery, to which he applied, refused to receive him under their care. But this solemn rebuff, instead of humbling him, only provoked his indignation, and, as if in despite of them, he turned at once to the study of another profession, in which he might have succeeded had he remained moral and temperate in his habits; but falling into bad company—he became dissipated and soon came, without any known reformation, to a premature death. Now suppose this man had been permitted to enter the ministry, the probability is that, though his unchristian temper would have done much evil, yet he would have continued in the sacred office to his dying day. "Let him that thinks he stands take heed lest he fall." (1 Cor 10:12)

Chapter 2: Piety in children—Comparatively few renewed in childhood—Soul awakened in different ways—Legal conviction not a necessary part of true religion—Progress of conviction

Many believe that infants are naturally free from moral pollution and, therefore, need no regeneration. But this opinion is diametrically opposite to the doctrine of Scripture, and inconsistent with the acknowledged fact that, as soon as they are capable of moral action, all do go astray and sin against God. If children were not depraved, they would be naturally inclined to love God and delight in His holy law; but the reverse is true.

There is no ground for those who are still impenitent to comfort themselves with the notion that they were regenerated in early childhood—for piety in a child will be as manifest as in an adult; and in some respects, more so, because there are so few young children who are pious, and because they have more simplicity of character and are much less liable to play the hypocrite than people of mature age. Mere decency of external behavior, with a freedom from gross sins, is no evidence of regeneration; for these things may be found in many whose spirit is proud and self-righteous, and entirely opposite to the religion of Christ. And we know that outward regularity and sobriety may be produced by the restraints of a religious education and good example, where there are found none of the internal characteristics of genuine piety.

Suppose then, that in a certain case grace has been communicated at so early a period that its first exercises cannot be remembered, what will be the evidences which we should expect to find of its existence? Surely, we ought not to look for wisdom, judgment, and the stability of adult years, even in a pious child. We should expect, if I may say so, a childish piety—a simple, devout, and tender state of heart. As soon as such a child should obtain the first ideas of God as its Creator, Preserver, and Benefactor, and of Christ as its Savior, who shed His blood and laid down His life for us on the cross—it would be piously affected with these truths, and would give manifest proof that it possessed a susceptibility of emotions and affections of heart corresponding with the conceptions of truth which it was capable of taking in. Such a child would be liable to sin, as all Christians are—but when made sensible of faults, it would manifest tenderness of conscience and genuine sorrow, and would be fearful of sinning afterwards. When taught that prayer was both a duty and a privilege, it would take pleasure in drawing near to God, and would be conscientious in the discharge of secret duties. A truly pious child would be an affectionate and obedient child to its parents and teachers; kind to brothers and sisters, and indeed to all other people; and would take a lively interest in hearing of the conversion of sinners, and the advancement of Christ's kingdom in the world.

We ought not to expect from a regenerated child uniform attention to serious subjects, or a freedom from that gaiety and volatility which are characteristic of that tender age; but we should expect to find the natural propensity moderated, and the temper softened and seasoned, by the commingling of pious thoughts and affections with those which naturally flow from the infant mind. When such children are called, in Providence, to leave the world, then commonly their piety breaks out into a flame, and these young saints, under the influence of divine grace, are enabled so to speak of their love to Christ and confidence in Him, as astonishes, while it puts to shame aged Christians. Many examples of this kind we have on record, where the evidence of genuine piety was as strong as it well could be. There is a peculiar sweetness, as well as tenderness, in these early buddings of grace. In short, the exercises of grace are the same in a child as in an adult, only modified by the peculiarities in the character and knowledge of a child. Indeed, many adults in years who are made the subjects of grace are children in knowledge and understanding, and require the same indulgence, in our judgments of them, as children in years.

To those who cannot fix any commencement of their pious exercises—but who possess every other evidence of a change of heart, I would say: Be not discouraged on this account—but rather be thankful that you have been so early placed under the tender care of the great Shepherd, and have thus been restrained from committing many sins to which your nature, as well as that of others, was inclined. The habitual evidences of piety are the same, at whatever period the work commenced. If you possess these, you are safe. And early piety is probably more steady and consistent when matured by age, than that of later origin, though the change, of course, cannot be so evident to yourselves or others.

The education of children should proceed on the principle that they are in an unregenerate state, until evidences of piety clearly appear, in which case they should be sedulously cherished and nurtured. These are Christ's lambs—"little ones, who believe in Him" (Matt 18:6; Mark 9:42)—whom none should offend or mislead upon the peril of a terrible punishment. But though the religious education of children should proceed on the ground that they are destitute of grace, it ought ever to be used as a means of grace. Every lesson, therefore, should be accompanied with the lifting up of the heart of the instructor to God for a blessing on the means. "Sanctify them through your truth; your word is truth." (John 17:17)

Although the grace of God may be communicated to a human soul at any period of its existence in this world, yet the fact manifestly is, that very few are renewed in early childhood. Most people with whom we have been acquainted grew up without giving any decisive evidence of a change of heart. Though religiously educated, yet they have evinced a lack of love to God, and an aversion to spiritual things. Men are very reluctant, it is true, to admit that their hearts are wicked and at enmity with God. They declare that they are conscious of no such feeling—but still the evidence of a dislike to the spiritual worship of God they cannot altogether disguise; and this is nothing else but enmity to God. They might easily be convicted of loving the world more than God, the creature more than the Creator; and we know that he who will be the friend of the world is the enemy of God.

Let the most moral and amiable of mankind, who are in this natural state, be asked such questions as these: Do you take real pleasure in perusing the sacred Scriptures, especially those parts which are most spiritual? Do you take delight in secret prayer, and find your heart drawn out to God in strong desires? Do you spend much time in contemplating the divine attributes? Are you in the habit of communing with your own hearts, and examining the true temper of your souls? No unregenerate people can truly answer these, and suchlike questions, in the affirmative.

It is evident, then, that most people whom we see around us and with whom we daily converse, are in the gall of bitterness and bond of iniquity, and, continuing in that state, where Christ is they never can come. And yet, alas! they are at ease in Zion, and seem to have no fear of that wrath which is coming. Their case is not only dangerous—but discouraging. Yet those who are now in a state of grace, yes those of our race who are now in heaven, were once in the same condition. You, my reader, may now be a member of Christ's body and heir of His glory; but you can easily look back and remember the time when you were as unconcerned about your salvation as any of the mirthful, who are now fluttering around you. The same power which arrested you is able to stop their mad career. Still hope and pray for their conversion.

But tell me, how were you brought to turn from your wayward, downward course? This, as it relates to the external means of awakening, would receive a great variety of answers. One would say, "While hearing a particular sermon, I was awakened to see my lost estate, and I never found rest or peace until I was enabled to believe in the Lord Jesus Christ." Another would answer, "I was brought to consideration, by the solemn and pointed conversation of a pious friend who sought my salvation." While a third would answer, "I was led to serious consideration, by having the hand of God laid heavily upon me in some affliction." In regard to many, the answer would be, that their minds were gradually led to serious consideration, they scarcely know how.

Now in regard to these external means or circumstances, it matters not whether the attention was arrested and the conscience awakened, by this or that means, gradually or suddenly. Neither do these things at all assist in determining the nature of the effect produced. All who ever became pious must have begun with serious consideration, whatever means were employed to produce this state of mind. But all who, for a season, become serious, are not certainly converted. There may be solemn impressions and deep awakenings which never terminate in a saving change— but end in some delusion, or the person returns again to his old condition, or rather to one much worse; for it may be laid down as a maxim, that religious impressions opposed, leave the soul in a more hardened state than before; just as iron, heated and then cooled, becomes harder. In general, those impressions which come gradually, without any unusual means, are more permanent than those which are produced by circumstances of a striking and alarming nature. But even here there is no general rule. The nature of the permanent effects is the only sure criterion. "By their fruits you shall know them." (Matt 7:20)

That conviction of sin is a necessary part of experimental religion, all will admit; but there is one question respecting this matter, concerning which there may be much doubt; and that is, whether a law-work, prior to regeneration, is necessary; or, whether all true and beneficial conviction is not the effect of regeneration. I find that a hundred years ago this was a matter in dispute between the two parties into which the Presbyterian church was divided, called the old and new side. The Tennents and Blairs insisted much on the necessity of conviction of sin by the law, prior to regeneration; while Thompson and his associates were of opinion that no such work was necessary, nor should be insisted on. As far as I know, the opinion of the necessity of legal conviction has generally prevailed in all our modern revivals: and it is usually taken for granted, that the convictions experienced are prior to regeneration. But it would be very difficult to prove from Scripture, or from the nature of the case, that such a preparatory work was necessary.

Suppose an individual to be, in some certain moment, regenerated; such a soul would begin to see with new eyes, and his own sins would be among the things first viewed in a new light. He would be convinced, not only of the fact that they were transgressions of the law—but he would also see that they were intrinsically evil, and that he deserved the punishment to which they exposed him. It is only such a conviction as this that really prepares a soul to accept of Christ in all His offices; not only as a Savior from wrath—but from sin. And it can scarcely be believed, that that clear view of the justice of God in their condemnation, which most people sensibly experience, is the fruit of a mere legal conviction on an unregenerate heart. For this view of God's justice is not merely of the fact that this is His character—but of the divine excellency of His attributes, which is accompanied with admiration of it, and a feeling of acquiescence or submission. This view is sometimes so clear, and the equity and propriety of punishing sin are so manifest, and the feeling of acquiescence so strong, that it has laid the foundation for the very absurd opinion, that the true penitent is made willing to be damned for the glory of God. When such a conviction as this is experienced, the soul is commonly near to comfort, although at the moment it is common to entertain the opinion, that there is no salvation for it. It is wonderful, and almost unaccountable, how calm the soul is in the prospect of being forever lost.

An old lady of the Baptist denomination was the first person I ever heard give an account of Christian experience, and I recollect that she said that she was so deeply convinced that she should be lost, that she began to think how she should feel and be exercised in hell; and it occurred to her, that all in that horrid place were employed in blaspheming the name of God. The thought of doing so was rejected with abhorrence, and she felt as if she must and would love Him, even there, for His goodness to her; for she saw that she alone was to blame for her destruction, and that He could, in consistency with His character, do nothing else but inflict this punishment on her. Now surely her heart was already changed, although not a ray of comfort had dawned upon her mind.

But is there not before this, generally, a rebellious rising against God, and a disposition to find fault with His dealings? It may be so in many cases—but this feeling is far from being as universal as some suppose. As far as the testimony of pious people can be depended on, there are many whose first convictions are of the evil of sin, rather than of its danger, and who feel real compunction of spirit for having committed it, accompanied with a lively sense of their ingratitude. This question, however, is not of any great practical importance; but there are some truly pious people who are distressed and perplexed, because they never experienced that kind of conviction which they hear others speak of, and the necessity of which is insisted on by some preachers. Certainly that which the reprobate may experience—which is not different from what all the guilty will feel at the day of judgment—cannot be a necessary part of true religion; and yet it does appear to be a common thing for awakened people to be at first under a mere legal conviction.

Though man, in his natural state, is spiritually dead, that is, entirely destitute of any spark of true holiness, yet is he still a reasonable being, and has a conscience by which he is capable of discerning the difference between good and evil, and of feeling the force of moral obligation. By having his sins brought clearly before his mind, and his conscience awakened from its stupor, he can be made to feel what his true condition is as a transgressor of the holy law of God. This sight and sense of sin, under the influence of the common operations of the Spirit of God, is what is usually styled conviction of sin. And there can be no doubt that these views and feelings may be very clear and strong in an unrenewed mind. Indeed, they do not differ in kind from what every sinner will experience at the day of judgment, when his own conscience will condemn him, and he will stand guilty before his Judge. But there is nothing in this kind of conviction which has any tendency to change the heart, or to make it better.

Some indeed have maintained, with some show of reason, that under mere legal conviction the sinner grows worse and worse; and certainly he sees his sins to be greater in proportion as the light of truth increases. There is not, therefore, in such convictions, however clear and strong, any approximation to regeneration. It cannot be called a preparatory work to this change, in the sense of disposing the person to receive the grace of God. The only end which it can answer is to show the rational creature his true condition, and to convince the sinner of his absolute need of a Savior. Under conviction there is frequently a more sensible rising of the enmity of the heart against God and His law; but feelings of this kind do not belong to the essence of conviction. There is also sometimes an awful apprehension of danger; the imagination is filled with strong images of terror, and hell seems almost uncovered to the view of the convinced sinner. But there may be much of this feeling of terror, where there is very little real conviction of sin; and on the other hand, there often is deep and permanent conviction, where the passions and imagination are very little excited.

When the entrance of light is gradual, the first effect of an awakened conscience is, to attempt to rectify what now appears to have been wrong in the conduct. It is very common for the conscience, at first, to be affected with outward acts of transgression, and especially with some one prominent offence. An external reformation is now begun: for this can be effected by mere legal conviction. To this is added an attention to the external duties of religion, such as prayer, reading the Bible, hearing the Word, etc. Everything, however, is done with a legal spirit; that is, with the wish and expectation of making amends for past offences; and if painful penances should be prescribed to the sinner, he will readily submit to them if he may, by this means, make some atonement for his sins. But as the light increases, he begins to see that his heart is wicked, and to be convinced that his very prayers are polluted for lack of right motives and affections. He, of course, tries to regulate his thoughts and to exercise right affections; but here his efforts prove fruitless. It is much easier to reform the life, than to bring the corrupt heart into a right state.

The case now begins to appear desperate. The sinner knows not which way to turn for relief and, to cap the climax of his distress, he comes at length to be conscious of nothing but unyielding hardness of heart. He fears that the conviction which he seemed to have is gone, and that he is left to total obduracy. In these circumstances he desires to feel keen compunction and overwhelming terror, for his impression is that he is entirely without conviction. The truth is, however, that his convictions are far greater than if he experienced that sensible distress which he so much courts. In this case, he would not think his heart so incurably bad, because it could entertain some right feeling—but as it is, he sees it to be destitute of every good emotion and of all tender relentings. He has got down to the core of iniquity, and finds within his bosom a heart unsusceptible of any good thing. Does he hear that others have obtained relief by hearing such a preacher, reading such a book, conversing with some experienced Christian? He resorts to the same means—but entirely without effect. The heart seems to become more insensible, in proportion to the excellence of the means enjoyed. Though he declares he has no sensibility of any kind, yet his anxiety increases; and perhaps he determines to give himself up solely to prayer and reading the Bible; and if he perishes, to perish seeking for mercy.

But however strong such resolutions may be, they are found to be in vain; for now, when he attempts to pray, he finds his mouth as it were shut. He cannot pray. He cannot read. He cannot meditate. What can he do? Nothing. He has come to the end of his legal efforts; and the result has been the simple—deep conviction that he can do nothing; and if God does not mercifully interpose, he must inevitably perish. During all this process he has some idea of his need of divine help—but until now he was not entirely cut off from all dependence on his own strength and exertions. He still hoped that, by some kind of effort or feeling he could prepare himself for the mercy of God. Now he despairs of this, and not only so—but for a season he despairs, it may be, of salvation—gives himself up for lost. I do not say that this is a necessary feeling, by any means—but I know that it is very natural, and by no means uncommon, in real experience.

But conviction having accomplished all that it is capable of effecting, that is, having emptied the creature of self-dependence and self-righteousness, and brought him to the utmost extremity—even to the borders of despair, it is time for God to work. The proverb says, "Man's extremity is God's opportunity." So it is in this case; and at this time, it may reasonably be supposed, the work of regeneration is wrought, for a new state of feeling is now experienced. Upon calm reflection, God appears to have been just and good in all His dispensations; the blame of its perdition the soul fully takes upon itself, acknowledges its ill-desert, and acquits God. "Against you, you only, have I sinned and done this evil in your sight, that you might be justified when you speak, and be clear when you judge." (Psalm 51:4) The sinner resigns himself into the hands of God, and yet is convinced that if he does perish, he will suffer only what his sins deserve. He does not fully discover the glorious plan according to which God can be just and the Justifier of the ungodly who believe in Jesus Christ.

The above is not given as a course of experience which all real Christians can recognize as their own—but as a train of exercises which is very common. And as I do not consider legal conviction as necessary to precede regeneration—but suppose there are cases in which the first serious impressions may be the effect of regeneration, I cannot, of course, consider any particular train of exercises under the law as essential. It has been admitted, however, that legal conviction does in fact take place in most instances, prior to regeneration; and it is not an unreasonable inquiry—'why is the sinner thus awakened?' What good purpose does it answer? The reply has been already partially given; but it may be remarked, that God deals with man as an accountable, moral agent, and before he rescues him from the ruin into which he is sunk, he would let him see and feel, in some measure, how wretched his condition is; how helpless he is in himself, and how ineffectual are his most strenuous efforts to deliver himself from his sin and misery. He is therefore permitted to try his own wisdom and strength. And finally, God designs to lead him to the full acknowledgment of his own guilt, and to justify the righteous Judge who condemns him to everlasting torment.

Conviction, then, is no part of a sinner's salvation—but the clear practical knowledge of the fact that he cannot save himself, and is entirely dependent on the saving grace of God.

Chapter 3: The new birth an event of great importance—The evidences of the new birth—Diversities of experience in converts—Examples—Causes of diversity

There is no more important event which occurs in our world than the new birth of an immortal soul. Heirs to titles and estates, to kingdoms and empires, are frequently born—and such events are blazoned with imposing pomp, and celebrated by poets and orators. But what are all these honors and possessions but the gewgaws of children—when compared with the inheritance and glory to which every child of God is born an heir! But this being a birth from above, and all the blessings and privileges of the young heir, of a hidden and spiritual nature, the world around cannot be expected to take a lively interest in the event. It is with the children of God as with the divine Savior; "the world knows them not, as it knew him not". (1 John 3:1) The night on which He was born, there was a great crowd of the descendants of David, collected from every part of the Holy Land, where they were scattered abroad; but none of all these knew that a Savior was born that night. Yet the angels celebrated the event in a truly celestial hymn, and announced the glad tidings to a company of simple shepherds, who were watching their flocks in the open field. So these celestial inhabitants, the messengers of God, take a lively interest still in events in which a mirthful and ungodly world feel no concern. For "there is joy in the presence of the angels of God over one sinner that repents". (Luke 15:10)

How they know certainly when a soul is born to God, we need not inquire; for they have faculties and sources of knowledge unknown to us. We know that "they are all ministering spirits, sent forth to minister for those who shall be heirs of salvation"; (Heb 1:14) but how they carry on their ministry we cannot tell. If the evil spirit can inject evil thoughts into our minds, why may not good spirits suggest pious thoughts, or occasionally make sudden impressions for our warning, or change, by some means, the train of our thoughts? No doubt the devil soon learns the fact, when a sinner is converted unto God; for he has then lost a subject, and perhaps no conversion ever takes place which he does not use every effort to prevent.

But, to return to our subject, the implantation of spiritual life in a soul which is dead in sin, is an event the consequences of which will never end. When you plant an acorn, and it grows, you do not expect to see the maturity, much less the end of the majestic oak, which will expand its boughs and strike deeply into the earth its roots. The fierce blasts of centuries of winters may beat upon it and agitate it—but it resists them all. Yet finally this majestic oak, and all its towering branches, must fall. Trees die of old age, as well as men. But the plants of grace shall ever live. They shall flourish in everlasting verdure. They will bear transplanting to another climate—to another world. They shall bloom and bear fruit in the paradise of God. At such an hour one is born in Zion unto God. Few know it. Few care for the event, or consider it of much importance. But, reader, this feeble germ, this incipient bud, will go on to grow and flourish for infinitely more years than there are sands upon the seashore.

To drop the figure—this renewed soul will be seen and known among the saints in heaven, and assisting in the never-ceasing songs of those who surround the throne of God and the Lamb, millions of ages hereafter. Pure and holy shall it be—"without spot or wrinkle or any such thing". (Eph 5:27) Bright as an angel, and as free from moral taint—but still distinguished from those happy beings, to whom it is equal, by singing a song in which they can never join; in wearing robes made white in the blood of the Lamb; and claiming a nearer kindred to the Son of God than Gabriel himself. Can that event be of small import, which lays a foundation for immortal bliss?—for eternal life?

Let us, then, patiently and impartially inquire into some of the circumstances and evidences of the new birth. And here I cannot but remark, that among all the preposterous notions which a new and crude theology has poured forth so profusely in our day, there is none more absurd, than

> *If you eat from this tree you will surely die! We were already dead!*

that a dead sinner can beget new life in himself. The very idea of a man's becoming his own father in the spiritual regeneration is as unreasonable as such a supposition in relation to our first birth. Away with all such soul-destroying, God-dishonoring sentiments! "Who were born, not of blood, nor of the will of the flesh, nor of the will of man—but of God" (John 1:13)—"Born of the Spirit" (John 3:8)—"And you has He quickened who were dead in trespasses and sins". (Eph 2:1)

But who can trace the work of the Spirit in this wonderful renovation? Can we tell how our bones and sinews were formed in our mothers' wombs? Surely, then, there must be mystery in the second birth! As our Lord said to Nicodemus when discoursing on this very subject: "If I have told you earthly things, and you believe not, how shall you believe if I tell you of heavenly things?" (John 3:12) "The wind blows where it wills, and you hear the sound thereof—but cannot tell whence it comes, and where it goes." (John 3:8)

There are, doubtless, great diversities in the appearances of the motions and actings of spiritual life in its incipient stages. The agent is the same, the deadness of the subject the same, the instrument the same, and the nature of the effect the same—in every case. But still, there are many differing circumstances, which cause a great variety in appearance and expression; such as the degree of vigor in the principle of life communicated. I know, indeed, that there are some who entertain the opinion, that the new creature as it comes from the hand of God—if I may so speak—is in all respects identical or of equal value. But this is not the fact. There is as much difference in the original vigor of spiritual as of natural life. Now, who does not perceive what a remarkable difference this will make in all the actings and external exhibitions of this principle?

As in nature, some children as soon as born are active and vigorous and healthy, and let all around know quickly that they are alive and have strong feeling too; whereas others come into the world with so feeble a spark of life, that it can hardly be discerned whether they breathe or have any pulsation in their heart and arteries; and when it is ascertained that they live, the principle of vitality is so weak, and surrounded with so many untoward circumstances and symptoms, that there is a small prospect of the infant reaching maturity; just so it is in the new birth. Some are brought at once into the clear light of day. They come "out of darkness into the marvelous light" (1 Pet 2:9) of the gospel. "Old things are" consequently "passed away, and all things are become new". (2 Cor 5:17) The change is most obvious and remarkable. They are as if introduced into a new world. The Sun of righteousness has risen upon them without an intervening cloud. Their perception of divine things is so new and so clear, that they feel persuaded that they can convince others, and cause them to see and feel as they do. Indeed, they wonder why they did not always see things in this light, and they do not know why others do not see them as they do. Such people can no more doubt of their conversion than of their existence. Such a case was that of Saul of Tarsus. Such also was the case of Colonel James Gardiner.

Now this bright day may be clouded over, or it may not. In the case of the two people mentioned, there does not seem ever to have arisen a passing cloud to create a doubt whether indeed they had been brought to enjoy the light of a heavenly day. But many a day which begins with an unclouded sun is deformed by dark and lowering clouds, and even agitated with tremendous storms, before it closes. So it may be in the spiritual life. Some commence their pilgrimage under the most favorable auspices and seem to stand so firmly on the mount that they are ready to say,

"I shall never be moved." (Psalm 30:6) Yet when their Lord hides His face they are soon troubled, and may long walk in darkness, and enjoy no light or comfort. And commonly this change is brought about by our own spiritual pride and carelessness.

The opinion commonly entertained, that the most enormous sinners are the subjects of the most pungent convictions of sin and the most alarming terrors of hell, is not correct. In regard to such, the commencement of a work of grace is sometimes very gradual, and the impressions apparently so slight, that they afford very little ground of optimistic expectations of the result. On the other hand, some people of an unblemished moral character, and who, from the influence of a religious education, have always respected religion and venerated its ordinances, when brought under conviction, are more terribly alarmed and more overwhelmed with distress than others whose lives have been stained by gross crimes. Pastor John Newton, 1725-1807, when awakened to some sense of his sinful and dangerous condition, which occurred during a violent and long-continued storm at sea, though his judgment was convinced that he was the greatest of sinners, and he doubted whether it was possible for him to be saved, yet seems to have had no very deep feelings or agitating fears. He says, "It was not until long after (perhaps several years), when I had gained some clear views of the infinite righteousness and grace of Christ Jesus my Lord, that I had a deep and strong apprehension of my state by nature and practice; and perhaps until then I could not have borne the sight. So wonderfully does the Lord proportion the discoveries of sin and grace. For He knows our frame, and that if He were to put forth the greatness of His power, a poor sinner would be instantly overwhelmed, and crushed as a moth."

And though from this time there was a sensible change, and his mind was turned towards true religion, yet it is evident from the history of his life, as well as his experiences afterwards, that grace existed during several years in the feeblest state of which we can well conceive. It appeared so much so to himself, that he warns all people from considering his experience a model for them. "As to myself," says he, "every part of my case has been extraordinary—I have hardly met a single instance resembling it. Few, very few have been rescued from such a dreadful state, and those few that have been thus favored have generally passed through the most severe convictions; and, after the Lord has given them peace, their future lives have been usually more zealous, bright, and exemplary than common."

Now this is the opinion which I think, is taken up rather from theory than an observation of facts. I think that those people who have been most conversant with exercised souls will say that there is no general rule here—that very pungent convictions and deep distress are found as frequently in those who have been preserved from outbreaking transgressions, as in those noted for their immoralities. There seems, indeed, more reason for severe convictions in the latter case—but convictions are not uniformly proportioned to the magnitude of crimes. And in truth, we are incapable of comparing together the heinousness of the sins of different people. The moral man, as we call him, may be the greater sinner of the two, when weighed in the balances of the sanctuary. I heard a popular preacher once undertake to prove that moral men and formal professors must, in all cases, be far more wicked than the blaspheming infidel and gross debauchee. The argument was plausible—but labored under one essential defect; and I was of opinion, and still am, that such a doctrine is highly dangerous, and calculated to encourage men to go to all lengths in wickedness.

When I was a very young preacher, I expressed the opinion, in a sermon preached in North Carolina, that the mere moralist and formalist were more out of the way of conviction than the openly profane. When the sermon was ended, a fierce-looking man came up to me and said that I had delivered precisely his opinion on one point, and mentioned the above sentiment. I inquired, when he was gone, who he was, and found that he was the most notorious profligate in all the country; and not long afterwards he was apprehended and imprisoned, at the head of a company engaged in felonious acts. This taught me a lesson which I never forgot.

Mr. Newton proceeds thus: "Now as, on the one hand, my convictions were very moderate, and far below what might have been expected from the dreadful review I had to make; so, on the other, my first beginnings in a pious course were as faint as can well be imagined. I never knew that season alluded to (Jer 2:2; Rev 2:4), usually called the time of 'first love'." And then he relates facts which give sad evidence of a very low state of grace; and if it had never risen higher, we would certainly have been inclined to believe that he was not a subject of saving grace. But this leads me to remark a fact analogous to what is common in the natural world; that the infant which, when born, barely gives evidence of life, may not only grow to maturity—but in size and strength may far exceed those who commenced life with more activity and vigor; and so in the spiritual life, when the incipient motions and affections are very feeble, the person may eventually become a mature and eminent Christian, as we have no doubt John Newton did.

Another instance of a similar kind, if my memory serves me, was Richard Cecil, who had also been for many years a profane infidel—but who, in process of time, became one of the most eminent Christians, as well as spiritual ministers of his day. Dr. Thomas Scott, also, was a Socinian, and yet a preacher in the established Church; but the progress of illumination and conviction in his mind was very gradual. His 'Force of Truth' is an admirable little work, and furnishes a full illustration of the sentiment which I wish to inculcate—that grace, in the commencement, is often exceedingly faint and feeble, and yet may grow into a state of maturity and comparative perfection.

In the experience of Jonathan Edwards, as recorded by himself, we find no account of any deep and distressing convictions of sin at the commencement of his religious course, though afterwards, perhaps few men ever attained to such humbling views of the depth and turpitude of the depravity of the heart. But his experience differs from that of those mentioned above, in that his first views of divine things were clear and attended with unspeakable delight. "The first instance that I remember of that sort of inward, sweet delight in God and divine things, that I have lived much in since, was on reading those words, 1 Tim 1:17, 'Now unto the King eternal, immortal, invisible, the only wise God, be honor and glory forever and ever. Amen.' As I read these words, there came into my soul, and was as it were diffused through it, a sense of the glory of the Divine Being; a new sense, quite different from anything I ever experienced before. Never had any words of Scripture seemed to me as these words did. I thought with myself, how excellent a Being that was, and how happy I would be, if I might enjoy that God, and be enrapt up to Him in heaven, and be as it were swallowed up in Him forever!" "From about that time I began to have a new kind of apprehension and ideas of Christ, and the work of redemption, and the glorious way of salvation by Him. An inward, sweet sense of these things, at times, came into my heart; and my soul was led away in pleasant views and contemplations of them. ... After this, my sense of divine things gradually increased, and became more and more lively, and had more of that inward sweetness. The appearance of everything was altered. There seemed to be, as it were, a calm, sweet cast or appearance of divine glory, in almost everything. God's excellency, His wisdom, His purity, and His love seemed to appear in everything."

The difference between this and many other cases of incipient piety is very striking. And yet these views and exercises do not come up to the standard which some set up in regard to Christian experience, because they are so abstract, and have such casual reference to Christ, through Whom alone God is revealed to man as an object of saving faith. And if there be a fault in the writings of this great and good man on the subject of experimental religion, it is, that they seem to represent renewed people as at the first occupied with the contemplation of the attributes of God with delight, without ever thinking of a Mediator. But few men ever attained, as we think, higher degrees of holiness, or made more accurate observations on the exercises of others. His Treatise concerning Religious Affections is too abstract and tedious for common readers; but it is an excellent work, although I think his fourteen signs of truly gracious Affections might with great advantage be reduced to half the number, on his own plan. The experimental exercises of religion are sure to take their complexion from the theory of doctrine entertained, or which is inculcated at the time.

The VARIETY which appears in the exercises of real converts does not depend alone on the different degrees of vigor in the principle of spiritual life—but on many other circumstances, some of which will now be noticed. The benefit of sound doctrinal instruction to the newborn soul has already been mentioned—but demands a more particular consideration. What degree of knowledge is absolutely necessary to the existence of piety cannot be accurately determined by man—but we know that genuine faith may consist with much ignorance and error. Suppose two people, then, to have received the principle of spiritual life in equal vigor—but let the one be ignorant and the other well instructed; it is easy to see what a difference this will make in the exercises of the two converts, and also in the account which they are able respectively to give to others of the work of grace on their hearts.

It is here taken for granted, that nothing but divine truth can be the object of holy affections, or furnish the motives from which true Christians are bound to act, and that faith in all its actings has respect to revealed truth. That which is unknown can be the object neither of faith nor love; and that which is known obscurely, and viewed indistinctly, can never operate with the same effect as that which is clearly understood. Accordingly, our missionaries inform us that we ought not to expect the same consistency of maturity in the religion of real converts from heathenism as from religiously educated people in our own country. It is a lamentable fact that in this land of churches and of Bibles there are many who know little more of the doctrines of Christianity than the pagans themselves.

The proper inference from the fact stated is, that they are flagrantly in error, who think that the religious education of children is useless or even injurious; and their opinion is also condemned who maintain that it matters little what men believe provided their lives are upright. All good conduct must proceed from good principles—but good principles cannot exist without a knowledge of the truth. "Truth is in order to holiness", and between truth and holiness there is an indissoluble connection. It would be as reasonable to expect a child born into an atmosphere corrupted with pestilential vapor, to grow and be healthy, as that spiritual life should flourish without the nutriment of the pure milk of the Word, and without breathing in the wholesome atmosphere of truth. The new man often remains in a dwarfish state, because he is fed upon husks; or he grows into a distorted shape by means of the errors which are inculcated upon him. It is of unspeakable importance that the young disciple have sound, instructive, and practical preaching to attend on. It is also of consequence that the religious people with whom he converses should be discreet, evangelical, and intelligent Christians; and that the books put into his hands should be of the right kind.

There is what may be called a 'sectarian peculiarity' in the experimental religion of all the members of a religious denomination. When it is required, in order that people be admitted to communion, that they publicly give a narrative of the exercises of their minds, there will commonly be observed a striking similarity. There is a certain mold into which all seem to be cast. By the way, this requisition is unwise; few people have humility and discretion enough to be trusted to declare in a public congregation what the dealings of God with their souls have been. When ignorant, weak, and fanciful people undertake this, they often bring out such crude and ludicrous things as greatly tend to bring experimental religion into discredit.

The practice seems also to be founded on a false principle, namely, that real Christians are able to tell with certainty whether others have religion, if they hear their experience. Enthusiasts have always laid claim to this 'discernment of the spirits', and this enthusiasm is widely spread through some large sects; and when they meet with any professing piety, they are always solicitous to hear an account of their conviction, conversion, etc.

Sincere dialogs of this kind among intimate friends are no doubt profitable; but a frequent and indiscriminate disclosure of these secret things of the heart is attended with many evils. Among the chief is the fostering of spiritual pride, which may often be detected when the person is boasting of his humility. In those social meetings in which every person is questioned as to the state of his soul, the very sameness of most of the answers ought to render the practice suspect. Poor, weak, and ignorant people often profess to be happy, and to be full of the love of God—when they know not what they say. It is amazing how little you hear of the spiritual conflict in the account which many professors give of their experience. The people know what kind of answers is expected of them, and they come as near as they can to what is wished; and it is to be feared that many cry "peace", when there is no peace, (Jer 6:14; Jer 8:11) and say that they are happy, merely because they hear this from the lips of others. Hypocrisy is a fearful evil, and everything which has a tendency to produce it should be avoided.

Among some classes of religious people, all 'doubting about the goodness and safety of our state' is scouted as inconsistent with faith. It is assumed as indubitably true, that every Christian must be assured of his being in a state of grace, and they have no charity for those who are distressed with almost perpetual doubts and fears. This they consider to be the essence of unbelief; for faith, according to them, is a full persuasion that our sins are forgiven. No painful process of self-examination is therefore requisite, for every believer has possession already of all that could be learned from such examination.

Among other groups, doubting, it is to be feared, is too much encouraged; and serious Christians are perplexed with needless scruples originating in the multiplication of the marks of conversion, which sometimes are difficult of application, and, in other cases, are not scriptural—but arbitrary, set up by the preacher who values himself upon his skill in detecting the close hypocrite; whereas he wounds the weak believer, in ten cases, where he awakens the hypocrite in one. I once heard one of these preachers, whose common mode was harsh and calculated to distress the feeble-minded, attempt to preach in a very different style. He seemed to remember that he should not "bruise the broken reed", nor "quench the smoking flax". (Isa 42:3; Matt 12:20) A person of a contrite spirit heard the discourse with unusual comfort—but at the close the preacher resumed his harsh tone, and said, "Now you hypocrites will be snatching at the children's bread"; on hearing which, the broken-hearted hearer felt himself addressed, and instantly threw away all the comfort which he had received. And though there might be a hundred hypocrites present, yet not one of them cared anything about the admonition.

In some places, anxious inquirers are told that, if they will hold on praying and using the means, God is bound to save them; as though a dead, condemned sinner could so pray as to bring God under obligation to him, or could secure the blessings of the covenant of grace by his selfish, legal striving. These instructions accord very much with the self-righteous spirit which is naturally in us all; and one of two things may be expected to ensue: either that the anxious inquirer will conclude that he has worked out his salvation, and cry peace; or that he would sink into discouragement and charge God foolishly, because He does not hear his prayers, and grant him his desires.

There is another extreme—but not so common among us. It is, to tell the unconverted, however anxious, not to pray at all—that their prayers are an abomination to God, and can answer no good purpose, until they are able to pray in faith. The writer happened once to be cast into a congregation where this doctrine was inculcated, at the time of a considerable revival, when many sinners were cut to the heart and were inquiring, 'What must we do to be saved?' He conversed with some who appeared to be under deep and solemn convictions—but they were directed to use no means—but to believe, and they appeared to remain in a state of passivity, doing nothing—but confessing the justice of their condemnation, and appearing to feel that they were entirely at the disposal of Him who "has mercy on whom he will have mercy". (Exod 33:19; Rom 9:15,18) The theory, however, was not consistently carried out, for while these people were taught not to pray, they were exhorted to hear the gospel, and were frequently conversed with by their pastor.

But this extreme is not so dangerous as the former, which encourages sinners to think that they can do something to recommend themselves to God by their unbelieving prayers. The fruits of this revival, I have reason to believe, were very precious. Even among the same people and under the same minister—the exercises of the awakened in a revival are very different. In some seasons of this sort, the work appears to be far deeper and more solemn than in others.

Chapter 4: Causes of diversity in experience continued—Effect of temperament—Melancholy—Advice to the friends of people thus affected—Illustrative cases—Causes of melancholy and insanity

We have before shown how the principle of spiritual life is affected in its appearance by two circumstances—the degree of vigor given to it in its commencement, and the degree of knowledge and maturity of judgment which one may possess above another. We now come to another pregnant cause of the great variety which is found in the exercises and comforts of real Christians, and that is the difference of temperament which is so familiar, and which so frequently modifies the characters, as well as the feelings of men in other matters. There can be no doubt, I think, that the susceptibility of lively emotion is exceedingly different in men under the same circumstances. People of strong affections and ardent temperament, upon an unexpected bereavement of a beloved wife or child, are thrown into an agony of grief which is scarcely tolerable; while those of a cold, phlegmatic temperament seem to suffer no exquisite anguish from this or any other cause. Not that they possess more fortitude or resignation, for the contrary may be the fact; but their susceptibilities are less acute. And this disparity appears in nothing more remarkably than in the tendency to entertain different degrees of hope or fear in similar circumstances. For while some will hope whenever there is the smallest ground for a favorable result, others are sure to fear the worst which can possibly happen; and their apprehensions are proportioned to the magnitude of the interest at stake.

Now, is it amazing that men's religious feelings should be affected by the same causes? When two exercised people speak of their convictions, their sorrows and their hopes, is it not to be expected that with the same truths before their minds, those of a optimistic temperament will experience more sensible emotions, and, upon the same evidence, entertain more confident hopes than those of a contrary disposition? And, of necessity, the joy of the one will be much more lively than that of the other. Thus, two people may be found, whose experience may have been very similar as to their conviction of sin and exercise of faith and repentance; and yet the one will express a strong confidence of having passed from death unto life, while the other is afraid to express a trembling hope. Of these two classes of Christians, the first is the more comfortable; while the latter the safer, as being unwilling to be satisfied with any evidence but the strongest.

But there is not only a wide difference from this natural cause of the liveliness of the emotions of joy and sorrow, and of the confidence of the hopes entertained—but usually a very different mode of expression. Optimistic people, from the very impulse of ardent feeling, have a tendency to express things in strong language constantly verging on exaggeration. They are apt to use superlatives and strong emphasis, as wishing to convey a full idea of their feelings, while those of a colder temperament and more timid disposition fall below the reality in their descriptions, and are cautious not to convey to others too high an idea of what they have experienced. This diversity, as the cause is permanent, characterizes the religious experience of these respective classes of Christians through their whole pilgrimage, and may be equally manifest on a dying bed. Hence it appears how very uncertain a knowledge of the internal state of the heart we obtain from the words and professions of serious people. It should also serve to shake the vain confidence of those who imagine that they can decide with certainty whether another is a truly converted person, merely from hearing a narrative of his religious experience.

Two people may employ the same words and phrases to express their feelings, and yet those feelings may be specifically different. Each may say, "I felt the love of God shed abroad in my heart", (Rom 5:5) which in the one case may be the genuine affection described in these words, while in the other it may be a mere transport of natural feeling, a mere selfish persuasion of being a favorite of heaven, or a high state of nervous exhilaration, produced by a physiological cause. Both these people may be sincere, according to the popular acceptance of that term; that is, both have really experienced a lively emotion, and both mean to express the simple fact; and yet the one is a real Christian, while the other may be in an unregenerate state.

Another thing which ought to destroy this foolish persuasion that we can certainly determine the true spiritual condition of another person by hearing from him a narrative of his experience, is that any words or phrases which can be used by a really pious man may be learned by a designing hypocrite. What is to hinder such a one from using the very language and imitating the very manner in which true Christians have been heard to relate their experience? What can prevent deceivers from catching up the narrative of godly exercises so abundantly found in religious biography, and applying it to themselves, as though they had experience of these things? While only two classes of Christians have been mentioned, yet in each of these there are many subordinate divisions, to describe all of which would be tedious and not for edification. The reader can readily apply the general principles to every variety of experience, modified by this cause.

In the preceding remarks, the healthy, constitutional temperament has alone been brought into view; but by far the most distressing cases of conscience with which the spiritual physician has to deal, are owing to a morbid temperament. As most people are inclined to conceal their spiritual distresses, few have any conception of the number of people who are habitually suffering under the frightful malady of melancholy. With some, this disease is not permanent—but occasional. They have only periodical paroxysms of deep religious depression; and they may be said to have their compensation for the dark and cloudy day, by being favored with one of peculiar brightness, in quick succession. If their gloom was uninterrupted, it would be overwhelming—but after a dark night, rises a lovely morning without the shadow of a cloud.

This rapid and great alternation of feeling is found in those who possess what may be called a mercurial temperament. It is connected with a nervous system peculiarly excitable, and exceedingly liable to temporary derangement. A rough east wind is sufficient to blow up clouds which completely obscure the cheerful sunshine of the soul; while the wholesome zephyrs as quickly drive all these gloomy clouds away. Such people always have a stomach easily disordered, and one ounce of improper food, or one too much of wholesome food, is cause sufficient to derange the nerves and depress the spirits. The lack of refreshing sleep, or wakefulness, is another cause of the same effects; and in its turn, is an effect from disordered nerves.

But physical causes are not the only ones which produce this painful state of feeling. It is often produced, in a moment, by hearing some unpleasant news, or by the occurrence of some disagreeable event. But as was hinted, when these people of nervous temperament are relieved from a fit of depression, their sky is uncommonly free from clouds; their hopes are lively, their spirits buoyant, and nothing can trouble them. These alternations of day and night, of sunshine and darkness, must of necessity affect the feelings in regard to all matters, temporal and spiritual; for as in a dark night every object appears black, so when the mind is overcast with gloomy clouds, every view must partake of the same aspect. To many people this description will be unintelligible; but by others, it will be recognized at once as a just view of their own case. But when religious melancholy becomes a fixed disease, it may be reckoned among the heaviest calamities to which our suffering nature is subject. It resists all argument and rejects every topic of consolation, from whatever source it may proceed. It feeds upon distress and despair and is displeased even with the suggestion or offer of relief. The mind thus affected seizes on those ideas and truths which are most awful and terrifying. Any doctrine which excludes all hope, is congenial to the melancholy spirit; it seizes on such things with an unnatural avidity, and will not let them go.

There is no subject on which it is more vain and dangerous to theorize than our religious experience. It is therefore of unspeakable importance that ministers of the gospel, who have to deal with diseased consciences, should have had some experience themselves in these matters. This, no doubt, is one reason why some, intended to be "sons of consolation" (Acts 4:36) to others, have been brought through deep waters, and have been buffeted by many storms, before they obtained a settled peace of mind. It is a proper object of inquiry, why, in our day, so little is heard about the spiritual troubles of which we read so much in the treatises of writers of a former age. It can scarcely be supposed that the faith of modern Christians is so much stronger than that of believers who lived in other days, that they are enabled easily to triumph over their melancholy fears and despondency.

Neither can we suppose that Satan is less busy in casting his fiery darts, and in attempts to drive the children of God to despair. There is reason to fear, that among Christians of the present time, there is less deep, spiritual exercise than in former days; and as little is said on this subject in public discourses, there may be greater concealment of the troubles of this kind than if these subjects were more frequently discussed. It is observable that all those who have experienced this sore affliction and have been mercifully delivered from it, are very solicitous to administer relief and comfort to others who are still exposed to the peltings of the pitiless storm; and these are the people who feel the tenderest sympathy with afflicted consciences, and know how to bear with the infirmities and waywardness which accompany a state of religious melancholy. It is also remarkable that very generally, those who have been recovered from such diseases, attribute no small part of their troubles to a morbid temperament of body, and accordingly, in their counsels to the melancholy—they lay particular stress on the regular, healthy state of the body.

About the close of the seventeenth century, Timothy Rogers, 1658-1728, a pious and able minister of London, fell into a state of deep melancholy; and such was the distressing darkness of his mind, that he gave up all hope of the mercy of God, and believed himself to be a vessel of wrath, designed for destruction, for the praise of the glorious justice of the Almighty. His sad condition was known to many pious ministers and people throughout the country, who, it is believed, were earnest and incessant in their supplications in his behalf. And these intercessions were not ineffectual; for it pleased God to grant a complete deliverance to His suffering servant. And having received comfort of the Lord, he was exceedingly desirous to be instrumental in administering the same comfort to others, with which he himself had been comforted. He therefore wrote several treatises with this object in view, which are well calculated to be of service to those laboring under spiritual distress. One of these is entitled, 'Recovery from Sickness', another, 'Consolation for the Afflicted', and a third, 'A Discourse on Trouble of Mind, and the Disease of Melancholy'. In the preface to this last, the author gives directions to the friends of people laboring under religious melancholy, how to treat them. The substance of these, I will now communicate to the reader.

"1. Look upon your distressed friends as under one of the worst distempers to which this miserable life is exposed. Melancholy incapacitates them for thought or action: it confounds and disturbs all their thoughts and fills them with vexation and anguish. I verily believe, that when this malignant state of mind is deeply fixed and has spread its deleterious influence over every part, it is as vain to attempt to resist it by reasoning and rational motives—as it is to oppose a fever or the gout or pleurisy. One of the very worst attendants of this disease is the lack of sleep, by which in other distresses men are relieved and refreshed; but in this disease, either sleep flies far away, or is so disturbed that the poor sufferer, instead of being refreshed, is like one on the rack. The faculties of the soul are weakened, and all their operations disturbed and clouded; and the poor body languishes and pines away at the same time.

And that which renders this disease more formidable is its long continuance. It is a long time often before it comes to its height; and it is usually as tedious in its declension. It is, in every respect, sad and overwhelming; a state of darkness that has no discernible beams of light. It generally begins in the body and then conveys its venom to the mind. I pretend not to tell you what medicines will cure it, for I know of none. I leave you to advise with such as are skilled in medicine, and especially to such doctors as have experienced something of it themselves; for it is impossible to understand the nature of it in any other way than by experience. There is danger, as Richard Greenham says, 'that the bodily physician will look no further than the body; while the spiritual physician will totally disregard the body, and look only at the mind'.

"2. Treat those who are under this disease with tender compassion. Remember also that you are liable to the same affliction; for however brisk your spirits and lively your feelings now, you may meet with such reverses, with such long and sharp afflictions, as will sink your spirits. Many, not naturally inclined to melancholy, have, by overwhelming and repeated calamities, been sunk into this dark gulf.

"3. Never use harsh language to your friends when under the disease of melancholy. This will only serve to fret and perplex them the more—but will never benefit them. I know that the counsel of some is to rebuke and chide them on all occasions; but I dare confidently say that such advisers never felt the disease themselves; for if they had, they would know that thus they do but pour oil into the flames, and chafe and exasperate their wounds, instead of healing them. John Dod, 1549-1645, by reason of his mild, meek and merciful spirit, was reckoned one of the fittest people to deal with those thus afflicted. Never was any person more tender and compassionate, as all will be convinced, who will read the accounts of Mr. Peacock and Mrs. Drake, both of whom were greatly relieved by his conversation.

"4. If you would possess any influence over your friends in this unhappy state of mind, you must be careful not to express any lack of confidence in what they relate of their own feelings and distresses. On this point there is often a great mistake. When they speak of their frightful and distressing apprehensions, it is common for friends to reply, 'that this is all imaginary'—'nothing but fancy', 'an unfounded whim'. Now the disease is a real one, and their misery is as real as any experienced by man. It is true, their imagination is disordered—but this is merely the effect of a deeper disease. These afflicted people never can believe that you have any real sympathy with their misery, or feel any compassion for them, unless you believe what they say.

"5. Do not urge your melancholy friends to do what is out of their power. They are like people whose bones are broken, and who are incapacitated for action. Their disease is accompanied with perplexing and tormenting thoughts; if you can innocently divert them, you would do them a great kindness; but do not urge them to anything which requires close and intent thinking; this will only increase the disease. But you will ask, ought we not to urge them to hear the Word of God? I answer, if they are so far gone in the disease as to be in continual, unremitting anguish, they are not capable of hearing, on account of the painful disorder of their minds. But if their disorder is not come to such a distressing height, you may kindly and gently persuade them to attend on the preaching of the Word; but beware of using an overbearing and violent method. The method pursued by John Dod with Mrs. Drake should be imitated. 'The burden which overloaded her soul was so great, that we never dared add any thereunto—but fed her with all encouragements, she being too apt to overload herself, and to despair upon any addition of fuel to that fire which was inwardly consuming her. And so, wherever she went to hear, notice was given to the minister officiating, that he had such a hearer, and by this means she received no discouragement from hearing.'

"6. Do not attribute the effects of mere disease to the devil; although I do not deny that he has an agency in producing some diseases; especially, by harassing and disturbing the mind to such a degree, that the body suffers with it. But it is very unwise to ascribe every feeling and every word of the melancholy man to Satan; whereas, many of these are as natural consequences of bodily disease, as the symptoms of a fever, which the poor sufferer can no more avoid, than the sick man can keep himself from sighing and groaning. Many will say to such an one, 'Why do you so pore over your case and thus gratify the devil?', whereas it is the very nature of the disease to cause such fixed musings. You might as well say to a man in a fever, 'Why are you not well, why will you be sick?' Some, indeed, suppose that the melancholy hug their disease, and are unwilling to give it up—but you might as well suppose that a man would be pleased with lying on a bed of thorns, or in a fiery furnace. No doubt the devil knows how to work on minds thus diseased, and by shooting his fiery darts he endeavors to drive them to utter despair. But if you persuade them that all which they experience is from the devil, you may induce the opinion in them that they are actually possessed of the evil one; which has been the unhappy condition of some whose minds were disordered. I would not have you to bring a railing accusation even against the devil, neither must you falsely accuse your friends by saying that they gratify him.

"7. Do not express much surprise or wonder at anything which melancholy people say or do. What will not they say, who are in despair of God's mercy? What will not they do, who think themselves lost forever? You know that even such a man as Job cursed his day, so that the Lord charged him with 'darkening counsel by words without knowledge'. Do not wonder that they give expression to bitter complaints; the tongue will always be speaking of the aching tooth. Their soul is sore vexed, and although they get no good by complaining, yet they cannot but complain, to find themselves in such a doleful case. And they can say with David, 'I am weary with my groaning: all the night make I my bed to swim. I water my couch with my tears'; yet they cannot forbear to groan and weep more, until their very eyes be consumed with grief. Let no sharp words of theirs provoke you to talk sharply to them. Sick people are apt to be peevish, and it would be a great weakness in you not to bear with them, when you see that a long and sore disease has deprived them of their former good temper.

"8. Do not tell them any frightful stories, nor recount to them the sad disasters which have overtaken others. Their hearts already meditate terror, and by every alarming thing of which they hear they are the more terrified, and their disordered imagination is prepared to seize upon every frightful image which is presented. The hearing of sad things always causes them more violent agitations. Yet you must avoid merriment and levity in their presence, for this would lead them to think that you have no sympathy with them, nor concern for them. A mixture of gravity and affableness will best suit them; and if I might advise, I would counsel parents not to put their children, who are naturally inclined to melancholy, to learning, or to any employment which requires much study; lest they should at length be preyed upon by their own thoughts.

"9. Do not, however, think it needless to talk with them. But do not speak as if you thought their disease would be of long continuance; for this is the prospect which appears most gloomy to the melancholy. Rather encourage them to hope for speedy deliverance. Endeavor to revive their spirits by declaring that God can give them relief in a moment, and that He has often done so with others; that He can quickly heal their disease, and cause His amiable and reconciled face to shine upon them.

"10. It will be useful to tell them of others who have been in the same state of suffering and yet have been delivered. It is, indeed, true, that they who are depressed by such a load of grief are with difficulty persuaded that any were ever in such a condition as they are. They think themselves to be more wicked than Cain or Judas, and view their own cases to be entirely singular. It will, therefore, be important to relate real cases of deliverance from similar distress and darkness. Several such cases have been known to me, as that of Mr. Rosewell, and also Mr. Porter, both ministers of the gospel. The latter was six years under the pressure of melancholy; yet both these experienced complete deliverance, and afterwards rejoiced in the light of God's countenance. I myself was near two years in great pain of body, and greater pain of soul, and without any prospect of peace or help; and yet God recovered me by His sovereign grace and mercy. Robert Bruce, 1554-1631, minister in Edinburgh, was twenty years in terrors of conscience, and yet delivered afterwards. And so of many others, who after a dark and stormy night, were blessed with the cheerful light of returning day. John Foxe, in his Book of Martyrs, gives an account of a certain John Glover, who was worn and consumed with inward trouble for five years, so that he had no comfort in his food, nor in his sleep, nor in any enjoyment of life. He was so perplexed, as if he had been in the deepest pit of hell, and yet this good servant of God, after all these horrid temptations and buffetings of Satan, was delivered from all his trouble, and the effect was such a degree of mortification of sin, that he appeared as one already in heaven.

"11. The next thing which you are to do for your melancholy friends is to pray for them. As they have not light and composure to pray for themselves, let your eyes weep for them in secret, and there let your souls melt in fervent holy prayers. You know that none but God alone can help them. Mr. Peacock said to John Dod, and his other friends, "Take not the name of God in vain, by praying for such a reprobate." Mr. Dod replied, "If God stirs up your friends to pray for you, He will stir up Himself to hear their prayers." You ought to consider that nothing but prayer can do them good. It is an obstinate disease that nothing else will overcome. Those who can cure themselves by resorting to wine and company, were never under this disease.

"12. Not only pray for them yourself—but engage other Christian friends also to pray for them. When many good people join their requests together, their cry is more acceptable and prevailing. When the church united in prayer for Peter in chains, he was soon delivered, and in the very time of their prayers. All believers have, through Christ, a great interest in heaven, and the Father is willing to grant what they unitedly and importunately ask in the name of His dear Son. I myself have been greatly helped by the prayers of others, and I heartily thank all those especially who set apart particular days to remember at a throne of grace my distressed condition. Blessed be God that He did not turn away His mercy from me, nor turn a deaf ear to their supplications!

"13. Put your poor afflicted friends in mind, continually—of the sovereign grace of God in Jesus Christ. Often impress on their minds that He is merciful and gracious; that as far as the heavens are above the earth, so far are His thoughts above their thoughts; His thoughts of mercy above their self-condemning, guilty thoughts. Teach them, as much as you can, to look unto God, by the great Mediator, for grace and strength; and not too much to pore over their own souls, where there is so much darkness and unbelief. And turn away their thoughts from the decrees of God. Show them what great sinners God has pardoned, and encourage them to believe and to hope for mercy. When Mrs. Drake was in her deplorable state of darkness, she would send a description of her case to distinguished ministers, concealing her name, to know whether such a creature, without faith, hope, or love to God or man—hardhearted, without natural affection, who had resisted and abused all means, could have any hope of going to heaven? Their answer was, that such like, and much worse, might by the mercy of God be received into favor, converted and saved; which did much allay her trouble. 'For,' said she, 'the fountain of all my misery has been that I sought that in the 'law'—which I should have found in the 'gospel'; and for that in myself, which was only to be found in Christ.' 'From my own experience, I can testify,' says Mr. Rogers, 'that the mild and gentle way of dealing with such is the best.'"

A volume might be written on the subject of religious melancholy, and such a volume is much needed; but it would be difficult to find a person qualified for the undertaking. We have some books written by pious men; and the subject is handled in medical treatises on insanity; but, to do it justice, physiological knowledge must be combined with an accurate acquaintance with the experience of Christians. The spiritual physician, who has the cure of diseased souls, takes much less pains to inquire minutely and exactly into the maladies of his patients, than is observable in physicians of the body. I have often admired the alacrity and perseverance with which medical students attend upon anatomical and physiological lectures, although often the exhibitions are extremely repulsive to our natural feelings. The patience and ingenuity with which the men of this profession make experiments, are highly worthy of imitation.

Many of our young preachers, when they go forth on their important errand, are poorly qualified to direct the doubting conscience or to administer safe consolation to those troubled in spirit. And in modern preaching there is little account made of the various distressing cases of deep affliction under which many serious people are suffering. If we want counsel on subjects of this kind, we must go back to the old writers; but as there is now small demand for such works, they are fast sinking into oblivion; and their place is not likely to be supplied by any works which the prolific press now pours forth. It is, however, a pleasing circumstance, that the writings of so many of our old English divines have recently been reprinted in London. But still, many valuable treatises are destined to oblivion.

The only object which I have in view in introducing this subject is to inquire, what connection there is between real experimental religion and melancholy. And I must in the first place endeavor to remove a prevalent prejudice, that in all religious people there is a strong tendency to melancholy. Indeed, there are not a few who confound these two things so completely, that they have no other idea of becoming religious, than sinking into a state of perpetual gloom. Such people as these are so far removed from all just views of the nature of religion, that I shall not attempt at present to correct their errors. There are others, who entertain the opinion that deep religious impressions tend to produce that state of mind called melancholy; and not only so—but they suppose that in many cases insanity is the consequence of highly raised religious affections.

The fact cannot be denied that religion is often the subject which dwells on the minds of both the melancholy and the insane. But I am of opinion that we are here in danger of reversing the order of nature, and putting the effect in the place of the cause. Religion does not produce melancholy—but melancholy turns the thoughts to religion. People of a melancholy temperament seize on such ideas as are most awful, and which furnish the greatest opportunity of indulging in despondency and despair. Sometimes, however, it is not religion which occupies the minds and thoughts of the melancholy—but their own health, which they imagine, without reason, to be declining; or their estates, which they apprehend to be wasting away, and abject poverty and beggary stare them in the face.

Frequently this disease alienates the mind entirely from religion, and the unhappy victim of it refuses to attend upon any religious duties, or to be present where they are performed. Frequently it assumes the form of monomania—or a fixed misapprehension in regard to some one thing. The celebrated and excellent William Cowper labored for years under one of the most absurd hallucinations respecting a single point; and in that point, his belief—though invincible—was repugnant to the whole of his religious creed. He imagined that he had received from the Almighty a command, at a certain time, when in a fit of insanity, to kill himself; and as a punishment for disobedience, he had forfeited a seat in paradise. And so deep was this impression, that he would attend on no religious worship, public or private; and yet at this very time took a lively interest in the advancement of Christ's kingdom; and his judgment was so sound on other matters, that such men as John Newton and Thomas Scott were in the habit of consulting with him on all difficult points. The case of this man of piety and genius was used by the enemies of religion, and particularly by the enemies of Calvinism, as an argument against the creed which he had embraced; whereas his disease was at the worst, before he had experienced anything of religion, or had embraced the tenets of Calvin. And let it be remembered that it was by turning his attention to the consolations of the gospel that his excellent physician was successful in restoring his mind to tranquility and comfort; and the world will one day learn that, of all the remedies for this malady, the pure doctrines of grace are the most effectual to resuscitate the melancholy mind.

This is, in fact, a bodily disease, by which the mind is influenced and darkened. Thus it was received by the ancient Greeks; for the term is compounded of two Greek words which signify black bile. How near they were to the truth in assigning the physical cause which produces the disease, I leave to others to determine. Philosophers have often erred egregiously by referring all such cases to mental or moral causes. It is probable, even when the disease is brought on by strong impressions on the mind, that by these, physical derangement occurs. To reason with a man against the views which arise from melancholy is commonly as inefficacious as reasoning against bodily pain! I have long made this a criterion, to ascertain whether the dejection experienced, was owing to a physical cause; for in that case, argument, though demonstrative, has no effect. Still such people should be affectionately conversed with; and their peculiar opinions and views should rarely be contradicted. Cases often occur in which there is a mixture of moral and physical causes; and these should be treated in reference to both sources of their affliction.

Melancholy is sometimes hereditary, and often constitutional. When such people are relieved for a while, they are apt to relapse into the same state as did William Cowper. The late excellent and venerable James Hall, of North Carolina, was of a melancholy temperament, and after finishing his education at Princeton, he fell into a gloomy dejection, which interrupted his studies and labors for more than a year. After his restoration, he labored successfully and comfortably in the ministry for many years, even to old age; but at last was overtaken again, and entirely overwhelmed by this terrible malady. Of all men that I ever saw, he had the tenderest sympathy with people laboring under religious despondency. When on a journey, I have known him to travel miles out of his way to converse with a sufferer of this kind; and his manner was most tender and affectionate in speaking to such.

I have remarked, that people who gave no symptoms of this disease until the decline of life, have then fallen under its power, owing to some change in the constitution at that period, or some change in their active pursuits. I recollect two cases of overwhelming melancholy in people who appeared in their former life as remote from it as any that I ever knew. The first was a man of extraordinary talents and eloquence, bold and decisive in his temper, and fond of company and good cheer. When about fifty-five years of age, without any external cause to produce the effect, his spirits began to sink, and feelings of melancholy to seize upon him. He avoided company; but I had frequent occasion to see him, and sometimes he could be engaged in conversation, when he would speak as judiciously as before; but he soon reverted to his dark melancholy mood. On one occasion he mentioned his case to me, and observed with emphasis, that he had no power whatever to resist the disease, and, said he, with despair in his countenance, "I shall soon be utterly overwhelmed." And so it turned out, for the disease advanced until it ended in the worst form of mania, and soon terminated his life. The other was the case of a gentleman who had held office in the American army during the revolutionary war. About the same age, or a little later, he lost his cheerfulness, which had never been interrupted before, and by degrees sank into a most deplorable state of melancholy which, as in the former case, soon ended in death. In this case, the first thing which I noticed was a morbid sensibility of the moral sense, which filled him with remorse for acts which had little or no moral turpitude attached to them.

I would state then, as the result of all my observation, that true religion, in its regular and rational exercise, has no tendency to melancholy or insanity—but the contrary; and that religion is the most effectual remedy for this disease, whatever be its cause. But melancholy people are very apt to seize on the dark side of religion, as affording food for the morbid state of their minds. True Christians, as being subject to like diseases with others, may become melancholic—but not in consequence of their piety: but in this melancholy condition they are in a more comfortable, as well as in a safer state than others. They may relinquish all their hopes—but they cannot divest themselves of their pious feelings.

I have said nothing respecting the supposed tendency of strong religious feelings to produce INSANITY, for what has been said respecting melancholy is equally applicable to this subject. Indeed, I am of opinion that melancholy is a species of insanity; and in its worst form, the most appalling species; for in most cases insane people seem to have many enjoyments, arising out of their strange misconceptions—but the victim of melancholy is miserable; he is often suffering under the most horrible of all calamities—black despair. When a child, I used to tremble when I read Bunyan's account, in his Pilgrim, of the man shut up in the iron cage. And in the year 1791, when I first visited the Pennsylvania Hospital, I saw a man there who had arrived a few days before, said to be in a religious melancholy and to be in despair. He had made frequent attempts on his own life, and all instruments by which he might accomplish that direful purpose were carefully removed. Having never been accustomed to see insane people, the spectacle of so many deprived of reason made a solemn impression on my mind; but although some were raving and blaspheming in their cells, and others confined in straitjackets, the sight of no one so affected me as that of this man in despair. Although near half a century has elapsed since I beheld his sorrowful countenance, there is still a vivid picture of it in my imagination. We spoke to him—but he returned no answer, except that he once raised his despairing eyes—but immediately cast them down again. Whether this man had been the subject of any religious impressions, I did not learn. But this one thing I must testify, that I never knew the most pungent convictions of sin to terminate in insanity; and as to the affections of love to God and the lively hope of everlasting life producing insanity, it is too absurd for any one to believe it.

I do not dispute, however, that wild enthusiasm may have a tendency to insanity; and some people are so ignorant of the nature of true religion as to confound it with enthusiasm. I will go further and declare that, after much thought on the subject of enthusiasm, I am unable to account for the effects produced by it, in any other way than by supposing that it is a case of real insanity. Diseases of this class are the more dangerous because they are manifestly contagious. The very looks and tones of an enthusiast are felt to be powerful by everyone; and when the nervous system of any one is in a state easily susceptible of emotions from such a cause, the dominion of reason is overthrown, and wild imagination and irregular emotion govern the infatuated person, who readily embraces all the extravagant opinions, and receives all the disturbing impressions which belong to the party infected.

Without a supposition such as the foregoing, how can you account for the fact, that an educated man and popular preacher, and a wife, intelligent and judicious above most, having a family of beloved children, should separate from each other, relinquish all the comforts of domestic life, and a pleasant and promising congregation, to connect themselves with a people who are the extreme of all enthusiasts—the Shakers? But such facts have been witnessed in our own times, and in no small numbers. In a town in New Hampshire, the writer, when in the neighborhood, was told of the case of a young preacher who visited the Shaker settlement out of curiosity to see them dance, in which exercise their principal worship consists: but, while he stood and looked on, he was seized with the same spirit, and began to shake and dance too; and never returned—but remained in the society. But, there being no demand for his learning or preaching talents, whatever they might be—and he being an able-bodied man, they employed him in building stone fences. This species of infatuation, which is called enthusiasm, is apt to degenerate into bitterness and malignity of spirit towards all who do not embrace it, and then it is termed fanaticism.

This species of insanity, as I must be permitted to call it, differs from other kinds in that it is social, or affects large numbers in the same way, and binds them together by the link of close fraternity. It agrees with other kinds of monomania, in that the aberration of mind relates to one subject, while the judgment may be sound in other matters. No people know how to manage their agricultural, horticultural, and mechanical business more skillfully and successfully than the Shakers. And the newer sect of Mormons would soon settle down to peaceable industry, if the people would let them alone. This country promises to be the theater of all conceivable forms of enthusiasm and fanaticism; and as long as these misguided people pursue their own course without disturbing other people, they should be left to their own delusions, as it relates to the civil power; but if any of them should be impelled by their fanatical spirit to disturb the peace, they should be treated like other maniacs.

The causes of melancholy and insanity, whether physical or moral, cannot easily be explored. The physician will speak confidently about a lesion of the brain—but when insane people have been subjected to a postmortem examination, the brain very seldom exhibits any appearance of derangement. The philosopher, on the other hand, thinks only of moral causes, and attributes the disease to such of this class as are known to have existed, or flees to 'hypothesis', which will account for everything.

There is a remarkable coincidence, however, which has fallen under my observation, between those who assign a moral and those who assign a physical cause for melancholy and madness, in regard to one point. Some forty or fifty years ago, the writer, about the same time, read Thomas Shepard's Sincere Convert, and James Robe on Religious Melancholy, and he noticed that they both ascribe the deep and fixed depression of spirits frequently met with, to a secret, reprehensible indulgence. In the statistics of several insane asylums and penitentiaries which have been published recently, the most of the cases of insanity are confidently ascribed to the same thing, as its physical cause. This increasing evil is of such a nature that we cannot be more explicit. Those who ought to know the facts will understand the reference. It must, after all, be admitted that the claims of intemperance in the use of intoxicating drinks, to a deleterious influence on the reason, stand in the foremost rank; but the madness produced by this cause is commonly of short duration. I do not speak of that loss of reason which is the immediate effect of alcohol on the brain—but of that most tremendous form of madness called delirium tremens. I have said that it was short, because it is commonly the last struggle of the human constitution, under the influence of a dreadful poison, which has now consummated its work—and death soon steps in and puts an end to the conflict.

After spending so much time in speaking of melancholy as a disease, I anticipate the thoughts of some good people, who will be ready to say, 'What, is there no such thing as spiritual desertion—times of darkness and temptation, which are independent of the bodily temperament?' To which I answer, that I fully believe there are many such cases; but they deserve a separate consideration, and do not fall within the compass of my present design. The causes, symptoms, and cure of such spiritual maladies are faithfully delineated by many practical writers; and although these cases are entirely distinct from melancholy, they assume, in many respects, similar symptoms, and by the unskillful philosopher are confounded with it. These two causes, as I have before intimated, may often operate together and produce a mixed and very perplexing case, both for the bodily and spiritual physician.

After all that has been said, the fact with which we commenced is that religious exercises are very much modified by the temperament, and in some cases, by the idiosyncrasy of the individual. The liquor put into an old cask commonly receives a strong tincture from the vessel. Old habits, although a new governing principle is introduced into the system, do not yield at once; and propensities, apparently extinguished, are apt to revive and give unexpected trouble.

It is a comfortable thought, that these vile bodies cannot go with the saints to heaven, until they are completely purified. What proportion of our present feelings will be dropped with the body, we cannot tell. How a disembodied spirit will perceive, feel, and act, we shall soon know by consciousness; but, if ever so many of the departed should return and attempt to communicate to us their present mode of existence, it would be all in vain; the things which relate to such a state are inconceivable, and unspeakable. What Paul saw in the third heaven he dare not, or he could not communicate; but he did not know whether he saw these wonderful things in the body or out of the body. This was a thing known, as he intimates—only to God.

Chapter 5: Effect of sympathy illustrated—Cautions in relation to this subject—A singular case in illustration.

The causes, already considered, which modify religious experience, relate to Christians as individuals—but man is constitutionally a social being; and religion is a social thing; so that we cannot have a complete view of this subject without considering them as they stand connected with others, and especially as they are influenced by one another. There is a mysterious bond, called sympathy, by which not only human beings, but some species of animals are connected. It is much easier, on this subject, to state facts than to account for them. A man cannot go into any company without being sensible of some change in his feelings. Whatever passion agitates those around him, he involuntarily participates in the emotion; and the mere external expression of any feeling often produces the same expression in himself, whether it be yawning, smiling, crying, or coughing; and this must be effected by an assimilation of the mind of the beholder to the state of mind which produced the external act. The wilder and stronger the passions which agitate others, the more are we affected by them. This operation of mutual sympathetic excitement, when many people are brought together under some agitating influence, produces a stream of emotion which cannot easily be resisted; and far above what any one of the crowd would have felt if the same cause had operated on him alone. Hence the ungovernable fury of mobs, carrying desolation and often murder in their train; and yet the ringleaders, had they been alone, would have experienced no such violence of passion; and hence the danger, in large cities, of permitting multitudes of undisciplined people to assemble promiscuously. A mob is an artificial body, pervaded by one spirit; by the power of sympathy, for which the French have an appropriate phrase, esprit de corps.

If there be anything in animal magnetism, which has of late made so much noise, beside sheer imposture, it must be grafted on this principle; for the extent to which human beings may influence one another by contact or proximity, in certain excitable states of the nervous system, has never been accurately ascertained. In those remarkable bodily affections called 'the jerks', which appeared in religious meetings some years ago, the nervous irregularity was commonly produced by the sight of other people thus affected; and if, in some instances, without the sight, yet by having the imagination strongly impressed by hearing of such things. It is a fact, as undoubted as it is remarkable, that, as this bodily affection assumed a great variety of appearances in different places, nothing was more common than for a new species of the exercise, as it was called, to be imported from another part of the country by one or a few individuals. This contagion of nervous excitement is not unparalleled; for whole schools of young ladies have been seized with spasmodic or epileptic fits, in consequence of a single scholar being taken with the disease. There are many authentic facts ascertained in relation to this matter, which I hope some person will collect and give to the public, through the press.

It will not be thought strange, then, that sympathy should have a powerful influence in increasing and modifying the feelings which are experienced in religious meetings; nor is it desirable that it should be otherwise. This principle, no doubt, is liable to abuse, and when unduly excited may be attended with disagreeable and injurious effects—but without it how dull and uninteresting would social worship be. When a whole assembly, in listening to the same evangelical discourse, or praising God in the same divine song, or sitting together around the same sacramental table, are deeply affected, they form, as it were, one body, and the whole mass is melted down and amalgamated into one grand emotion. They seem to have but one heart and one soul; and as harmoniously as their voices mingle in the sacred song of praise to the Redeemer, do their feelings amalgamate in one ascending volume towards heaven.

The preacher who is privileged to address such an assembly seems to have before him one great body, having many eyes but one soul. Hence we see the reason why a company thinly scattered over a large house always appears cold and uncomfortable; while the same people brought near together, in a small house, have an entirely different appearance; and also we see why social meetings in private houses are felt by sincere Christians to be more profitable, often, than the more solemn assemblies of the church. And, upon the same principle, all worshipers feel more animated when surrounded by a multitude.

But it is in times of revival or general awakening that the power of this principle manifests itself most evidently; and it is no evidence of a spurious work that the sympathies of the people are much awakened, or that many are led to seriousness by seeing others affected. God often blesses this instinctive feeling in this very way. But is it not to be expected that, at such a time, many will be affected by mere sympathy? And will not such as are thus affected be in great danger of being deceived, by taking these tender emotions of sympathy to be the exercises of true repentance, especially as they fall in with those convictions of conscience which all who hear the gospel experience? Is it then judicious, by impassioned discourses addressed to the sympathies of our nature, to raise this class of feelings to a flame? or to devise measures by which the passions of the young and ignorant may be excited to excess? That measures may be put into operation which have a mighty influence on a whole assembly is readily admitted; but are excitements thus produced really useful? They may bring young people, who are diffident, to a decision, and as it were, constrain them to range themselves on the Lord's side—but the question which sticks with me is—does this really benefit the people? In my judgment, not at all—but the contrary. If they have the seed of grace, though it may come forth slowly, yet this principle will find its way to the light and air, and the very slowness of its coming forward may give it opportunity to strike its roots deep in the earth.

If I were to place myself on what is called an 'anxious seat', or should kneel down before a whole congregation to be prayed for, I know that I would be strangely agitated—but I do not believe that it would be of any permanent utility. But if it should produce some good effect, am I at liberty to resort to anything in the worship of God which I think would be useful? If such things are lawful and useful, why not add other circumstances and increase the effect? Why not require the penitent to appear in a white sheet, or to be clothed in sackcloth, with ashes on his head? and these, remember, are Scriptural signs of humiliation. And on these principles, who can reasonably object to holy water, to incense, and the use of pictures or images in the worship of God? All these things come into the church upon this same principle, of devising new measures to do good; and if the 'anxious seat' is so powerful a means of grace, it may soon come to be reckoned among the sacraments of the church. The language of experience is, that it is unsafe and unwise to bring people who are under religious impressions too much into public view. The seed of the Word, like the natural seed, does not vegetate well in the sun. Be not too impatient to force into maturity the plant of grace. Water it, cultivate it—but handle it not with a rough hand.

The opinion entertained by some good people that all religion obtained in a revival is suspect, has no just foundation. At such times, when the Spirit of God is really poured out, the views and exercises of converts are commonly more clear and satisfactory than at other times, and the process of conversion more speedy. But doubtless there may be expected a considerable crop of spurious conversions, and these may make the greatest show; for the seed on the stony ground seems to have vegetated the quickest of any. And this is the reason that, after all revivals, there is a sad declension in the favorable appearances; because that which has no root must soon wither. In looking back after a revival season, I have thought, how would matters have been if none had come forward—but such as persevere and bring forth fruit? Perhaps things would have gone on so quietly that the good work would not have been called a revival.

But ministers cannot prevent the impressions which arise merely from sympathy—neither should they attempt it; but when they are about to gather the wheat into the garner, they should faithfully winnow the heap; not that they can discern the spirits of men—but the Word of God is a discerner of the thoughts and intents of the heart. The church is no place of safety for the unconverted. Hundreds and thousands are shielded from beneficial convictions by their profession and situation in the church. Let ministers be "wise as serpents", as well as "harmless as doves". (Matt 10:16) "Be not many masters, knowing that we shall receive the greater condemnation." (James 3:1) "They watch for souls as those who must give account" (Heb 13:17)—solemn account!

From what has been said about the power of sympathy, some may be ready to conclude that all experimental religion and all revivals may be accounted for on this principle, without the necessity of supposing any supernatural agency to exist; and if no effects were produced but those excitements which often mingle with religious exercises, this would be no irrational conclusion. But under the preaching of the gospel we find a permanent change of moral character taking place: so great a change that, even in the view of the world who observe it, the subject appears to be "a new man". An entire revolution has taken place in his principles of action as well as in his sentiments respecting divine things. Now those who would ascribe all experimental religion to mere natural feelings, artificially excited, must believe that there are no such transformations of character as have been mentioned, and that all who profess such a change are false pretenders. But this ground is manifestly untenable, for no facts are more certain than such reformations; and if there are men of truth and sincerity in the world, they are to be found among those who have undergone this moral transformation. Surely there are no phenomena now taking place in our world half so important and worthy of consideration, as the repentance of an habitual sinner; so that he utterly forsakes his wicked courses, and takes delight in the worship of God and obedience to His will.

Let it be remembered that these are effects observed only where the gospel is preached, and in some instances, numerous examples of such conversions from sin to holiness occur about the same time and in the same place. No series of miracles could give stronger evidence of the divine origin and power of the gospel than the actual and permanent reformation of wicked men; and the skeptic may be challenged to account for such effects on any natural principles.

But it may still be asked how the person who is the subject of these new views and exercises can know that they are the effects of a supernatural agency. It is readily admitted that we cannot be conscious of the agency of another spirit on ours, because our consciousness extends only to our thoughts, and often when new feelings arise in our minds we are unable to trace them to their proper cause. In this case, if we had no revelation from God, we might not be able with certainty to account for such effects; but in the Word of God we are distinctly and repeatedly informed that God by His Spirit will continue to operate on the minds of men, to turn them from iniquity, and to cause them to engage with delight in His service. And when we find these very effects taking place in connection with the means appointed to produce them, we can have no doubt about their divine origin; and our faith is confirmed in this doctrine of divine agency by observing the wonderful change produced by the preaching of the gospel upon the most depraved and degraded of the heathen.

The transformation of character, in thousands of instances now existing, is enough to produce conviction in any mind not rendered obdurate by the prejudices of infidelity. It may be objected that, in many instances, the change professed is not permanent—but temporary, and they who appear saints today may be found wallowing in the mire of iniquity tomorrow. These are facts which we cannot gainsay; but we do deny that they go to invalidate the argument from the examples of a permanent and thorough change which do really take place. If there were only one real, sound conversion and reformation in a hundred of those who may be religiously impressed, still, the conclusion in favor of a divine influence would be valid. In the spring we behold the trees clothed and adorned with millions of blossoms which never produce mature fruit; but when in autumn we find here and there apples, large, sweet, and mellow, do we hesitate to believe that this is a good tree which produces good fruit?

For reasons already given, it ought not to be expected that all serious impressions should eventuate in a sound conversion. External appearances may be the same to our view, where the causes are entirely diverse. This is especially to be expected when a great many are affected at once, and meet in the same assembly. And if these transient appearances did not take place under the preaching of the gospel, our Savior's doctrine of the various effects of the Word would not be verified. Ministers of the gospel cannot be blamed for these temporary impressions, unless they use unauthorized means to work upon the sympathies of their hearers. That, through ignorance, vanity and enthusiastic ardor, many preachers in our day have attempted to produce such excitements, cannot be denied; and by the true friends of vital piety is greatly lamented. Perhaps nothing has so much prejudiced the minds of sensible men against experimental religion as the extravagance and violence of those 'staged excitements' which have been promoted in various places by measures artfully contrived to work upon the passions and imagination of weak and ignorant people. And as the preacher must have his reward of glory for his efforts, all this must be so brought out, that their number may be counted and published to the world. Alas! alas! poor human nature!

I believe that all respectable denominations among us are becoming more and more sensible, that something more is requisite in the ministry than fiery zeal. Some who, within our remembrance, disparaged a learned ministry are now using noble exertions to erect seminaries, and encourage their young preachers to seek to be learned. This is a matter of rejoicing, and bodes well for the American Church hereafter. I would be unwilling to bring before the public all the scenes that I have witnessed under the name of religious worship. But as the subject of sympathy is still under consideration, I will relieve the reader by a short narrative.

Being in a part of the country where I was known, by face, to scarcely anyone, and hearing that there was a great meeting in the neighborhood, and a good work in progress, I determined to attend. The sermon had commenced before I arrived, and the house was so crowded that I could not approach near to the pulpit—but sat down in a kind of shed connected with the main building where I could see and hear the preacher. His sermon was really striking and impressive, and in language and method far above the common run of extempore discourses. The people were generally attentive, and so far as I could observe, many were tenderly affected, except that in the extreme part of the house where I sat, some old tobacco-planters kept up a continual conversation in a low tone about tobacco-plants, seasons, etc. When the preacher came to the application of his discourse he became exceedingly vehement and boisterous, and I could hear sounds in the center of the house which indicated strong emotion. At length a female voice was heard, in a piercing cry, which thrilled through me and affected the whole audience. It was succeeded by a low murmuring sound from the middle of the house; but, in a few seconds, one and another arose in different parts of the house, under extreme and visible agitation. Casting off bonnets and caps, and raising their folded hands, they shouted to the utmost extent of their voice; and in a few seconds more, the whole audience was agitated, as a forest when shaken by a mighty wind. The sympathetic wave, commencing in the center, extended to the extremities; and at length it reached our corner, and I felt the conscious effort of resistance as necessary as if I had been exposed to the violence of a storm. I saw few people through the whole house who escaped the prevailing influence; even careless boys seemed to be arrested and to join in the general outcry. But what astonished me most of all was that the old tobacco-planters whom I have mentioned and who, I am persuaded, had not heard one word of the sermon, were violently agitated. Every muscle of their brawny faces appeared to be in tremulous motion, and the big tears chased one another down their wrinkled cheeks.

Here I saw the power of sympathy. The feeling was real, and propagated from person to person by the mere sounds which were uttered; for many of the audience had not paid any attention to what was said—but nearly all partook of the agitation. The feelings expressed were different, as when the foundation of the second temple was laid; for while some uttered the cry of poignant anguish, others shouted in the accents of joy and triumph. The speaker's voice was soon silenced, and he sat down and gazed on the scene with a complacent smile.

When this tumult had lasted a few minutes, another preacher, as I suppose he was, who sat on the pulpit steps, with his handkerchief spread over his head, began to sing a soothing and yet lively tune, and was quickly joined by some strong female voices near him; and in less than two minutes the storm was hushed, and there was a great calm. It was like pouring oil on the troubled waters. I experienced the most sensible relief to my own feelings from the appropriate music; for I could not hear the words sung. But I could not have supposed that anything could so quickly allay such a storm; and all seemed to enjoy the tranquility which succeeded. The disheveled hair was put in order, and the bonnets, etc., gathered up, and the irregularities of the dress adjusted, and no one seemed conscious of any impropriety. Indeed, there is a peculiar luxury in such excitements, especially when tears are shed copiously, which was the case here.

I attended another meeting in another place where there had been a remarkable excitement—but the tide was far on the ebb; and although we had vociferation and out-crying of a stunning kind, I did not hear one sound indicative of real feeling—and I do not think that one tear was shed during the meeting.

Chapter 6: Erroneous views of regeneration—The correct view—The operation of faith—Exercises of mind, as illustrated in Jonathan Edwards's narrative—The operations of faith still further explained

It is proper now to inquire, what are the precise effects of regeneration, or the exercises of a newly converted soul? As the restoration of depraved man to the image of God, lost by the fall, is the grand object aimed at in the whole economy of salvation, it can easily be said, in the general, that by this change—a principle of holiness is implanted, spiritual life is communicated, the mind is enlightened, the will renewed, and the affections purified and elevated to heavenly objects. Such general descriptions do not afford full satisfaction to the inquiring mind; and as we have taken into view many of those circumstances which diversify the exercises of grace in different subjects, let us now endeavor to ascertain, with as much precision as we can, what are those things which are essential to the genuineness of this work and which, therefore, will be found in every sincere Christian.

But in this attempt, great difficulty will be met in conveying our ideas with precision. Even those terms which are most used in the Holy Scriptures to designate the essential exercises of piety are differently understood, and when used, convey different ideas to different people. I will endeavor, however, to avoid this difficulty as much as possible, by defining the terms which I employ. I have all along admitted that the mode of the Spirit's operation in regeneration is altogether inscrutable: and an attempt to explain it is worse than folly. We may, however, without intruding into things unseen, or attempting to dive into the unsearchable nature of the divine operations, say that God operates on the human mind in a way perfectly consistent with its nature, as a spirit, and a creature of understanding and will. On this principle some suppose that there can be no other method of influencing a rational mind but by the exhibition of truth, or the presentment of motives: any physical operation, they allege, would be unsuitable. Their theory of regeneration, therefore, is that it is produced by the moral operation of the truth, contemplated by the understanding, and influencing the affections and the will, according to the known principles of our rational nature. But respecting what is necessary to bring the truth fairly before the mind, the abettors of this theory divide into several parts.

The Pelagian, believing human nature to be uncontaminated, and needing nothing but a correct knowledge of the truth, rejects all supernatural aid, and maintains that every man has full ability to perform all good actions, and to reform what is amiss, by simply attending to the instructions of the Word, and exercising his own free will, by which he is able to choose and pursue what course he pleases.

The semi-Pelagian agrees with this view, except in one particular. He believes that the truth, if seriously contemplated, will produce the effects stated—but that mankind are so immersed in the world of sensible objects, and so occupied and filled with earthly thoughts and cares, that no man will, or ever does, contemplate the truth so impartially and steadily as to produce a change in his affections and purposes, until he is influenced by the Holy Spirit; and, according to him, the only need of divine agency in regeneration is to direct and fix the attention on divine things. This being done, the truth as contained in the divine Word, and as apprehended by the natural understanding, is adequate to produce all the desired effects on the active principles of our nature.

There is still a third party who attribute regeneration to the simple operation of the truth on the mind, whose views are neither Pelagian nor semi-Pelagian. They hold that the natural man cannot discern the things of the Spirit of God, and that if a man should ever so long contemplate the truth with such views as natural reason takes of it, it would never transform him into the divine likeness; but that, by the illumination of the Holy Spirit, the sinner must obtain new and spiritual views of divine things, by which he is renovated or regenerated. Yet these deny that any operation on the mind itself is necessary, as they allege that these spiritual views of truth will certainly draw after them the exercise of those affections in which holiness essentially consists.

Now, in my judgment, this theory is defective in one point only, and that is, it supposes the mind, which is already in possession of doctrinal knowledge of the truth, to have this same truth presented to it in an entirely new light, without any operation on the soul itself. Just as if a man was blind—but standing in the clear shining of the sun's rays. These he feels, and can talk philosophically about the sensation of light and colors; while he has not in his mind the first simple perception of any object of sight. Could this man be made to perceive the visible objects around him, without an operation on the eyes to remove the obstruction, or to rectify the organ?

The case of the soul is entirely analogous. Here is light enough; the truth is viewed by the intellect of unregenerate man—but has no transforming efficacy. The fault is not in the truth, which is perfect—but the blindness is in the mind, which can only be removed by an influence on the soul itself; that is, by the power of God creating "a new heart", (Ezek 18:31; Ezek 36:26) to use the language of Scripture. The apostle Paul was sent to the Gentiles "to open their eyes, and to turn them from darkness to light". (Acts 26:18) Two things are always necessary to distinct vision, the medium of light, and a sound organ; either of these without the other, would be useless; but combined, the beauties of nature, and the glory of God in the visible world, are seen with delight.

It is so in the spiritual world. The truth is necessary—but until the mind is brought into a state in which it can perceive it in its beauty and glory, it is heard and read and contemplated without any transforming effect—without drawing the affections to God, or subduing the power of selfish and sensual desires. The fault existing in the person, there must be such an exertion of divine power as will remove it, and this is regeneration. Then all the effects of the truth will take place, as according to the former theory.

But I seem to hear the common objection, that if the soul be the subject of any operation, this must be 'physical', and what is this but to make man a mere machine, or to deal with him as if he were a block? I believe that a more ambiguous, unhappy word could not be used than physical. The best way to get clear of the mists which surround it, is to drop its use altogether in this connection. Indeed, it is a term which properly belongs to another science—to natural philosophy. If the operation must have a name, let it receive it from the nature of the effect produced; this being spiritual, let it be called a 'spiritual' operation; or as the effect produced is confessedly above the powers of unassisted nature, let us call it supernatural, which is the precise technical term used by the most accurate theologians. Can the Almighty, who made the soul, operate upon it in no other way than by a mechanical force? Cannot He restore its lost power of spiritual perception and susceptibility of holy feeling, without doing any violence to its free and spiritual nature?

But I shall be told, that there neither is, nor can be, any moral or spiritual nature, or disposition prior to volition, in the mind—for morality consists essentially in choice; and to suppose morality to have any other existence than in the transient act is an absurdity. If this be sound moral philosophy, then my theory must fall. This is a question not requiring or admitting of much reasoning. It is a subject for the intuitive judgment of the moral faculty. If there are minds so constituted that they cannot conceive of permanent, latent dispositions in the soul, both good and evil, I can do no more than express my strong dissent from their opinion, and appeal to the common sense of mankind.

Some of my most serious readers, I know, will object to my theory of the mind's operations, in one important particular. They are so far from thinking that any illumination of the mind will produce holy affections, that it is a radical principle in their philosophy of religion, that light always increases or stirs up the enmity of an unregenerate heart; that the more unholy beings know of God, the more they will hate Him, as is supposed to be proved by the experience of thousands under conviction of sin; and by the case of the devils who believe and tremble—but never love. The difference between me and these people is not so great as at first view it seems. Their error consists, if I am right, in making too wide a severance between the understanding and the will; between the intellect and the affections. I am ready to admit that all the knowledge which you can communicate to a man remaining unregenerate, may have the tendency of increasing or stirring up his enmity to God and His law; but observe that I make illumination the first effect of regeneration. And I hold that no unregenerate man is, while in that state, any more capable of spiritual perception than a blind man is of a perception of colors. The blind man, however, has his own ideas about colors, and may understand their various relations to each other, and all the laws which regulate the reflection and refraction of light, as well as those who see. This was remarkably exemplified in the case of Dr. Sanderson, who, though blind from his early infancy, delivered an accurate course of lectures on light and colors, in the University of Oxford. Just so, an unregenerate man may be able to deliver able lectures on all the points of theology, and yet not have one glimpse of the beauty and glory of the truth with which he is conversant.

The sacred Scriptures represent all unconverted men as destitute of the true knowledge of God. If there be a clear truth in the laws of mental operation, it is that the affections are in exact accordance with the views of the understanding. If men are unaffected with the truth known, it must be because they do not know it aright: neither can they perceive it in its true nature until they are regenerated. Did any man ever see an object to be lovely and not feel an emotion corresponding with that quality? And what unconverted man ever beheld in Christ, as represented in Scripture, the beauty and glory of God? Hence that doctrine is not true which confines depravity or holiness to the will, and which considers the understanding as a natural and the will as a moral faculty. The soul is not depraved or holy by departments; the disease affects it, as a soul; and of course all faculties employed in moral exercises must partake of their moral qualities. There is, however, no propriety in calling either of them a moral faculty; for although both understanding and will are concerned in every moral act, yet not one hundredth part of the acts of either partakes of a moral nature. The will is just as much a natural faculty as the understanding, and the understanding is as much a moral faculty as the will. But in strict propriety of speech, the only faculty which deserves to be called a moral faculty is conscience, because by it only are we capable of moral perceptions or feelings.

I am afraid that I have gone too far into abstruse distinctions for most of my readers; but there are thousands of plain, private Christians in our country, who not only can enter into such disquisitions—but will relish them.

I come now to what I intended, when I began this subject, to describe as exactly as I can, what are the exercises of the new heart, or the regenerate man. And here my appeal is to no theories—but to experience, combined with the Word of God.

Every man on whom this divine operation has passed, experiences new views of divine truth. The soul sees in these things that which it never saw before. It discerns in the truth of God a beauty and excellence of which it had no conception until now. Whatever may be the diversity in the clearness of the views of different people, or in the particular truths brought before the mind, they all agree in this, that there is a new perception of truth; whether you ascribe it to the head or the heart, I care not. It is a blessed reality, and there are many witnesses of sound mind and unquestionable veracity, who are ready to attest it as a verity, known in their own delightful experience. But as the field of truth is very wide, and divine things may be perceived under innumerable aspects and relations, and as there is no uniformity in the particular objects which may first occupy the attention of the enlightened mind, it is impossible to lay down any particular order of exercises which take place.

The case may be illustrated by supposing a great multitude of blind people restored to sight by an act of divine power. Some of them would be so situated, that the first object seen would be the glorious luminary of day; another might receive the gift of sight in the night, and the moon and stars would absorb his wondering attention; a third might direct his opened eyes to a beautiful landscape; and a fourth might have but a ray of light shining into a dark dungeon without his knowing whence it came. Of necessity, there must be the same endless variety in the particular views of new converts; but still they all partake of new views of divine truth; and the same truths will generally be contemplated, sooner or later—but not in the same order, nor exhibited to all with the same degree of clearness.

Now, according to the views which I entertain, this spiritual knowledge granted to the regenerated soul is nothing else but saving faith; for knowledge and belief involve each other. To know a thing and not believe it is a contradiction; and to believe a thing and not know it is impossible. Faith is simply a belief of the truth, when viewed as distinct, and discriminated from all other mental acts. Some will be startled at this nakedness of faith; and many will be ready to object, that it is to make faith to be no more than a bare assent of the understanding to the truth: well, if it be uniformly accompanied by all holy affections and emotions, what is the difference? But I deny that, as described, it is a naked assent of the understanding, as those words are commonly understood. The wide distinction between the understanding and will, which has very much confounded our mental philosophy, has come down to us from the schoolmen. But in making the distinction, they made simple verity the object of the understanding. And that is what we commonly mean by bare assent; it relates to the simple truth; but the will has respect, they said, to good—every species of good.

Now the faith of which I have spoken, at the same time contemplates the truth, and the beauty, excellency, and goodness of the object, and also its adaptedness to our necessities: all these things are comprehended in the views which the Holy Spirit gives to the mind. Therefore, though faith be a simple uncompounded act, a firm belief or persuasion, it comprehends the objects ascribed both to the understanding and the will.

Here I shall be met by a definition of faith, which makes the act simple also—but considers that act to be trust or confidence. This the reader will remember is Dr. Dwight's definition of faith. And the only objection to it is, that it is too narrow to comprehend all that belongs to the subject. Trust is nothing else than the firm belief or persuasion of the truth of a promise. When we say that we trust or have confidence in a person, it relates to some promise. This definition comprehends all acts of faith which have a promise of God for their object, and these are certainly the most important acts, and accompanied with the most sensible emotions. But all divine truth is not in the form of a promise. The whole Word of God is the proper object of a true faith; and a large part of divine revelation is taken up with histories, prophecies, doctrines, and precepts. The Christian believes all these, as well as the promises.

Here faith is the first act of the regenerated soul; and the most important act, for it draws all holy affections and emotions in its train. But though it sweetly mingles with every other grace, it is distinct from them all. All its diversified acts arise from the nature of the truths believed, and men may enumerate and name as many of these acts as they please; still the nature of faith remains simple. It is a firm persuasion or belief of the truth, apprehended under the illumination of the Holy Spirit. It necessarily works by love and purifies the heart, for divine things thus discerned cannot but excite the affections to holy objects, by which sinful desires and appetites will be subdued; and when we are persuaded of the truth of God's gracious promises, there will always be a sweet repose of soul, because the promises contain the very blessings which we need; and to be assured that there are such blessings for all who will receive them, and especially if the soul is conscious that it is exercising faith, will produce sweet consolation—There is "joy and peace in believing". (Rom 15:13)

According to the view of faith now given, there is nothing mysterious about it. To believe in divine truth is an act of the mind, precisely the same as to believe in other truth; and the difference between a saving faith and a historical or merely speculative faith consists not in the truths believed, for in both they are the same; nor in the degree of assent given to the proposition—but in the evidence on which they are respectively founded. A saving faith is produced by the manifestation of the truth in its true nature to the mind, which now apprehends it, according to the degree of faith, in its spiritual qualities, its beauty, and glory, and sweetness; whereas a historical or speculative faith may rest on the prejudices of education, or the deductions of reason; but in its exercise there is no conception of the true qualities of divine things. The humblest, weakest believer possesses a knowledge of God, hidden from the wisest of unenlightened men; according to that saying of Christ, "I thank you, O Father, Lord of heaven and earth, that you have hidden these things from the wise and prudent, and have revealed them to babes." (Luke 10:21)

On the subject of experimental religion our dependence must not be on the theories of men—but on the unerring Word of God, and on the facts which have been observed in the experience of true Christians. In the exercises of new converts there is, in some respects, a remarkable similarity, and in others a remarkable variety. All are convinced of sin, not only of life but of heart. All are brought to acknowledge the justice of God in their condemnation, and to feel that they might be left to perish, without any derogation from the perfections of God; and that they have no ability to bring God under any obligations to save them, by their prayers, tears, or other religious duties. All true Christians, moreover, love the truth which has been revealed to their minds, and are led to trust in Christ alone for salvation; and they all hunger and thirst after righteousness, and resolve to devote themselves to the service of God, and prefer His glory above their chief joy. But besides those varieties already described, as arising from several causes, there is often much difference in their exercises, arising from the particular truths which they are led to contemplate when their eyes are first opened.

I do not mean to go over the ground which we have already passed, otherwise than by a statement of facts from authentic sources, which may serve to corroborate and illustrate the statements already given. Perhaps no man who has lived in modern times has had a better opportunity to form an accurate judgment of facts of this kind than Jonathan Edwards; and few men who ever lived were better qualified to discriminate between true and false religion. It is a thing much to be prized, that this great and good man has left a record of that most remarkable revival which took place in Northampton, New England, in the year 1734 and onwards. This narrative was written soon afterwards, and was communicated to Dr. Watts and Dr. Guyse, who united in a preface which accompanied the narrative, when published in London. In this account, carefully drawn up, we have a satisfactory account of the exercises of the subjects of the work, with the varieties which were observed in the experience of different people. The leading facts have here been selected from the narrative, so as to occupy the least possible room. To any who take an interest in this subject these facts cannot but be gratifying; and however the narrative may have been perused by some, yet it will not be disagreeable to them to have some of the prominent traits of the religious exercises at that time presented to them in a condensed form.

Edwards informs us, "that there was scarcely a single person in the town, old or young, left unconcerned about the great things of the eternal world"; and although he does not pretend to know the precise number of converts, he is of opinion that it could not be less, in the judgment of charity, than three hundred. Our object is not to abridge the narrative—but merely to select the account of the variety of exercises experienced, as there given. "There is a great variety," says he, "as to the degree of trouble and fear that people are exercised with before they attain any comfortable evidence of pardon and acceptance with God. Some are from the beginning carried on with abundantly more hope and encouragement than others. Some have had ten times less trouble than others, in whom the work yet appears the same in the outcome. ... The solemn apprehensions people have had of their misery have, for the most part, been increasing, the nearer they have approached to deliverance. Sometimes they think themselves wholly senseless, and fear that the Spirit of God has left them, and that they are given up to judicial hardness, yet they appear very deeply exercised with that fear, and in great earnestness to obtain conviction again. Many times, people under great awakenings were concerned because they thought they were not awakened—but miserably hardhearted, senseless, sottish creatures still, and sleeping on the brink of hell. ... People are sometimes brought to the borders of despair, and it looks as black as midnight to them, a little before the day dawns on their souls.

"The depravity of the heart has revealed itself in various exercises, in the time of legal convictions. Sometimes it appears as in a great struggle, like something roused by an enemy. Many in such circumstances have felt a great spirit of envy towards the godly, especially towards those thought to have been recently converted. As they are gradually more and more convinced of the corruption and wickedness of their hearts, they seem to themselves to grow worse and worse, harder and blinder, more desperately wicked, instead of growing better. ... When awakenings first begin, their consciences are commonly more exercised about their outward wicked courses—but afterwards are much more burdened with a sense of heart sins, the dreadful corruption of their nature, their enmity against God, the pride of their hearts, their unbelief, their rejection of Christ, the stubbornness of their will, and the like. ... Very often, under first awakenings, they set themselves to walk more strictly, confess their sins, and perform many religious duties, with a secret hope of appeasing God's anger. And sometimes, at first setting out, their affections are so moved that they are full of tears in their confessions and prayers, which they are ready to make much of, as if they were some atonement, and conceive that they grow better apace, and shall soon be converted; but their affections and hopes are short-lived, for they quickly find that they fail, and then they think themselves to be grown worse again. When they reflect on the wicked working of their hearts against God, they have more distressing apprehensions of His anger, and have great fears that God will never show mercy to them; or perhaps, that they have committed the unpardonable sin, and are often tempted to leave off in despair. ...

"When they begin to seek salvation, they are commonly profoundly ignorant of themselves. They are not sensible how blind they are, and how little they can do, to bring themselves to see spiritual things aright, and towards putting forth gracious exercises in their own souls. When they see unexpected pollution in themselves, they go about to wash their own defilements and make themselves clean; and they weary themselves in vain, until God shows them that it is in vain; and that their help is not where they have sought it. But some people continue to wander in such a labyrinth ten times as long as others, before their own experience will convince them of their own insufficiency—so that it is not their own experience at last that convinces them—but the Spirit of God.

"There have been some who have not had great terrors—but yet have had a very quick work. Some, who have not had very deep conviction before their conversion, have much more of it afterwards. God has appeared far from limiting Himself to any certain method in His proceedings with sinners under legal convictions. There is in nothing a greater difference in different people, than with respect to the time of their being under trouble: some but a few days, and others for months and years. As to those in whom legal convictions seem to have a saving outcome, the first thing that appears after their trouble is a conviction of the justice of God in their condemnation, from a sense of their exceeding sinfulness. Commonly, their minds, immediately before the discovery of God's justice, are exceedingly restless—in a kind of struggle or tumult; and sometimes in mere anguish; but commonly, as soon as they have this conviction, it immediately brings their minds to a calm and unexpected quietness and composure; and most frequently then, though not always, the pressing weight upon their spirits is taken off; or a general hope arises that some time God will be gracious, even before any distinct, particular discoveries of mercy. Commonly, they come to a conclusion that they will lie at God's feet and wait His time. ...

"That calm of spirit which follows legal conviction, in some instances continues some time before any special and delightful manifestation is made to the soul of the grace of God as revealed in the Gospel. But very often some comfortable and sweet views of a merciful God, of a sufficient Redeemer, or of some great and joyful things of the gospel, immediately follow, or in a very little time. And in some, the first sight of their desert of hell, of God's sovereignty in regard to their salvation, and a discovery of all-sufficient grace, are so near that they seem to go together. The gracious discoveries whence the first special comforts are derived, are in many respects very various. More frequently, Christ is distinctly made the object of the mind, in His all-sufficiency and willingness to save sinners; but some have their thoughts more especially fixed on God, in some of His sweet and glorious attributes manifested in the Gospel and shining forth of Jesus Christ. Some view the all-sufficiency of the grace of God—some chiefly, the infinite power of God and His ability to save them, and to do all things for them—and some look most to the truth and faithfulness of God. In some, the truth and certainty of the Gospel in general is the first joyful discovery they have: in others, the certain proof of some particular promise. In some, the grace and sincerity of God in His invitations, very commonly in some particular invitation, is before the mind. Some are struck with the glory and wonderfulness of the dying love of Christ; and others with the sufficiency of His blood, as offered to make an atonement for sin; and others again, with the value and glory of His obedience and righteousness. In many, the excellency and loveliness of Christ chiefly engage their thoughts, while in some, His divinity; being filled with the idea that He is indeed the Son of the living God; and in others, the excellency of the way of salvation by Christ, and the suitableness of it to their necessities. ... There is often in the mind some particular text of Scripture, holding forth some particular ground of consolation; at other times, a multitude of texts, gracious invitations, and promises, flowing in one after another, filling the soul more and more with comfort and satisfaction. Comfort is first given to some while reading some portion of Scripture; but in others it is attended with no particular Scripture at all. In some instances many divine things seem to be discovered to the soul at once, while others have their minds fixed on some one thing, and afterwards a sense of others is given; in some, with a slower, in others, a swifter succession.

"It must be confessed, that Christ is not always distinctly and explicitly thought of in the first sensible act of grace—though most commonly He is—but sometimes He is the object of the mind only implicitly. Thus when people have evidently appeared stripped of their own righteousness, and have stood condemned, as guilty of death, they have been comforted with a joyful and satisfactory evidence that the mercy and grace of God is sufficient for them—that their sins, though ever so great, shall be no hindrance to their being accepted—that there is mercy enough in God for the whole world, etc.—while they give no account of any particular or distinct thought of Christ; but yet it appears that the revelation of mercy in the Gospel is the ground of their encouragement and hope; yet such people afterwards obtain distinct and clear discoveries of Christ, accompanied with lively and special actings of faith and love towards Him. Frequently, when people have had the Gospel ground of relief opened to them, and have been entertaining their minds with the sweet prospect, they have thought nothing at that time of their being converted. The view is joyful to them as it is in its own nature glorious; gives them quite new and delightful ideas of God and Christ, and greatly encourages them to seek conversion, and begets in them a strong resolution to devote themselves to God and His Son. There is wrought in them a holy repose of soul in God through Christ, with a secret disposition to fear and love Him, and to hope for blessings from Him in this way, yet they have no conception that they are now converted; it does not so much as come into their minds. They know not that the sweet complacence they feel in the mercy and complete salvation of God, as it includes pardon and sanctification and is held forth to them through Christ, is a true receiving of this mercy, or a plain evidence of their receiving it. Many continue a long time in a course of gracious exercises and experiences, and do not think themselves to be converted—but conclude otherwise; and none knows how long they would continue so, were they not helped by particular instructions. There are undoubted instances of some who lived in this way for many years together. Those who, while under legal convictions, have had the greatest terrors, have not always obtained the greatest light and comfort; nor has the light always been most speedily communicated; but yet I think the time of conversion has been most sensible in such people. Converting influences commonly bring an extraordinary conviction of the certainty and reality of the great things of religion; though in some this is much greater, some time after conversion, than at first."

The religious exercises contained in the preceding statement will not be new to those who have been at all conversant with revivals. Such will recognize, in the account, what they have observed, and will be gratified to find the same facts which they have observed, recorded and published by such a master in Israel. Almost the only remark which I feel disposed to make is, that it is too commonly supposed that the time of receiving comfort is always the time of regeneration; whereas this might rather be termed the time of conversion; for then the exercises of the renewed soul come to a crisis, and faith, which was before weak and obscure, shines forth with vigor. Perhaps it is the prevalent opinion among orthodox writers that the first views of the renovated soul are views of Christ; and when mere legal convictions are immediately followed by such views and their attendant consolations, this opinion may be correct; but in many cases it is reasonable to believe that the convictions experienced are those of the true penitent. And as, in almost all cases here recorded and observed by others, there is a distinct view and approbation of God's justice in the condemnation of the sinner, I cannot but think, agreeably to what was stated in a former chapter, that the soul has passed from death unto life before these feelings are experienced; and that may help to account for the remarkable calm which now follows the dark and stormy night. This revelation of Jesus Christ in the believer may be compared to the birth of a child into the light of this world; but its conception was long before. And so this interesting point in experience is the new birth—but the principle of spiritual life commonly exists before. Besides, comfort is no sure evidence of a genuine birth; some who become strong men in the Lord are born in sorrow. They weep before they are able to smile; but in the spiritual birth, joy and sorrow often sweetly mingle their streams.

There are two reasons why faith, though one of the simplest exercises of the mind, is represented as having so many different acts; the one is the great variety in the truths believed; and the other that, commonly, various exercises are included in the account of faith, which do always accompany or follow a true faith—but do not appertain to its essence. As faith has all revealed truth for its object, the feelings produced in the mind correspond with the particular nature of the truth which is at any time in the contemplation of the mind. If, by the soul under the illumination of the Holy Spirit, the law is viewed in its spirituality and moral excellence, while there will be experienced an approbation of the will of God thus expressed, yet a lively sense of the sinfulness of our hearts and lives must be the predominant feeling. This discovery of the purity of the law, and this deep feeling of the evil of sin, commonly precede any clear view of Christ and the plan of salvation; and this has given rise to the prevalent opinion that repentance goes before faith in the natural order of pious exercises. But, according to our idea of faith, as given above, it must necessarily precede and be the cause of every other gracious exercise. Commonly, indeed, when we speak of faith, we describe its maturity; but there are often many obscure but real acts of faith, before the soul apprehends the fullness and excellency and suitableness of Christ. And in many cases, when some view of the plan of salvation is obtained, the single truth believed is the ability of Christ to save; and even the full persuasion of this gives rise to joy, when the soul has been long cast down with gloomy forebodings of everlasting misery, and with the apprehension that, for such a sinner, there was no salvation.

As faith does no more than bring the truth before the mind in its true nature, every act of faith must, of course, be characterized by the qualities of the truth thus presented, and by its adaptation to the circumstances and convictions of the sinner. All those acts of faith which bring the extent and spirituality of the law of God fully into view must be accompanied with painful emotions, on account of the deep conviction of lack of conformity to that perfect rule, which cannot but be experienced when that object is before the mind. But all those invitations, promises, and declarations which exhibit a Savior and the method of recovery, when truly believed under a just apprehension of their nature, must be accompanied, not only with love—but joy and hope, and a free consent to be saved in God's appointed way; and when the previous distress and discouragement have been great, and the views of Gospel truth clear, the joy is overflowing, and as long as these views are unclouded, peace flows like a river.

But even in the discoveries which faith makes of Christ, there is a great variety in the extent and combination of divine truth which comes before the mind at any one time. Probably no two people, in believing, have precisely the same truths in all their relations, presented to them; and not only so—but it is hardly credible that the same believer, in his various contemplations of divine truth, takes in exactly the same field of view at different times. Hence it appears that the whole power of faith is derived from the importance, excellence, amiableness, and suitableness of the truths believed. And when faith is "imputed for righteousness", (Rom 4:22) it is not the simple act of faith which forms a righteousness. If any exercise of the renewed mind could constitute a righteousness, it would be love, which, according to its strength, is "the fulfilling of the law"; (Rom 13:10) but when the soul by faith is fully persuaded that Christ is the end of the law for righteousness, this righteousness of the Surety, when received by faith, is imputed; and by this alone, which is perfect, can God be just in justifying the ungodly. "Faith thus receiving and resting on Christ and His righteousness, is the solitary instrument of justification; yet is it not alone in the person justified—but is ever accompanied with all other saving graces, and is no dead faith—but works by love." (WCF 11.2)

"By this faith, a Christian believes to be true whatever is revealed in the Word, for the authority of God Himself speaking therein; and acts differently upon that which each particular passage thereof contains; yielding obedience to the commands, trembling at the threatenings, and embracing the promises of God for this life, and that which is to come. But the principal acts of faith are, accepting, receiving, and resting upon Christ alone for justification, sanctification, and eternal life, by virtue of the covenant of grace." (WCF 14.2) This quotation; taken from a formulary known to many of my readers, contains as just and comprehensive a view of the nature of saving faith as could be given in words.

But another reason why so many divine acts are attributed to faith is, because other exercises are included in the description of faith, which though they always accompany it, ought not to be confounded with it. It was, two hundred years ago, a question much agitated among the divines of Holland, whether love entered into the essence of faith. And in our own country, faith and love have not been kept distinct. A very prevalent system of theology makes the essence of faith to be love. Much evil arises from confounding what are so clearly distinguished in the Word of God. If faith and love were identical, how could it be said that "faith works by love"? (Gal 5:6) The apostle Paul speaks of faith, hope, and love, as so distinct, that, although they are all necessary, they may be compared as to excellency—"The greatest of these is charity". (1 Cor 13:13) The celebrated Witsius, in his Economy of the Covenants, in describing faith, among the various acts which he attributes to this divine principle, reckons "love of the truth", (2 Thess 2:10) and "hungering and thirsting after Christ". (Matt 5:6) Now, it is an abuse of language to say that faith loves or desires; faith works by love, and excites hungering and thirsting desires after Christ.

But, it may be asked, if these graces are inseparably connected, why be so solicitous to distinguish them? First, because in so doing we follow the sacred writers; secondly, because it has a bad effect to use a Scriptural word to express what it was never designed to express; and, thirdly, because of the special office of faith in a sinner's justification; in which neither love nor any other grace has any part, although they are the effects of faith. When love is confounded with a justifying faith, it is very easy to slide into the opinion that as love is the substance of evangelical obedience, when we are said to be justified by faith, the meaning is, that we are justified by our own obedience. And accordingly, in a certain system of divinity valued by many, the matter is thus stated: faith is considered a comprehensive term for all evangelical obedience. The next step is—and it has already been taken by some—that our obedience is meritorious, and when its defects are purged by atoning blood it is sufficient to procure for us a title to eternal life. Thus have some, boasting of the name of Protestants, worked around, until they have fallen upon one of the most offensive tenets of Popery. But it would be difficult to bring a true penitent to entertain the opinion that his own works were meritorious, or could in the least recommend him to God. The whole of God's dealings with the souls of His own people effectually dispel from their minds every feeling of this kind. The very idea of claiming merit is most abhorrent to their feelings.

But while it is of importance to distinguish faith from every other grace, yet it is necessary to insist on the fact that that faith which does not produce love and other holy affections is not a genuine faith. In the apostles' days a set of libertines arose who boasted of their faith—but they performed no good works to evince the truth of their faith. Against such the apostle James writes, and proves that such a faith was no better than that of devils, and would justify no man; that the faith of Abraham and other believers, which did justify, was not a dead faith—but living; not a barren faith—but productive of good works, and proved itself to be genuine by the acts of duty which it induced the believer to perform.

While then faith stands foremost in the order of gracious exercises because it is necessary to the existence of every other, love may be said to be the center around which all the virtues of the Christian revolve, and from which they derive their nature. Love of some kind is familiar to the experience of all people; and all love is attended with some pleasure in its exercise; but it varies on account of the difference of the objects of affection. Divine love is itself a delightful and soul-satisfying exercise. The soul which has tasted the goodness of God is convinced that nothing more is necessary to complete felicity than the perfection of love. This supposes, however, that our love to God is ever accompanied with some sense of His love to us. Love, unless reciprocated, would not fill up the cup of human happiness. But to love God, and be loved by Him—this is heaven! And "we love Him because he first loved us". (1 John 4:19) In the first exercises of a renewed mind, love to God and love to man are both brought into action; but often the prospect of deliverance from eternal misery which threatened may absorb the attention. It is indeed a marvelous deliverance, to be snatched from the verge of hell and assured of everlasting life; what a tumult of feeling must it create? But notwithstanding this, it frequently happens that in the first discoveries of the plan of salvation, the soul loses sight of its own interest, and is completely occupied in contemplating and admiring the wisdom, love, and justice of God, as exhibited in the cross of the Lord Jesus Christ. Indeed, the believer, when these spiritual discoveries are afforded, thinks nothing of the nature of those acts which he is exercising; and it may not be until long afterwards that he recognizes these outgoings of soul to be true love to the Savior.

There are two affections, distinct from each other in their objects, which are included under the term love; the one terminates on the goodness or moral excellence of its object, and varies according to the particular view, at any time enjoyed, of the divine attributes. This comprehends all pious affections and emotions arising from the contemplation of the perfections of God; and some of them, such as reverence and humility, would not fall under the name of love, when taken in a strict sense; but when used as a general term for our whole obedience, it must comprehend them all. This may, for convenience, be called the love of delight, in which the rational soul delights in the character of God as revealed in His word.

The other affection called love has not the character of the person beloved for its object—but his happiness. It may be intensely exercised towards those in whose moral qualities there can be no delight, and is called the love of benevolence. God's love to sinners is of this kind; and this is the kind of love which Christians are bound to exercise to all men in the world, even to those that hate and persecute them. Though the love of benevolence may exist without the love of delight, yet the converse cannot be asserted. No one ever felt love to the character of another without desiring his happiness. Before conversion, the soul is sordidly selfish—but no sooner does this change take place than the heart begins to be enlarged with an expansive benevolence. The whole world is embraced in its charity. "Good will to man" (Luke 2:14) is a remarkable characteristic of the "new creature"; (2 Cor 5:17; Gal 6:15) and this intense desire for the salvation of our fellow men, and ardent wish that they may all become interested in that Savior whom we have found to be so precious, is the true source of the missionary spirit, and is the foundation, often, of laborious and long continued exertions to prepare for the holy ministry; and prompts and inclines delicate females to consent to leave all the endearments of home, for arduous labor in a foreign and sometimes a savage land.

But however lively the affection of love in the exercises of the real Christian, he never can lose sight of his own unworthiness. Indeed, the brighter his discoveries of the divine glory, and the stronger his love, the deeper are his views of the turpitude of sin. The more he is elevated in affection and assured hope, the deeper is he dismayed in humility and self-abasement. His penitential feelings, from the nature of the case, keep pace with his love and joy; and when his tears flow in copious showers, he would be at a loss to tell whether he was weeping for joy or for sorrow. He might say, for both; for in these pious exercises, these opposite emotions sweetly mingle their streams; and so delightful is this mingling of affections naturally opposite, that the person could hardly be persuaded that the sweet would be as agreeable without, as with, the bitter. One hour spent under the cross, while the soul is thus elevated, thus abased—thus joyful, and thus sorrowful—is better than a thousand of earthly delights.

Observe, Bunyan does not make the burden of Christian fall off instantly on his entering in at the strait gate; but when, as he traveled, he came in sight of the cross. Then, in a moment, those cords which had bound it to his back, and which none could loose, were burst asunder, and his burden fell off and never was fastened on him again, although he lay so long in the prison of Giant Despair. The feelings of a renewed heart are never afterwards the same as under legal conviction. There are scenes, in the experience of the lively Christian, of which the wise men of the world never dream; and which, if they were told of them, they would not believe; and these things, while they are hidden from the wise and prudent, are revealed unto babes. The secret of the Lord is with those who fear him. The soul which has thus returned from its wanderings to its Bishop and Shepherd feels under the strongest obligations to live for God—to deny itself—to forsake the world—to do anything—be anything—or suffer anything, which may be for the honor of its divine Master. Hence a new life commences—a new spirit is manifested—and the new man, in spite of all his remaining ignorance and imperfection, gives lucid evidence to all who carefully observe him that he has been with Jesus, and has been baptized with the Holy Spirit; and the more frequently these views and exercises are reiterated, the more spiritual and heavenly is his conversation. This is a light which cannot be hid, and which ought to shine more and more unto the perfect day. Hear then the exhortation of the apostle Jude, "But you, beloved, building up yourselves on your most holy faith, praying in the Holy Spirit, keep yourselves in the love of God, looking for the mercy of our Lord Jesus Christ unto eternal life." (Jude 20-21)

Chapter 7: Considerations on dreams, visions, etc. Remarkable conversion of a blind infidel from hearing the Bible read

There are many professors of religion in our country who, if they should peruse this work, would imagine a great defect in the account given of a sinner's conversion, because nothing has been said about dreams and visions, or voices and lights, of a supernatural kind. During the various religious excitements which extended over the Southern States, under the preaching of different denominations, there was mingled with the good influence by which sinners were converted and reformed, no small degree of enthusiasm, which led the people to seek and expect extraordinary revelations, which were supposed to be granted in dreams or visions. Indeed, at one time, the leaders in a very general excitement which occurred in Virginia about the commencement of the Revolutionary war were impressed with the idea that they possessed precisely the same gifts and powers which had been bestowed upon the apostles; and this enthusiastic idea would have spread widely if they had not failed, in some private attempts, to work miracles.

But the opinion that certain people had an extraordinary call from God to preach, and that they needed neither learning nor study to enable them to preach the gospel, continued to prevail for a long time; and this species of enthusiasm is not entirely passed away even to this day. Such preachers were much in the habit of declaiming in every sermon against letter-learned and college-bred ministers, and they seldom failed to inform their hearers that they had selected the subject of discourse after entering the pulpit; and some of them even gloried that they had never learned to read, as they believed that all learning interfered with the inspiration of the Spirit, which they were confident that they possessed. While this notion of an extraordinary call and immediate inspiration was common, it is not surprising that the people should have entertained wild opinions respecting the nature of conversion. As it was customary to give the narratives of religious experience in public, not only in the presence of the church—but of a promiscuous assembly, there was a strong temptation to tell an extraordinary story; and the more miraculous it was, the higher evidence it was supposed to afford of being the work of God, concerning the genuineness of which the subject never expressed a doubt. Seldom was a narrative of experience heard which did not contain something supernatural; such as a remarkable prophetic dream; a vision; a sudden and brilliant light shining around, as in the case of Paul; or an audible voice, calling them by name, or uttering some text of Scripture, or some other encouraging words. Sometimes, however, the cause of experimental religion was sadly dishonored by the ludicrous stories of poor ignorant people—especially the unlettered slaves; for this religious concern seized upon them with mighty force, and many of them, I doubt not, were savingly converted.

The philosophy of dreams is very little understood: and it is not our purpose to entertain or perplex the reader with any theories on the subject. Dreams have by some been divided into natural, divine, and diabolical. The wise man says, "A dream comes through the multitude of business." Most dreams are undoubtedly the effect of the previous state of the mind, and of the peculiar circumstances and state of the body at the time. Most people find their thoughts, in sleep, occupied with those things which gave them concern when awake; and every cause which disorders the stomach or nerves gives a character to our dreams. Most people have experienced the distress of feverish dreams. But there are sometimes remarkable dreams, which leave on the mind the strong impression that they have a meaning, and portend coming events. And that there have been dreams of this description, we learn from the authority of the Bible; and these prophetic dreams were not confined to the servants of God, as we learn from the instances of the butler and baker, in the prison of Pharaoh, and from the remarkable dream of Pharaoh himself. All these must have proceeded from some supernatural influence, as, when interpreted by Joseph, they clearly predicted future events, of which the people dreaming had not the least knowledge. So, Nebuchadnezzar's dream contained a symbolical representation of future events of great importance, which, however, neither he nor his wise men understood, but which was interpreted by Daniel by divine inspiration.

Why God so frequently made His communications to His servants by dreams, is not easily explained. Perhaps the mind is better prepared for such revelations when external objects are entirely excluded; or it might have been to obviate that terror and perturbation to which all men were subject when an angel or spirit appeared to them. Whether God ever now communicates anything by dreams is much disputed. Many, no doubt, deceive themselves by fancying that their dreams are supernatural; and some have been sadly deluded by trusting to dreams; and certainly people ought not to be encouraged to look for revelations in dreams. But there is nothing inconsistent with reason or Scripture in supposing that, on some occasions, certain communications, intended for the warning or safety of the individual himself, or of others, may be made in dreams. To doubt of this is to run counter to a vast body of testimony in every age. And if ideas received in dreams produce a beneficial effect, in rendering the careless serious, or the sorrowful comfortable, in the view of divine truth, very well; such dreams may be considered providential, if not divine. But if any are led by dreams to pursue a course repugnant to the dictates of common sense or the precepts of Scripture, such dreams may rightly be considered diabolical.

Some people have supposed that they experienced a change of mind while asleep. They have gone to rest with a heart unsubdued and unconverted, and their first waking thoughts have been of faith and love. Some have sunk to sleep, worn down with distress, and in their sleep have received comfort, as they supposed, from a believing view of Christ. Such changes are suspicious; but if they are proved to be genuine by the future life of the person, we should admit the possibility of God's giving a new heart. Or truth may be as distinctly impressed on people's minds in sleep as when they are awake. Some people appear to have their faculties in more vigorous exercise, in some kinds of sleep, than when their senses are all exercised.

John Fletcher of Madeley, 1729-1785, relates that he had a dream of the judgment day, the effect of which was a deep and abiding impression of eternal things on his mind. As the scene was vividly painted on his imagination, and the representation of truth was as distinct and coherent as if he had been awake, it may be gratifying to the reader to have the account of it set before him.

Fletcher had been variously exercised about religion before this. "I was," says he, "in this situation, when a dream, in which I am obliged to acknowledge the hand of God, roused me from my security. Suddenly the heavens were darkened and clouds rolled along in terrific majesty, and a thundering voice like a trumpet, which penetrated to the center of the earth, exclaimed, "Arise, you dead, and come out of your graves." Instantly the earth and the sea gave up the dead which they contained, and the universe was crowded with living people who appeared to come out of their graves by millions. But what a difference among them! Some, convulsed with despair, endeavored in vain to hide themselves in their tombs, and cried to the hills to fall on them, and the mountains to cover them from the face of the holy Judge; while others rose with seraphic wings above the earth which had been the theater of their conflicts and their victory. Serenity was painted on their countenances, joy sparkled in their eyes, and dignity was impressed on every feature. My astonishment and terror were redoubled when I perceived myself raised up with this innumerable multitude into the vast regions of the air, from whence my affrighted eyes beheld this globe consumed by the flames, the heavens on fire, and the dissolving elements ready to pass away. But what did I feel, when I beheld the Son of man coming in the clouds of heaven, in all the splendor of His glory, crowned with the charms of His mercy, and surrounded with the terrors of His justice; ten thousand thousands went before him, and millions pressed upon his footsteps. All nature was silent. The wicked were condemned, and the sentence was pronounced—the air gave way under the feet of those who surrounded me, a yawning gulf received them and closed upon them. At the same time He who sat upon the throne exclaimed, 'Come, you blessed of my Father, inherit the kingdom prepared for you from the foundation of the world.' (Matt 25:34) Happy children of God! I cried, You are exalted in triumph with your Redeemer, and my dazzled eyes will soon lose sight of you, in the blaze of light which surrounds you. Wretch that I am, what words can express the horrors of my situation! A fixed and severe look from the Judge, as He departed, pierced me to the heart, and my anguish and confusion were extreme, when a brilliant personage despatched from the celestial throng thus addressed me: 'Slothful servant, what are you doing here? Do you presume to follow the Son of God, whom you have served merely with your lips, while your heart was far from Him? Show me the seal of your salvation and the pledge of your redemption. Examine your heart, and see if you can discover there a real love to God, and a living faith in His Son? Ask your conscience what were the motives of your pretended good works? Do you not see that pride and self-love were the source of them? Do you not see that the fear of hell rather than the fear of offending God, restrained you from sin?' After these words he paused; and regarding me with a compassionate air, seemed to await my reply. But conviction and terror closed my mouth, and he thus resumed his discourse, 'Withhold no longer from God the glory which is due to Him. Turn to Him with all your heart, and become a new creature. Watch and pray, (Matt 26:41; Mark 13:33) was the command of the Son of God; but instead of having done this by working out your salvation with fear and trembling, (Phil 2:12) you have slept the sleep of security. At this very moment—do you not sleep in that state of lethargy and spiritual death, from which the Word of God, the exhortations of His servants, and the strivings of His grace have not been sufficient to deliver you? Time is swallowed up in eternity. There is no more place for repentance. You have obstinately refused to glorify God's mercy in Christ Jesus—go then, slothful servant and glorify His justice.' Having uttered these words he disappeared, and, at the same time, the air gave way under my feet—the abyss began to open—dreadful wailings assailed my ears, and a whirlwind of smoke surrounded me. The agitation of my mind and body awoke me, the horror of which nothing can equal, and the mere recollection of which still makes me tremble. O how happy I felt on awaking to find that I was still in the land of mercy, and the day of salvation! O my God, I cried, grant that this dream may continually influence my sentiments and my conduct! May it prove a powerful stimulus to excite me to prepare continually for the coming of my great

Master!"

By this dream Fletcher was convinced that he had been indulging vain hopes, and that his mind was still unrenewed. His conviction of this truth, however, did not rest entirely nor chiefly on what had been told him in his dream—but he now set to work in sober earnest to examine his religious principles and motives by the Scriptures; and the more he examined the more fully was he convinced that he was yet in an unconverted state. From this time he began with all earnestness to seek for justification through the blood of Christ; and never rested until he found peace with God by a living faith in the truth and promises of God.

I will conclude this discussion by citing the words of that remarkable young sage of remote antiquity, Elihu, the reprover of both Job and his friends, and the sublime defender of God and His dispensations. "For God speaks once, yes twice, yet man perceives it not. In a dream, in a vision of the night, when deep sleep falls upon men, in slumberings upon the bed. Then he opens the ears of men and seals their instruction." (Job 33:14-16)

Sometime in the year 1811, the substance of the following narrative was put into my hands by Dr. William M. Tennent of Abington, Pennsylvania, when this excellent man was on his deathbed and near his end. It will be seen that it was drawn up with a view to publication as soon as the subject of the memoir, who was then alive in Dr. Tennent's congregation, should be called home to his rest. That event occurred some time since; and in communicating this memoir to the public, the writer considers himself as fulfilling an implied promise when he accepted the manuscript.

Having, however, ascertained that Mrs. Ann Snowden of Philadelphia was the lady at whose house this gentleman resided, and that she was the person by whom the Scriptures were read; and knowing, also, that she was both pious and intelligent, I requested her to put down on paper an exact account of this pleasing and remarkable event; which she did with the utmost readiness. From these authentic sources the following narrative is derived; and will be given, with very slight verbal alterations, in the very words of the respected people named.

Mr. Tennent's narrative proceeds as follows: "George Inglis was born in the city of Philadelphia, of honorable parentage, and received a liberal education in the university of that city, which was completed between his 16th and 17th year. Having served a regular apprenticeship to a merchant, he entered into the mercantile business and settled in the island of Jamaica, where he continued about eleven years. Very early in life he began to drink in iniquity like water, manifested strong prejudices against serious people and serious things; associated with the mirthful, libertine, and dissipated. His propensities to sinful indulgences increased with his years, and in the island where he resided, temptations being increased, and the means of restraint from wicked courses diminished, he became more and more confirmed in the habits of sin, until at length he was given up to almost every species of iniquity. Amidst his open and avowed enmity to God and true religion, an awful tornado fell upon that part of the island where he resided, by which he lost the greater part of his property, and was compelled to return to the American continent. This happened during the revolutionary war. All this made no alteration in his morals for the better—but the more he was corrected, the more hardened he grew, casting off the fear of God, and putting to defiance the scourges of Jehovah. Thus he continued, until some years afterwards, being in the town of Manchester, Virginia, without any natural (known) cause to produce the effect, he was smitten by the immediate hand of God while in the possession of good health, with the total loss of sight within a few days. In this situation his mind was all distraction. His cry was to man only for help; but to God his Maker, who gives songs in the night to the afflicted and oppressed, he had not learned to cry. This lesson, however, he was taught not long afterwards."

Thus far the narrative has been given in the words of Dr. Tennent; it will now be proper to hear Mrs. Snowden's account of the conversion of this man, as she was the only human instrument made use of in bringing him to the knowledge of the truth. It is in the form of a letter addressed to the writer.

"Pastor and Dear Sir—I will now endeavor to fulfill the promise made to you some time ago, by giving such information as is within my recollection, respecting the case of George Inglis. That gentleman, a native of Philadelphia, had received a classical education, and with it every indulgence which a father's partiality could bestow. Brought up in the mirthful world, it is to be feared there was but little attention paid to his immortal interests. After spending the time necessary to acquire the knowledge of mercantile affairs, he left the city for the West Indies, where he was, for a while, successful in business, and found himself in circumstances to visit England; and, while in London, throwing aside every restraint, he indulged himself in all the amusements and levities of that mirthful metropolis. Returning to America, he engaged in business in the State of Virginia. After residing some time there, it pleased the Lord to deprive him of his sight, an affliction at that time looked upon by him as insupportable, for he saw not the hand from whence it came; but after he was made sensible that he was a brand snatched from the burning, often have I heard him bless the chastisement as that of a tender Father.

"Inglis had weak eyes from an early age—but his blindness came on him suddenly. Finding no relief from the physicians where he resided, he left Virginia for Philadelphia; and upon the application of his friends, was received, with his servant, into my house as a boarder. I found him a man of strong passions, impatient under sufferings, and not willing to submit to restraints of any kind. When the physicians of the city were consulted, they gave his friends no hope of the recovery of his eyesight: they soothed him with the promise of a further consideration of his case. A few weeks after he came to my house, a gentleman very much celebrated as an eye doctor came to the city. Inglis applied to him for advice. He did not tell him that his was an incurable case—but said that he would see him again. He bore this very impatiently, observing to me that life was now becoming an intolerable burden; but that he had this consolation, that he had it in his power at any time to lay it down. It was but to increase the quantity of opium (he was in the habit of taking opium) and all his sufferings would be at an end; and that, after another visit from the doctor, if he found there was no hope of his recovering his sight, he would certainly take that method of putting an end to his existence.

I remonstrated with him on the impropriety of his behavior, alleging that he had no more right to take away his own life than he had to take away the life of his neighbor; asking him if he had considered the consequences of rushing uncalled into the presence of his Maker. His answer was, that he had considered it well; and he advocated his opinion on this principle, that he was by a merciful Creator placed on this earth to enjoy the good things of this life as far as it was in his power honestly to obtain them—that the duties required of him were, to be as useful to his friends in particular, and society at large, as his circumstances would admit of—that having lost his sight, he would no longer enjoy any happiness here, would become a burden to his friends, and could be of no use in the world. He alleged that the purposes for which life was given to him were now defeated; of course there would be no impropriety in laying it down. I made some remarks on what he had advanced as his sentiments and, to strengthen what I said, quoted some passages of Scripture. These he treated in a very light manner—spoke of the Bible as the work of men—contrived to keep the ignorant in awe—with many other observations too common with men of deistical principles. I then inquired if he had ever read the Bible; he frankly acknowledged that he had not since he left school. Upon asking him if he had not read the works of those that were opposed to the Scriptures, he admitted that he had. If so, I observed, he must have formed his opinions from the avowed enemies of that sacred book. Was this a fair method of proceeding? I said that I thought he would not act thus, on any other occasion. This book you acknowledge you have not read since you were a boy. All that you know about it, you have from the enemies of the Christian religion. Taking these things into consideration, I hope you will no more speak against the Bible, as it is a book that you have never read since you were capable of forming a judgment of its contents. He apologized in a sincere manner for what he had said, acknowledged that he was wrong in speaking as he had done, and expressed a wish to have it read to him. This I declined, and gave my reasons for so doing, which were, that a man so prejudiced as he appeared to be, was not likely to profit by the reading of the Bible, that he would most probably cavil at, and perhaps ridicule it; in so doing, he would wound my feelings without benefitting himself; for I considered it as the Word of God, and my hopes of eternal salvation rested on the truths contained in it. He then assured me on the word of a gentleman, that if I would read it to him, whatever his opinions might be, he would carefully avoid saying anything that might have a tendency to wound my feelings, or give offence, in the smallest degree. There was an earnestness in his manner of addressing me which satisfied my mind that he was sincerely desirous to have the Scriptures read to him, and the next day was fixed upon for that purpose.

"It appeared to me that he waited impatiently for the arrival of the appointed hour, for no sooner did the time come than he sent for me. Before we began, I observed to him that, as in the New Testament he would find the fulfilment of the promises of the Savior, I would point out those promises as they occur in reading the Old Testament, which it would be necessary for him to take notice of as we proceeded. Beginning then with Gen 1, before we had gone through the chapter he stopped me to express his admiration of the language. 'It was sublime beyond anything he had ever read.' While I was reading, he was all attention; and when the time arrived when I was under the necessity of stopping, it was with regret that he observed that I had finished; putting me in mind, at the same time, of my promise to attend to him, on the next day.

"I think it was on the second day of my reading to him, that he cried out, 'What a wretch am I to have spoken against such a book! a book that I knew nothing of, having never given it an attentive perusal.' I went on for a few days, reading to him according to the plan laid down, which was one hour every day; when the distress of his mind greatly increased. There was now no more said about a second visit to the doctor—no complaints—no murmurings on account of the loss of sight. He now saw the hand of God in the dispensation of His providence, and would acknowledge that it was less, far less, than he deserved. My family duties preventing me from being with him as much as I wished, I now called in the aid of some of my pious friends, among whom was Joseph Eastburn, to converse with him and to assist in reading to him. Several religious books were now occasionally read to him, among which were Boston's Fourfold State, Newton's Works, Hervey's Dialogues, etc. The descriptive parts of the last mentioned author were at his request passed over, except where it more fully served to explain the doctrines of free grace—a subject to him of the deepest interest. Though totally deprived of sight, and unaccustomed to go out, he now neglected no opportunity of hearing the Word of God, attending sermons on Sabbaths, and weekly societies as often as was in his power. As might be expected, his natural disposition, sometimes getting the better of the good resolutions he had formed, would betray him into a fretfulness that was troublesome to his friends and occasioned much uneasiness to himself. On such occasions I have heard him lament deeply over his sinful nature, accusing himself of ingratitude to that God who had mercifully stopped him in his career of vice, by depriving him of the light of day and enlightening his darkened mind, and had enabled him to understand the truths contained in His blessed word. I do not recollect how long he stayed with me—but it was something less than a year, when his friends thought it would be best to remove him to the country; and boarding was obtained for him in the neighborhood of the Rev. Dr. Tennent of Abington."

Dr. Tennent, in the memoir already quoted, after mentioning some circumstances which have been given in detail in a former page, goes on to say, "It pleased God by these means to bring him to very serious and deep impressions of His moral character, and to constrain him, after some time, to attempt to pray. This change was effected in the gentleness, kindness, and tenderness of infinite mercy, and without those horrors which often precede the conversion of highhanded and daring sinners. In his case, all was mercy, without extraordinary terror. He was embraced in the arms of redeeming love, and delivered from the fiery pit without beholding its awful flames. In his first attempt to supplicate God, he was principally affected with a sense of the wickedness of his conduct, and his vile ingratitude for the mercies bestowed, and this exercise was accompanied with an involuntary flow of tears and a desire to call God his Father, and afterwards to mention the blessed name of Jesus the Savior. Probably this was the beginning of his new birth, and the hour of his conversion; which was not long afterwards confirmed by a remarkable vision of two books, with a glorious light shining in the midst of them, as he was lying in his bed; which he apprehended to be the Old and New Testaments of the living God, presenting to, and impressing on his mind this sacred declaration—but without a voice, 'This is the Way,' and filling his soul at the same time with inexpressible joy."

What is here related is no doubt strictly true—but there is no propriety in calling it "a vision", since it can easily be accounted for by a vivid impression on the imagination. A vision is something supernatural seen with the bodily eyes; but this man was totally blind; the objects so clearly discerned must then have been from impressions on the imagination. But in saying this, it is not intended to deny that the cause was the Spirit of God. This divine Agent can and does produce vivid impressions on the imagination, which have so much the appearance of external realities, that many are persuaded that they do see and hear what takes place only in their own minds.

"In the year 1790, Inglis was removed to Abington, and became a boarder in the house of Dr. William M. Tennent, and soon afterwards was admitted to the communion of the church in that place, with which he has walked steadfastly in the faith ever since, exemplifying in a striking and high degree the power of God's grace in the 'new creation'. From the beginning of his turning to God, there was abundant proof that 'old things had passed away, and that all things had become new'. (2 Cor 5:17) Before, a blasphemer—but now a worshiper of the true God. Before, a drunkard and a Sabbath-breaker, unclean, a ridiculer of holy things, and indulging habitually in all ungodliness and wickedness—led captive by the prince of the power of the air, who rules in the children of disobedience—but now, freed from his bonds and made by sovereign grace to rejoice in the liberty of the Gospel. Before, a hater of godly men and godly things—but now a lover of both. He was made to hunger and thirst after righteousness—after the bread of life—after the knowledge of His will; and seemed only to be happy when he had a glimpse of His glory. For more than a year after his conversion, he could not bear to hear any other book read to him than the Holy Scriptures and the most practical authors on religion. He shunned all political conversation, the reading of newspapers, and whatever might divert his thoughts from holy meditations and a further knowledge of his Redeemer.

"While residing in his first permanent lodgings in the country, it may not be improper to mention a second remarkable vision which he had. Walking in the garden one day, as he usually did for sacred meditation, he was suddenly arrested and overcome with a most affecting view of his Savior, as suspended on the cross and bearing his very sins. In this vision of redeeming love he was so lost that he knew not where he was—overwhelmed with unutterable joy and the most affecting gratitude for the discharge of the immense debt which he owed to the justice of a holy God. The impressions then made are still kept in strong remembrance. How long he was in this state he knew not—but was finally conducted to the house, after having called for a guide—full of joy and gladness: a second remarkable proof of his interest in gospel redemption."

We will simply repeat our objection to the use of the word "vision" to represent what was nothing more than a strong, believing view of the scene of the crucifixion; accompanied, no doubt, with a vivid imagination of the bleeding, dying Savior suffering for his sins.

"The writer will only add that he has frequently, for some twenty years, heard Inglis say he would not, if it had been within the power of a wish, have had his natural sight restored, having found his eyes such an avenue to sin. His whole conduct since his conversion has corresponded with his profession as a Christian disciple. He has, in the view of his brethren where he resides, made a visible growth in grace, even in the knowledge of our Lord and Savior Jesus Christ. He has, with others traveling to the same blessed country, been on the mount and in the valley—an humble, meek, patient, self-denying Christian, rejoicing in the hopes of a better country—weeping on account of his own unfruitfulness—looking for strength to vanquish his enemies, and hoping for victory by the merits of the great Redeemer. Hitherto steadfast, may he hold fast unto the end! and may many such be added unto the Lord! Blessed be God for the gift of His Son, for the revelation of His incomprehensible love and grace, and for the crown of glory which is laid up for all who are looking and longing for His second appearance!"

The foregoing account was written about thirty years ago, and Inglis, who was then aged, did not depart this life until two or three years since. As Robert Steel had succeeded Dr. Tennent as pastor of the Presbyterian church at Abington, I requested him to give me notice of the old gentleman's death, with an account of his state of mind in his latter days. This he did, and I regret that I have mislaid his letter, so that I cannot at present put my hands on it. But I confess that I was much disappointed in not finding something more memorable in the closing scene of one who had been so manifestly snatched "as a brand from the burning". (Zech 3:2) As well as I recollect, Steel represents that the spirituality and ardor of Inglis's religion considerably declined in his later years; that he became somewhat worldly-minded, and appeared to be much concerned about his little property; and that he had nothing remarkable in the exercises of his mind while on his deathbed: but no one, I believe, ever doubted the reality of the change which he had experienced; neither was he ever left to do anything to bring discredit on the profession which he had made.

One reflection which occurred to me on reading Steel's letter was, that it usually is not desirable for a Christian to live to be very old; especially when all active service in the cause of Christ is precluded. Old age is a peculiarly unfavorable season for growth in grace. Many of the natural helps to piety are then removed; and at the same time, many infirmities cluster around us; so that a declension in religion is not uncommon in the protracted years of the aged.

Another solemn reflection was, that a man is never too old nor decrepit, to be covetous. Covetousness is peculiarly the vice of the aged, and when indulged, strikes its roots deeper, the older we grow. What Christ says to all, may with emphasis be addressed to the aged, "Take heed, and beware of covetousness." (Luke 12:15) The writer remembers to have seen and conversed with the old gentleman in the church at Abington, soon after Dr. Tennent's death. At that time he was always in his place in the house of God, and attracted attention by his venerable and solemn appearance. It was agreed that his taste and judgment in regard to preaching were uncommonly sound and good; but nothing would pass with him in which Christ was not made conspicuous. Purely evangelical preaching was that in which he delighted; and at that period his conversation was in a strain of warm and pious feeling.

My closing remark is that we should despair of the conversion of no one—and we should use all our efforts to prevail on skeptical men to read the Bible. The Bible has converted more infidels than all the books of "evidences" which exist.

Chapter 8: Religious conversation—Stress laid by some on the knowledge of the time and place of conversion—Religious experience of Halyburton

It is often a question among serious people, whether every person who is a real Christian knows not only that he is such—but the time and place of his conversion. This subject has already been partially discussed in these essays—but demands a more particular and extended consideration.

It is well known to all, that the Christian denominations which exist in this country differ from one another in their views of various doctrines and rites of religion; but the fact is not so well known, that the religious experience of the individuals of the several denominations is as various as their doctrines and external forms of worship. To those who view these things at a distance, and superficially, all religious people appear alike; and many, when they hear of a number converted, take it for granted that they have all passed through the same train of exercises, to whatever sect they belong. There are some serious people, well indoctrinated in the Scriptures, who, while they hold a sound theory respecting the nature of regeneration, never speak of their own religious exercises; believing that such exposures are not for edification, as they tend to foster spiritual pride and vain glory, and afford a temptation to hypocrisy, which is commonly too strong for the deceitful heart. Among such professors, you hear nothing of conviction and conversion; and when any of this class fall into a distressing case of conscience which urges them to seek spiritual counsel, they always propose the case in the third person. They will talk to you by the hour and the day about the doctrines of religion, and show that they are more conversant with their Bibles than many who talk much of their religious feelings.

There are two objections to this practice. The first is, that it has the effect of keeping out of view the necessity of a change of heart. The second is, that it is a neglect of one effectual means of grace. Religious conversation, in which Christians freely tell of the dealings of God with their own souls, has been often a powerful means of quickening the sluggish soul, and communicating comfort. It is in many cases a great consolation to the desponding believer to know that his case is not entirely singular; and if a traveler can meet with one who has been over the difficult parts of the road before him, he may surely derive from his experience some beneficial counsel and warning. The Scriptures are favorable to such communications. "Come and hear," says David, "all you who fear God, and I will declare what he has done for my soul." (Psalm 66:16) "Then those who feared the Lord spoke often one to another, and the Lord hearkened and heard it, and a book of remembrance was written before him for those who feared the Lord, and that thought upon his name." (Mal 3:16) Paul seldom makes a speech or writes a letter, in which he does not freely speak of his own religious joys and sorrows, hopes and fears.

There is, no doubt, an abuse of this means of grace, as of others; but this is no argument against its legitimate use—but only teaches that prudence should govern such religious fellowship. The opposite extreme is not uncommon in some denominations; as where professors are publicly called upon, and that periodically, for their experience; or where, when professors are met, it is agreed that everyone, in turn, shall give a narrative of his or her experience in religion. Such practices are not for edification.

There are, however, cases in which it may be expedient—it may be delightful—for a few select friends to enter into a full detail of the dealings of God with their souls. The writer, in another place, published an account of such a conference in Holland, which he received from the late Dr. Livingston of New Brunswick. A company of pious friends having met for religious conversation, the subject which came up was the striking similarity of the experience of God's people in all ages and in all countries; when someone observed that there were present four people from the four quarters of the world respectively, and who had embraced religion in their native country. One was from the Dutch settlements in the East Indies, a second from the Cape of Good Hope, the third a young nobleman of Holland, and the fourth Dr. Livingston himself, from the United States of America. It was then proposed, as an illustration of the subject of conversation, that each should give a narrative of his Christian experience. The company in attendance expressed the highest gratification, and were no doubt greatly edified.

It is much to be lamented that many people who are fond of religious conversation deal so much in cant phrases, and assume an air so affected and sanctimonious. This is the thing which disgusts grave and intelligent Christians, and often occasions the wicked to ridicule or blaspheme. "Let not your good be evil spoken of." (Rom 14:16) Be not public nor indiscriminate in your communications of this kind. "Take heed that you cast not your pearls before swine, lest they trample them under their feet, and then turn again and rend you." (Matt 7:6)

It is a fact, that what passes for conversion in one sect will be condemned as altogether insufficient in another. A few years since there was what was called a great revival in a Presbyterian congregation in New Jersey. The Presiding Elder of the Methodist Society for that district, having classes of his church mingled with the people of that congregation, so that he had the opportunity of conversing with a number of the subjects of this work, gave it as his opinion to a person who communicated the fact to me, that none with whom he spoke were converted, for he did not meet with one who would say that he knew his sins were pardoned. On the other hand, many of the conversions which take place at camp meetings, and other meetings where there is much excitement, though the subjects do profess to know that their sins are pardoned, are not believed to be cases of sound conversion by Presbyterians; and they are often confirmed in this opinion by the transitory nature of the reformation produced. We have known instances of people professing conversion at a camp meeting, and filling the camp with their rejoicing, who relapsed into their old habits of sin before reaching their own dwellings. In these strong excitements of the animal sensibilities there is great danger of deception. When feelings of distress are wound up to a very high pitch, there often occurs a natural reaction in the nervous system by which the bodily sensations are suddenly changed, and this, attended with some text of Scripture impressed on the mind, leads the person to believe that he was in that moment converted, when in reality no permanent change has been effected. It is one thing to be persuaded of the truth of the gospel, and quite another to be certain that I have believed, and that my sins are pardoned.

John Wesley was for several years in the ministry, and a missionary to America, before he had this joyful sense of the forgiveness of sins, and he seems to intimate that until this time he was an unconverted man; and most of his followers make this joyful sense of pardoned sin the principal evidence of conversion, and one which all must experience. Most serious, intelligent readers, however, will be of opinion that Wesley was as humble and sincere a penitent before this joyful experience, as afterwards; and that it is a dangerous principle to make a man's opinion of his own state, the criterion by which to judge of its safety. Certainly, we would greatly prefer to stand in the place of some brokenhearted contrite ones, who can scarcely be induced to entertain a hope respecting their acceptance, to that of many who boast that they never feel a doubt of their own safety. Men will not be judged in the last day by the opinion which they had of themselves. For this confidence, it would seem, never forsakes some to the last, who nevertheless will be cast into outer darkness. "Not everyone that says unto me, Lord, Lord, shall enter into the kingdom of heaven—but he that does the will of my Father who is in heaven. Many will say unto me in that day, Lord, Lord, have we not prophesied in your name, and in your name have cast out devils, and in your name done many wonderful works? And then will I profess unto them, I never knew you, depart from me you workers of iniquity." (Matt 7:22-23; Psalm 6:8)

In early life the writer knew some high professors of his own denomination who could tell the day and hour when God had mercy on them. One of these, a fair-spoken, plausible man, who had spent the former part of his life in pleasure and dissipation, gave such an account of his conversion as was adapted to produce envy and discouragement in professors who had been less favored; and not only could he designate the month and day of the month—but the hour of the day, when he obtained reconciliation with God. No one doubted of his piety—but mark the event. This high professor, a few years afterwards, was excommunicated from the church for manifest perjury! Another, whose experience was remarkable and his conversion sudden, became a preacher, then a fanatic—and finally an infidel. This man told me, that though often in great spiritual distress, he never doubted of the goodness of his state. They who believe that a man may be a saint today and a devil tomorrow, not in appearance only—but in reality, easily account for these apostasies. But we are inclined to hold fast by what the beloved disciple says about such, in his time. "They went out from us—but they were not of us, for if they had been of us they would no doubt have continued with us; but they went out, that they might be made manifest that they were not all of us." (1 John 2:19)

Few men in later times appear to have arisen to greater eminence in piety than Henry Martyn the missionary. The strength of the principle of holiness in his case was manifested in his habitual spirituality of mind, and constant exercise of self-denial; yet, as far as is related, his incipient exercises of religion were by no means strongly marked—but seem to have been rather obscure and feeble. The same is the fact respecting those two distinguished men of God, Philip and Matthew Henry, the father and the son. The early exercises of these men were not in any respect remarkable. Indeed, they both became pious when very young; and we rarely get a very distinct and accurate account of the commencement of piety in early life. But no one who is acquainted with the lives of these eminent ministers will deny that they grew up to an uncommon degree of piety, which in the experience of both, though characterized by genuine humility, was free from any mixture of gloom or austerity. True religion can rarely be found exhibiting so cheerful a deportment and so amiable an aspect, and yet, with these men everything became a part of their religion; to this one object their whole lives were devoted.

I have derived much satisfaction and, I hope, profit from the account which Thomas Halyburton, 1674-1712, gives of his religious experience; especially, because the account was given when the writer was advanced in years, and when his judgment was fully matured. Many youthful narratives of pious exercises are very fervent—but they are frothy, and marked with that kind of ignorance and self-confidence which arise from inexperience.

Halyburton is an example of a person brought up under religious discipline and instruction, and under constant restraint, whose convictions of sin were nevertheless exceedingly pungent and solemn. His conversion too was sudden, and his first exercises of faith clear and strong. "I cannot," says he, "be very positive about the day or the hour of this deliverance; nor can I satisfy many other questions about the way and manner of it. As to these things I may say with the blind man, 'One thing I know, that whereas I was blind, now I see.' (John 9:25)

"It was towards the close of January, or the beginning of February, 1698, that this seasonable relief came; and, so far as I can remember, I was at secret prayer, in very great extremity, not far from despair, when the Lord seasonably stepped in and gave this merciful turn to affairs. When I said there was none to save, then 'His arm brought salvation'. (Isa 59:16) God, who commanded the light to shine out of darkness, 'shined into my mind', to give the light of the knowledge of the glory of God in the face of Jesus Christ. That which afforded me relief was a discovery of the Lord as manifested in His Word. He said to me, 'You have destroyed yourself—but in me is your help.' (Hos 13:9) He let me see that there are forgivenesses with Him, that with Him is mercy and plenteous redemption. He made all His goodness pass before me, and proclaimed His name,

'The Lord, the Lord God, merciful and gracious, longsuffering, and abundant in goodness and truth, keeping mercy for thousands, forgiving iniquity and transgression and sin'; who will be gracious to whom He will be gracious, and will show mercy to whom He will show mercy.'

"This was a strange sight to one who before looked on God only as a 'consuming fire' (Deut 4:24; Heb 12:29) which I could not see and live. He brought me from Sinai and its thunderings, to Mount Zion, and to the Mediator of the new covenant, and to the blood of sprinkling that cleanses from all sin, and speaks better things than the blood of Abel. He revealed Christ in His glory. I now with wonder beheld His glory, the glory as of the only begotten of the Father, full of grace and truth. And I was made, by this sight, to say, 'You are fairer than the sons of men.' (Psalm 45:2) ... And I was hereby further satisfied, that not only was there forgiveness of sins and justification by free grace, through the redemption that is in Christ Jesus, whom God has set forth to be a propitiation through faith in His blood, to declare His righteousness for the remission of sins that are past, through the forbearance of God—but I saw moreover, with wonder and delight, how God by this means might be just even in justifying the ungodly who believe in Jesus. How was I ravished with delight when made to see that the God in whom, a little before, I thought there was no help for me, or any sinner in my case—if indeed there were any such—notwithstanding His spotless purity, His deep hatred of sin, His inflexible justice and righteousness, and His unimpeachable faithfulness pledged in the threatenings of the law, might not only pardon—but without prejudice to His justice or His other attributes, might be just, even in justifying the ungodly. ... And the Lord further opened the Gospel-call to me, and let me see that even to me, was 'the word of this salvation sent'. (Acts 13:26) All this was offered unto me, and I was invited to come and freely take of the waters of life, and to come in my distress unto the blessed rest. ... He, to my great satisfaction, gave me a pleasing discovery of His design in the whole, that it was, 'that no flesh might glory in his sight', (1 Cor 1:29) but that he who glories should glory only in the Lord; and that he might manifest the riches of His grace, and be exalted in showing mercy, and that we in the end might be saved. The Lord revealed to my soul the full and suitable provision made in this way against the power of sin—that as there is righteousness in Him, so there is strength, even 'everlasting strength' (Isa 26:4) in the Lord Jehovah, to secure us against all enemies. ... When this strange discovery was made of a relief, wherein full provision was made for all the concerns of God's glory, and my salvation in subordination thereto, my soul was, by a sweet and glorious power, carried out to rest in it, as worthy of God, and every way suitable and satisfying in my case. 'Those who know your name will put their trust in you.' (Psalm 9:10) All these discoveries were conveyed to me by the Scriptures only. It was not indeed by one particular promise or testimony of Scripture—but by the concurring light of a great many, seasonably set home, and most plainly expressing the truths above mentioned. The promises and truths of the Bible, in great abundance and variety, were brought to remembrance, and the wonders contained in them were set before my eyes in the light of the Word. 'He sent his word and healed me.' (Psalm 107:20) ...

"But it was not the Bible alone that conveyed the discovery; for most of these passages whereby I was relieved I had formerly, in my distress, read and thought upon, without finding any relief in them. But now the Lord shined into my mind by them. Formerly I was acquainted only with the letter, which profits not—but now the Lord's words were spirit and life, and in His light I saw light. God opened my eyes to see wonders out of His law. There was light in His words; a burning light by them shone into my mind, not merely some doctrinal knowledge—but 'the light of the knowledge of the glory of God in the face of Jesus Christ'. (2 Cor 4:6)

"The light that I now had shone from heaven; it was not a spark kindled by my own endeavors—but it shone suddenly about me; it came by the Word of God, a heavenly means. It opened heaven and discovered heavenly things, even the glory of God; and it led me up as it were to heaven. Its whole tendency was heavenward. It was a true light, giving manifestations of God, even the one true God, and the one Mediator between God and man; and giving a true view of my state with respect to God. ... It was a pleasant and a sweet light: it had a heavenly satisfaction in God attending it. It led to a pleasure in the fountain whence it came. It was a distinct and clear light, not only representing spiritual things—but manifesting them in their glory. It put all things in their proper place, in due subordination to God, and gave distinct views of their genuine tendency. It was a satisfying light. The soul rested in the discoveries that it made and was satisfied; it could not doubt of what it saw, and that things were as they were represented. It was a quickening, refreshing and healing light; when 'the Sun of Righteousness' (Mal 4:2) arose, there was 'healing under his wings'. It was a great light: it made discoveries which were easily distinguished from any former discoveries I had ever made. And it was a powerful light; it dissipated that thick darkness which had overspread my mind, and made all those frightful temptations, which had formerly disturbed me, fly before it. It was composing: not like a sudden flash of lightning, which fills the soul with fear and amazement—but it composed and quieted my soul and put all my faculties, as it were, in their due posture, and gave me the exercise of them. It destroyed not—but improved my former knowledge. But as the true idea of light is not conveyed by the ear, so no words can convey the idea of light to the blind. And he who has eyes will need no words to describe it. It is like the new name that none knows, but he who has it.

"The first discernible effect of this light was an approbation of God's way of saving sinners by Jesus Christ, to the glory of His grace. And this I take to be the true Scriptural notion of justifying faith; for it not only answers the Scripture descriptions of it, by receiving, coming, looking, trusting, believing, etc.—but it really gives God that glory which He designed by all this contrivance—the glory of His wisdom, grace, mercy, and truth. Now this discovery of the Lord's name brought me to trust in Him, and glory only in the Lord. I found my soul fully satisfied in these discoveries, as pointing out a way of relief, altogether and in all respects suitable to the need of a poor, guilty, self-condemned, self-destroyed sinner, driven from all other reliefs. In this I rested, as in a way of full peace, comfort, security, and satisfaction, and as providing abundantly for all those ends I desired to have secured. And this approbation was not merely for a time; but ever after in all temptations it discovered itself, by keeping in me a fixed assent and adherence of mind to this truth, and full persuasion of it, that God has granted unto us eternal life, and this life is in His Son.

"The next remarkable effect of this discovery was that it set me right as to my chief end, and made me look to the glory of God, for which formerly I had no real concern. Now my eye was made, in some measure, single in eyeing the Lord's honor. It manifested itself in frequent desires that the Lord might be honored and glorified in my life, or by my death. It kept my soul fixed in the persuasion that it was every way fit that I should take shame and confusion to myself as what truly and only belonged to me; and that the glory of my salvation was only and entirely the Lord's due.

"A third discernible effect was, that I was led to look upon His yoke to be easy and His burden light; and to count that His commandments were not grievous—but 'right concerning all things'. (Psalm 119:128) This was very contrary to my former temper. I now came to a fixed persuasion that the law was not only just, such as I could make no reasonable exception against—but holy, and such as became God; and good, such as was every way suited to my true interest and peace and advantage, which I could never think before. The duties to which my heart was most averse had now become agreeable and refreshing.

"A fourth remarkable effect of this discovery was the exercise of evangelical repentance, which was very different, in many respects, from that sorrow with which I was before acquainted. It differed in its rise. Sorrow before flowed from the discovery of sin as it brings on wrath; now it flowed from a sense of sin as containing wretched unkindness to One who was Himself astonishingly kind to an unworthy wretch. I looked on Him whom I had pierced, and did mourn. Sorrow formerly wrought death, alienated my heart from God, and thus dispirited me for duty, and made me fear hurt from Him; but this sorrow filled my heart with kindness to God and to His ways, sweetened my soul, and endeared God to it. It flowed from a sense of His favor to an unworthy wretch that deserved none, and was thus a godly sorrow leading to kindness to God, and a drawing near Him—but with much humble sense of my own unworthiness, like the returning prodigal. The more God manifested of His kindness, the more still did this feeling increase: when He was pacified, then was I ashamed and confounded. The sorrow I had before I looked on as a burden: it was nothing but selfish concern for my own safety, and a fear of the righteous resentment of God. But this sorrow was sweet and pleasant, as being the exercise of filial gratitude; and I took pleasure in the surprising manifestations of God's favor to one so unworthy, and in acknowledging my own unworthiness. This sorrow was a spring of activity, and I was glad to be employed in the meanest errand that might give opportunity to evidence how deeply I was grieved for my former disobedience. It resulted in a return to the way of life, and to such a course as upon a review I did not repent of—but delighted in, and in which I desired continually to advance. It wrought carefulness to avoid sin, concern to please God, indignation against sin, fear of offending God again, vehement desire of having sin removed, the Lord glorified, and obedience promoted.

"A fifth discernible effect was an humble—but sweet and comfortable hope and persuasion of my own salvation, answerable to the clearness of the discovery. When the Lord gave me this view of the way of salvation, He satisfied me that it was a way full of peace and security, the only way which I might safely venture. Hereby I was freed from the disquieting fear that the ground of my trust would fail. I was satisfied I could not fail, otherwise than by missing this way. While I held fast and reposed with satisfaction on what I was convinced was safe, I could not but be quiet and composed about the result. This shows how nearly allied faith and assurance are, though they are not the same, and therefore, no wonder the one should be taken for the other. This discovery manifested that salvation was in the way of self-denial, and trust in the Lord alone; for nothing so soon marred this hope as the least appearance of self and stirring of pride. Whenever the glory of the Lord appeared and He spoke peace, I was filled with shame, and the deeper this humiliation was, the more the humble confidence of my safety increased.

"A sixth discernible difference was with respect to the ordinances of the Lord's appointment. I was drawn to follow them as the Lord's institutions, and His appointed means of our obtaining discoveries of His beauty. I desired 'to behold the beauty of the Lord, and to inquire in His temple'. (Psalm 27:4) I was brought to exercise more liveliness; when the Lord revealed Himself, 'my soul then followed hard after Him'. (Psalm 63:8) When the Lord enlarged me and caused me to approach to Him and see His glory, He still humbled me, discovered self, and put me in opposition to it. I was now acquainted, in some measure, with that boldness and freedom of access, with humble confidence, to God as on a throne of grace, manifesting Himself in Christ. In a word, I was in some measure sensible of the Lord's hiding or manifesting Himself, according as I performed my duty, and of the necessity of the exercise of grace, particularly faith, in all approaches to God."

Although in the preceding authentic narrative of religious experience we have entered more into detail than usual, yet we are persuaded that the serious reader will not think the account too long or too particular. I have not met with any account of Christian experience which is so full and satisfactory as this; and when it is known to have been written by a man of sound understanding and most exemplary piety, at a late period of life, when his judgment was matured by much experience, it cannot but furnish a decisive proof of the reality of experimental religion, which cannot be gainsaid. In these exercises there is not a tincture of enthusiasm. Indeed, holy affections thus produced by the contemplation of truth are the very opposite of enthusiasm, which always substitutes human fancies or impulses for the truths of God, which it uniformly undervalues. In this case we see also how high the exercises of Scriptural piety may rise, without degenerating into any extravagance.

Many Christians seem not to know or believe that such spiritual discoveries of the beauty of holiness and the glory of the Lord are now attainable: but still there are some, and often those of the humbler class of society, who are privileged with these spiritual discoveries, and prize them above all price. The language of such is, "One day in your courts is better than a thousand. I would rather be a doorkeeper in the house of God, than dwell in the tents of sin." (Psalm 84:10) "Return unto your rest, O my soul, for the Lord has dealt bountifully with you." (Psalm 116:7)

It is delightful to trace the effects of God's truth in producing every holy affection, when it is discerned by the light of the Holy Spirit. Faith is almost identified with this view; love flows out sweetly and spontaneously; evangelical repentance is enkindled; the soul is clothed with humility; zeal for God's glory is predominant; His ordinances are sought with desire, and found to be channels which freely communicate with the rich fountain of grace beneath the throne of God. So far are right views of free grace from leading those who entertain them to indulge in indolence, or be careless about holy living, that they impart the only true cause of activity and diligence in the work of the Lord.

In the foregoing account, the reader may learn the nature of true religion more clearly than from many sermons and long treatises; but the humble, doubting Christian must not make the measure of grace which this favored saint enjoyed, the standard by which to judge of the reality of his own religious experience. The same light may shine with vastly different degrees of clearness, from the meridian blaze down to the faint dusky dawn—but the rays come from the same source; and that which is now but just discernible in the midst of shades of departing night, will go on to increase, until it shines more and more to the perfect day. Let not the extraordinary clearness and distinctness discourage those who are sincerely desirous to see "the beauty of the Lord", (Psalm

45:11) but let them rather take fresh courage in a pursuit, which from this example, they find may be crowned with glorious success. "Those who wait upon the Lord shall renew their strength; they shall mount up with wings as eagles—they shall run and not be weary, and they shall walk and not faint." (Isa 40:31)

Chapter 9: Christian experience of R C; Narrative of Sir Richard Hill's experience.

The following extracts, from a narrative of the Christian experience of R__ C__, will serve to illustrate some points which have heretofore been treated; particularly the gradual manner in which some people are brought to the knowledge of the truth; and the extreme difficulty of ascertaining, in many cases, where common grace ends and special grace commences.

"I grew up," says the narrator, "to manhood with very little thought of religion, and without experiencing any serious impressions, except the alarm occasionally produced by the death of a companion or relative. While I habitually cherished a great dislike to strict religion, which frowned upon a life of pleasure and amusement, I entertained a strong prejudice in favor of Christianity in general, and that particular denomination to which my parents and ancestors belonged. I call this a prejudice, for I knew nothing of the evidences of the truth of Christianity, and had only a very vague and confused notion of what the Scriptures contained; except that, when a child, I had read, frequently, many portions of the historical parts of the Bible. In this state of mind, I was exposed to the common objections of infidels, which arose from reading history, and finding that all nations had their respective religions, in which they believed as firmly as we did in ours; and the thought often occurred, 'Why may they not be in the right, and we in the wrong?' But about this time, infidelity began to prevail, and its abettors to be bold in declaring their opinions. My mind was so completely unfurnished with arguments in favor of Christianity, that the only thing on which I could fix was that it had come down from my ancestors, and the people with whom I was conversant generally believed in it. But this was far from satisfying my mind. I began to feel uneasy for fear that we were all wrong in our belief; but the thought was never pleasing to my mind. As to books of evidences, I knew nothing about them, and cannot remember that I had ever heard of such works. And I was so situated that I had no one to whom I could apply for instruction. The only person with whom I had any communication on literary subjects was a gentleman, who, though he said nothing to me on the subject, was deeply imbued with skeptical opinions. Being separated from the companions of my youth, and placed in a secluded situation, where, except on particular occasions, I saw little company, and where there were few opportunities of hearing instructive preaching, I was cast upon my own thoughts, and my reflections were often not very pleasing. One day—it was the Lord's day—as I was looking over some books which I had in a trunk, my eye caught the words, Internal Evidences of the Christian Religion. I had often seen the same book, and never so much as thought what the subject of it was; but in my present perplexity I seized it with avidity, and began to read. The work was the celebrated treatise of Soame Jenyns. I never removed from where I was sitting until I had finished it, and as I proceeded, the light of evidence poured in upon my mind with such power of demonstration, that at the conclusion I had the idea of the room being full of resplendent light. I enjoyed a pleasure which none can appreciate but those who have been led to the contemplation of the truth in like perplexing circumstances. Not only were all my doubts removed—but I wanted no more evidence. My conviction of the truth of Christianity was complete. I believe it could not have been increased.

"But still I knew scarcely anything of the method of salvation revealed in the gospel. I entertained the common legal notions of thousands of ignorant people, 'that at a convenient time I would become good', never doubting for a moment of my ability to do all that was requisite. The only thing which gave me uneasiness was the fear of a sudden death, which would not afford me the opportunity of repenting and making my peace with God. But the hope prevailed that I would die a lingering death, and be in my senses, and then I would do all that was requisite to prepare me for heaven; while at the same time I had no definite idea what that preparation was. During this period I was exposed to few temptations; but still some sins had dominion over me. One day a child brought to me a small book and said that Mrs. T. requested that I would read it and return it soon, as it was borrowed. The title was, Jenks on Submission to the Righteousness of God. I read the book through at a single sitting, and again a new light sprung up in my mind. The author, in the introduction, gives an account of his ignorance of the true method of a sinner's justification, until he had been for years a preacher. He was a minister of the Church of England. I now found that I likewise had been all my life ignorant of the way of salvation; for I entertained the same legal and unscriptural notions which he proves to be utterly erroneous. Although these new views seem to have been merely intellectual, yet they afforded me a great satisfaction. I had now a distinct knowledge of the gospel method of justification, which I ever afterwards retained. Another copy of this book I have never seen.

"The preaching to which I had access was mostly of a wild, fanatical kind, and the way in which I heard the new birth described, tended to prejudice me against the doctrine of regeneration. I had never before heard anything about this change, and yet I was sure that I knew some very good and religious people. I began to be troubled to know whether sober, intelligent Christians believed in this doctrine. It also became a subject of discussion in the little circle with which I was conversant, and I found that one person in the company professed to have experienced this change; another was convinced of its reality—but professed to be merely an inquirer; a third was of opinion that it related to the conversion of Jews and infidels, and that there was no other regeneration, except in baptism; and the fourth was the skeptical gentleman, already mentioned, who was incredulous about the whole matter. In these conversations, I, being young and ignorant, took no part—but I listened to them with intense interest. I had recourse to such books as I had access to—but could find nothing that was satisfactory; for my range of religious books was very narrow, and few of these of an evangelical cast. The person of my acquaintance who professed conversion, one day gave me a narrative of the various steps and changes experienced in this transition from darkness to light. As I entertained a favorable opinion of the veracity and sincerity of the individual, I began to think there might be something in it.

"Although I had experienced no remarkable change thus far, I knew that the subject of religion had become one of much more frequent thought, and excited much more interest in my mind than formerly. One evidence of this was that I commenced secret prayer, a duty utterly neglected until this time, except when some one of the family was dangerously sick. I had selected a retired spot, surrounded by a thick growth of trees and bushes, on the margin of a brook. Here I made a kind of arbor, over a little plat of green grass, and in the summer evenings I would resort to this sequestered spot. It was on the afternoon of a Sunday, I was reading a sermon on the longsuffering and patience of God, in waiting with delaying sinners; and so many things applied so exactly to my own case, that I became so much affected with a sense of the divine goodness and forbearance in sparing me and waiting so long with me, while I was living in neglect of Him, that I felt impelled to go out and weep. I was reading the sermon aloud to the family, by request. I laid down the book abruptly and hastened to my retirement, where I poured out a flood of tears in prayer. And suddenly I was overwhelmed with a flood of joy. It was ecstatic beyond anything which I had ever conceived; for though I thought religion a necessary thing, I never had an idea that there was any positive pleasure in its exercises. Whence this joy originated, I knew not. The only thing which had been on my mind was the goodness and patience of God, and my own ingratitude. Neither can I now say how long it continued; but the impression left was that I was in the favor of God and should certainly be happy forever. When the tumult of feeling had subsided, I began to think that this was conversion—this was the great change, of which I had recently heard so much.

"It occurred to me, when walking home, that if this was indeed the change called the new birth, it would be evinced by my forsaking all my sins. This suggestion appeared right, and I determined to make this the test of its reality. All the evening, my mind was in a delightful calm; but the next day my feelings had returned into their old channel. I was grieved at this, and resorted to the same place where I had experienced such a delightful frame, in hopes that by some kind of association the same scene would be renewed; but though there was the place and all the objects of yesterday, the soul-ravishing vision was not there; and after a feeble attempt at prayer, and lingering for some time, I returned without meeting with anything which I sought and desired.

"It was not long before I was subjected to the test which I had fixed; a temptation to a besetting sin was presented, and I had no strength to resist—but was instantly overcome. This failure gave me inexpressible pain, on reflection. I did not know how dear were my cherished hopes until they were wrested from me. I never felt a keener regret at any loss which I ever experienced.

"Although I was constrained to admit that I was not a regenerated person, I was sensible of a considerable change in my views and feelings on the subject of religion. I had no longer any doubt of the necessity of regeneration, and entertained some consistent notions of what its effects must be. I had, as before stated, acquired evangelical views of the way in which a sinner must be justified, and entertained different feelings from what I had formerly towards religious people. Formerly they were objects of dread and aversion, now I felt a sincere regard and high respect for the same characters; and was pleased when I heard of any of my friends becoming religious, or more serious than before. I had now an opportunity of hearing an able minister preach an evangelical sermon on the text, 'For our righteousnesses are as filthy rags', (Isa 64:6) etc., and I cannot tell the gratification I experienced, in hearing the doctrine of justification, which I had fully embraced, preached distinctly and luminously from the pulpit: but when I looked around on the audience, I had the impression that they were all, or nearly all, ignorant of what he was saying, and were still trusting to their own works. It now gave me pleasure, also, to converse on the doctrines of religion; and I felt a real abhorrence of wicked courses.

"This was my state of mind when Providence cast my lot where a powerful revival had been in progress for some time. I had witnessed something of this kind in a wild, fanatical sect, where bodily agitations were common and violent; but this was a different scene. The principal conductor and preacher was a man of learning and eloquence; and his views of experimental religion, as I think, most correct and scriptural. If he erred, it was on the safe side, in believing in the thorough conversion of but a small number of those who appeared impressed. In entering into this scene, I experienced various new and conflicting feelings. The young converts spoke freely, in my presence, of their conviction and conversion; but often with a degree of levity which surprised me. In their conversations I could take no part, and although my general purpose was to consider myself an unawakened, unconverted sinner, yet when I heard the marks of true religion laid down, and especially by the distinguished preacher before mentioned, I could not prevent the thought arising continually, 'If this is religion, then you have experienced it.' This seemed to me to be the suggestion of a false hope, by the enemy, to prevent my falling under conviction. Still the idea was continually presented to my mind, and with the appearance of truth. I took occasion to state the matter to the clergyman above alluded to, as soon as I could gain access to him; for I was diffident and timid, and had never opened my case to anyone freely. I told him all my former exercises, and stated distinctly that they had not been sufficient to break the habit of sinning to which I was addicted. As soon as I mentioned this part, he said in a peremptory tone, 'Then surely your exercises were not of the nature of true religion; you must seek a better hope or you will never be admitted into heaven.' This decisive answer drove away, from that moment, every idea of my being in a state of grace; and I felt relieved from what I had myself considered a temptation to entertain a false hope.

"Now I began to seek conviction as a necessary preliminary to conversion; and hoped that every sermon which I heard would be the means of striking terror into my soul. I read the most awakening discourses, went to hear the most arousing preachers; endeavored to work on my own mind by imagining the solemn realities of the judgment, and the torments of the damned. I strove to draw the covering off from the pit, that I might behold the lake of fire, and hear the wailings of the damned. But the more I sought these solemn feelings of conviction, the further they seemed to fly from me. My heart seemed to grow harder every day. I was sensible of nothing but insensibility. I became discouraged; and the more, because I was obliged to remove from the scene of the revival, to a place where there was no concern about religion in the people generally, and where I expected the preaching to be cold and lifeless. I spent a day before my departure, in secret, and in solemn reflection on my deplorable and hopeless case. I ran over all the kind dispensations of God's providence towards me, and reflected on the many precious means of grace, which I had recently enjoyed, without effect.

"The conclusion which seemed now to be forced on my mind was that God had given me up to a hard heart and that I never would be so happy as to obtain religion. This conclusion had, to my mind, all the force of a certainty; and I began to think about the justice of God in my condemnation: and no truth ever appeared with more lucid evidence to my mind. I fully justified God in sending me to hell. I saw that it was not only right—but I did not see how a just God could do otherwise. And I seemed to acquiesce in it, as a righteous and necessary thing. At this moment, my mind became more calm than it had been for a long time. All striving and effort on my part ceased, and being in the woods I recollected that it was time for me to return to the house, where I expected to meet some friends. Here I found a minister waiting for me, whom I had seen but never spoken to. He took me aside, and began to represent the many privileges which I had enjoyed, and expressed a hope that I had received some good impressions. I told him that it was true, that I had been highly favored; but that I had now come to a fixed conclusion that I would certainly be forever lost; for under all these means I had not received the slightest conviction, without which my conversion was impossible. He replied by saying, 'that no certain degree of conviction was necessary—that the only use of conviction was to make us feel our need of Christ as a Savior; and appealed to me whether I did not feel that I stood in need of a Savior'. He then went on to say, 'Christ is an advocate at the right hand of God, and stands ready to receive any case which is committed to His hands, and however desperate your case may now appear to be, only commit it to Him and He will bring you off safely, for He is able to save to the uttermost all who come unto God by Him.'

"Here a new view broke in on my mind. I saw that Christ was able to save even me, and I felt willing to give my cause into His hands. This discovery of the bare possibility of salvation was one of the greatest deliverances I ever experienced. I was affected exceedingly with the view which I had of this truth, so as to be unable to speak. Hope now sprung up in my desolate soul—not that I was pardoned or accepted. Such a thought did not occur—but that it was yet possible that I might be hereafter, and I was resolved never to give over seeking until I obtained the blessing. All that evening I was sweetly composed, and precious promises and declarations of the Word of God came dropping successively into my mind, as if they had been whispered to me. I never could have believed, unless I had experienced it, that the mere possibility of salvation would produce such comfort.

"About this time, next morning probably, when I retired to the woods where my secret devotions were usually performed, I experienced such a melting of heart from a sense of God's goodness to me, as I never felt before or since. It seemed as if my eyes—so hard to weep commonly—were now a fountain of tears. The very earth was watered with their abundance. Indeed, my heart itself seemed to be dissolved, just as a piece of ice is dissolved by the heat of the sun. Of the particular exercises of this melting season, my memory does not retain a distinct recollection.

"For some months I attended to religious duties, with various fluctuations of feeling. Sometimes I entertained a pleasing hope that I was indeed a Christian—a renewed person; but at other times I was not only distressed with doubts—but came to the conclusion that I was still in my sins. The only thing which I deem it important to mention during this period was a deeper discovery of the wickedness of my own heart. This conviction of deep-rooted, inherent depravity distressed me much; but I obtained considerable relief from reading Owen on Indwelling Sin. This book exhibited the state of my heart much better than I could have done myself. Still, however, I was much dissatisfied with myself, because after so long a time I had made so little progress. On one occasion, at the close of the exercises of the Sabbath, I was so deeply sensible that my soul was still in imminent danger of perdition, that I solemnly resolved to begin a new and more vigorous course of engagedness to secure my salvation. I had spent much time in reading accounts of Christian experience, and those which lay down the marks and evidences of true religion, such as Owen on Spiritual Mindedness, Edwards on Religious Affections, Guthrie's Trial of a Saving Interest in Christ, Newton's Letters, Pike and Hayward's Cases of Conscience, etc. I also conversed much with old and experienced Christians, as well as with those of my own age. But all these having, as it then seemed to me, very little facilitated my progress, and the evils of my heart seeming rather to increase, I hastily resolved to lay aside all books except the Bible, and to devote my whole time to prayer and reading, until I experienced a favorable change.

"In pursuance of this purpose, I withdrew into a deeply retired spot, where I knew I should be free from all intrusion from mortals, and began my course of exertion with fasting and strong resolution never to relinquish my efforts, until I found relief. For five or six hours I was engaged alternately in reading the Scriptures and attempting to pray; but the longer I continued these exercises, the harder did my heart become, and the more wretched my feelings, until at length I was exhausted and discouraged, and began to despair of help, and was about to leave my chosen retirement in gloomy despondence, when it occurred to me with peculiar force, that if I found I could do nothing to help myself, yet I might call upon God for mercy. Accordingly, I fell down before Him, and said little more than is contained in the publican's prayer, 'God be merciful to me a sinner'; (Luke 18:13) but this I uttered with a deep and feeling conviction of my utter helplessness. The words were scarcely out of my mouth, when God was pleased to give me such a manifestation of His love in the plan of redemption through Christ, as filled me with wonder, love, and joy. Christ did indeed appear to me as altogether lovely, and I was enabled to view Him as my Savior, and to see that His sufferings were endured for me. At no time before had I the full assurance of being in the favor of God; but now every doubt of this was dissipated. I could say for the first time with unwavering confidence, 'My beloved is mine, and I am his.' (Song 2:16) And this assurance of God's favor arose not from any suggestion or impulse directly made to my mind—but from the clear view that Christ as a Savior was freely offered, and from a conscious assurance that I did truly accept the offer. I now opened my Bible and began to read at John 18 and onward. Every word and sentiment appeared glorious. I seemed to be reading a book which was perfectly new, and truly, the sacred pages seemed to be illuminated with celestial light. And I rejoiced to think that the Sacred Scriptures would always be read in the same manner. How little did I know of the spiritual warfare! After my feelings had a little subsided—but while the glorious truths of the Gospel were still in full view, I made a formal and solemn dedication of myself to God, the Father, the Son, and the Holy Spirit; and having writing materials with me, I wrote down the substance of this covenant, and subscribed it with my hand.

"I now believed assuredly that I was reconciled to God through Jesus Christ; but being naturally inclined to be suspicious of myself, I resolved to make the Holy Scriptures the test of the genuineness of my exercises, and to leave the final determination to the fruits produced, as our Lord says, 'By their fruits you shall know them.' (Matt 7:20) I remembered that it was written that faith works by love and purifies the heart. I hoped, therefore, that I should now be delivered from those evils of the heart with which I had been lately so much affected. But, alas! in a few days I found that the 'old man' was not dead—but had power to struggle in a fearful manner. I must acknowledge, therefore, that after a few weeks I was in much the same spiritual condition in which I was before this remarkable manifestation."

Here the narration breaks off abruptly. It may be remarked, in the first place, on this narrative, that sometimes people are brought along very gradually in their acquisition of the knowledge of the truth. One discovery is made at one time, and another truth is revealed at another time; and between these steps there may be a long interval. It may again be remarked, that commonly before a person comes to the knowledge of a truth, the need of information is sensibly felt; and the appropriate means of communicating it are provided. A book, a sermon, a casual conversation, may be intimately connected with our salvation. Those who commence a pious life, though they may appear sincere, should always be urged to go forward; there is much before them which they have not yet experienced. If they are not yet in the right way they may arrive at it. In looking over the various exercises here detailed, I am utterly at a loss to say when the work of grace commenced. Perhaps scarcely any two people, taken at random, would agree in this point; for while some would scarcely admit that there was any exercising of saving faith until the last manifestation here described, others would be for carrying it back to the very beginning of the exercised soul's serious attention to religion.

However this matter may be decided, one thing, I think, is evident, that it is a great practical error to suppose that nothing connected essentially with the sinner's conversion is experienced or done until the moment of his conversion. He may have to unlearn many erroneous opinions taken up through prejudice or inclination. He must learn the truth of the Christian religion, if unhappily he has adopted skeptical notions. He must learn to know what the Bible teaches as to man's duty and the true method of salvation. God's methods of bringing His chosen into the paths of truth and holiness are often astonishing. They are, at every step, led in a way which they knew not. How remarkably true is this, as it relates to conviction of SIN! When the sinner is most convinced, he thinks he has no conviction at all. And in regard to conversion, what a different thing does it turn out to be in experience, from what it was conceived to be beforehand! While the anxious soul was expecting something miraculous, or entirely out of the way, he experiences a new train of thought, new and pleasing views of truth, with corresponding emotions, by which the mind is so occupied, that it has no time nor inclination to scrutinize the nature or cause of these pleasing exercises. He believes and hopes without asking himself whether these are the views and feelings of a renewed soul. Afterwards he can look back and see that faith was exercised in these very acts, and that the peace which he then enjoyed was the peace of reconciliation through our Lord Jesus Christ.

But when the love of God is shed abroad in the heart by the Holy Spirit, as described in the last part of this narrative, the distressed soul is made sensible at once of its happy state, and is made to rejoice in the smiles of the divine favor. Then he can no more doubt that God is reconciled and has lifted upon him the light of His countenance, than that the sun is shining at midday. All Christians, however, are not favored with these bright discoveries. Some always walk in a degree of darkness, or at best in a mere dusky light; yet they fear the Lord and obey of His voice. I have known instances of some people changing their opinion of the time of their own conversion several times, and fixing it at different periods of their experience, as their sentiments became more correct and mature; and those converts who shine forth more brightly at first are not always they who appear best after the lapse of years.

The following narrative of the experience of Sir Richard Hill, written by himself, is found in his biography by Edwin Sidney and has been inserted in the Christian Observer of London, for September, 1839. We make no apology for its length, as we are confident that all who have a taste for this kind of reading will be gratified to have the whole of this interesting account, without curtailment:

"It would not be an easy matter for me to ascertain the time when the first dawnings of divine light began to break in upon my soul; but I remember particularly that when I was about eight or nine years of age, being then at a neighboring school, and repeating the catechism one Sunday evening with some other boys, to the master, I found my heart sweetly drawn up to heavenly objects, and had such a taste of the love of God, as made everything else appear insipid and contemptible. This was but a transitory glimpse of the heavenly gift; and I was no sooner withdrawn with the rest of my schoolfellows, than my religious impressions vanished, and I returned to folly with the same eagerness as before. But God did not leave me to myself; I had frequent checks of conscience, and the thoughts of death sometimes came forcibly into my mind. I remained about two years at the school before mentioned, after which I was removed to Westminster, where my convictions still pursued me, and forced me to several superficial repentances and resolutions; but these being all made in my own strength, soon came to nothing.

"When I had been about four or five years at Westminster, I was to be confirmed with several more of my schoolfellows. I looked upon this as going into a new state, and therefore made the most solemn resolutions of becoming a new creature. But, alas! my happiness and conversion were far from beginning here, as I had fondly imagined. The adversary, now finding that he was not likely to make me continue any longer in a state of practical wickedness by his former stratagems, began to attack me on another side, namely, by suggesting horrible doubts concerning the very fundamentals of all religion—as the being of a God—the immortality of the soul, and the divine origin of the Scriptures. I endeavored to reason myself into the belief of these truths—but all in vain. However, I thought I might easily get some book that should convince me of their certainty. Accordingly, I borrowed Beveridge's Private Thoughts, of a clergyman's widow with whom I boarded, she having first read to me a few pages in that excellent work. It was, to the best of my remembrance, while she was reading, that such glorious instantaneous light and comfort were diffused over my soul, as no tongue can express; the love of God was shed abroad in my heart, and I rejoiced with joy unspeakable and full of glory. However, these comforts, I think, did not last above half an hour at most—but went off by degrees, when the same doubts followed; upon which I again had recourse to Beveridge's Thoughts, or to conversation on the subject of religion; and for several times as I did this, I experienced the same manifestations of divine love, which were sometimes of longer, sometimes of shorter duration.

"At length I began to be tired of this state of uncertainty, especially as the comforts I had before felt began to be few and faint. Add to this the bad example of my schoolfellows, and the despair I began to be in of obtaining satisfaction of the truth of what is called natural as well as revealed religion, contributed not a little to make me lay aside my inquiries, and to fall into many sins that youth and strong passions prompted me to; and this I did with the more eagerness, as I was desirous of laying hold of every opportunity of turning my thoughts from within myself.

"I believe I was now about eighteen years of age, when, having gone through the school at Westminster, I was entered at Magdalen College, Oxford, where I continued between four and five years. After which I went abroad for about two years more, returning to England in 1757, being then about the age of twenty-three or twenty-four. During my residence at Oxford and in foreign parts, notwithstanding all the wretched pains I took to lull conscience asleep, still my convictions pursued me; yes, the more I endeavored to put from me the thoughts of my soul by drinking deeper draughts of iniquity, the more strongly did the insulted Spirit plead with me, and often in the very act of sin would so embitter my carnal gratifications, and strike me with such deep remorse, that, oh! horrid to think! I have even been ready to murmur, because God would not let me alone, nor allow me to sin with the same relentless satisfaction which I observed in my companions.

"But He that has loved me with an everlasting love, had all this while thoughts of mercy towards me, and would not take His loving kindness utterly away from me. He therefore waited that He might be gracious unto me, and followed me with such loud and constant convictions as often brought me upon my knees, and sometimes forced me to break off my sins for a month, or a quarter of a year together; for though I still remained full of doubts as to the truth of religion, yet I thought that, if there was a God and a future state, and if Jesus Christ was indeed the true Messiah and the author of eternal salvation to those who obey Him, I could by no means be saved in the state I was in; and that, being uncertain whether these things were so or not, it was the highest infatuation to leave the eternal happiness or misery of my soul in question, especially as I could be no loser by admitting the truths of religion and living under their influence; whereas, were I to continue in sin under the supposition of their being false, I might find myself fatally mistaken when it would be too late to recant or retrieve my error. But, notwithstanding I came to this conclusion and plainly saw its reasonableness, yet were my religious fits of no long continuance—but every temptation that offered itself hurried me impetuously away, and I became seven times more the child of hell than before. Nevertheless, every new fall increased my anguish of spirit, and set me upon praying and resolving; insomuch that I frequently bound myself under the most solemn imprecations.

"But alas! alas! I was all this while as ignorant of my own weakness, as of Him on whom my strength was laid; and therefore no wonder all my attempts to make myself holy were attended with no better success than if I had tried to wash the Ethiopian white, and answered no other end than to distress my soul a thousand times more than if I had never made such solemn vows; for all this while I had no other notion of religion than that it consisted in something which I was to do in order to make amends to God for my past sins, and to please Him for the time to come; in consideration of which I should escape hell and be entitled to everlasting life.

"In this manner I went on vowing and breaking my vows, sinning and repenting, until my most merciful God and Savior, seeing that all His gracious calls would not overrule the horrible perverseness of my will, instead of giving me up, as in just judgment He might have done, or pronouncing against me that dreadful sentence, 'Cut it down, why does it cumber the ground?' (Luke 13:7)—I say, instead of this, He began to deal with me by a far more violent method than He had hitherto done, filling my soul with the most unimaginable terrors, insomuch that I roared for the very disquietness of my heart. The arrows of the Almighty stuck fast in me, the poison whereof drank up my spirits, and the pains of hell got hold upon me.

"From this time, which was about October, 1757, I may say that sin received its mortal blow, (I mean its reigning power, for God knows the body of sin yet is far from being done away), and I set myself to work with all the earnestness of a poor perishing mariner who is every moment in expectation of shipwreck. I fasted, prayed, and meditated; I read the Scriptures and gave much alms. But these things could bring no peace to my soul; on the contrary, I now saw, what I never had seen before, that all my works were mixed with sin and imperfection. Besides this, Satan furiously assaulted me with suggestions that I had committed the unpardonable sin against the Holy Spirit, and had let my day of grace slip; that therefore my prayers were cast out by God, and were an abomination to Him, and that it was too late to think of mercy when it was the time of judgment.

"It is beyond the power of conception, much more of expression, to form an idea of the dreadful agonies my poor soul was now in. What to do, or to whom to have recourse, I knew not; for, alas, I had no acquaintance with anybody who seemed to have the least experience in such cases. However, those about me showed the greatest concern for my situation, and offered their remedies for my relief, such as company, medicines, exercise, etc., which, in order to oblige them, I complied with; but my disorder not being bodily—but spiritual, was not to be removed by these carnal quackeries, as they were soon convinced.

"I determined to make my case known to Pastor John Fletcher, and accordingly wrote him a letter, without mentioning my name, giving him some account of my situation, and begging him for God's sake, if he had a word of comfort to offer to my poor, distressed, despairing soul, to meet me that very night at an Inn in Salop, in which place I then was. Though Mr. Fletcher had four or five miles to walk, yet he came punctually to the appointment, and spoke to me in a very comfortable manner, giving me to understand that he had very different thoughts of my state from what I had myself. After our discourse, before he withdrew, he went to prayer with me; and among other petitions that he put up in my behalf, he prayed that I might not trust in my own righteousness, which was an expression that, though I did not ask him its import, I knew not well what to make of.

"After my conversation with Mr. Fletcher, I was rather easier—but this decrease of my terrors was but for a few days' duration; for though I allowed that the promises and comforts he would have me apply to myself belonged to the generality of sinners, yet I thought they were not intended for me, who had been so dreadful a backslider, and who, by letting my day of grace slip, had sinned beyond the reach of mercy. Besides I concluded that they could be made effectual to none but such as had faith to apply them; whereas I had no faith, consequently they could avail me nothing. I therefore wrote again to Mr. Fletcher, telling him, as nearly as I can remember, that however others might take comfort from the Scripture promises, I feared none of them belonged to me, who had crucified the Son of God afresh, and sinned wilfully after having received the knowledge of the truth. I told him also, that I found my heart to be exceeding hard and wicked; and that, as all my duties proceeded from a slavish dread of punishment, and not from the principles of faith and love, and were withal so very defective, I thought it was impossible God should ever accept them. In answer to this, the kind and sympathizing Mr. Fletcher immediately wrote me a sweet and comfortable letter, telling me that the perusal of the account I had given him had caused him to shed tears of joy to see what great things the Lord had done for my soul, in convincing me experimentally of the insufficiency of all my own doings to justify me before God, and of the necessity of a saving faith in the blood of Jesus. He also sent me The Life and Death of Mr. Halyburton, Professor of Divinity in the University of St. Andrews, which book I read with the greatest eagerness, as the account Mr. Halyburton therein gives of himself seemed in a very particular manner to tally with my own experience. I therefore thought that what had been might be; that the same God who had showed Himself so powerfully, on the behalf of Mr. Halyburton, and delivered him out of all his troubles, was able to do the same for me.

"You will wonder how I could hold out under all these pressures, the half of which, I might say, has not been told; and indeed it was impossible I could have held out, had it not been that at those very times when I thought all was over with me, there would now and then dart in upon me some comfortable glimmering of hope, which kept me utterly from fainting.

"In this situation I continued from September 1757, to January 1758, when the Vinerian Professor of Oxford began to read a course of lectures upon the Common Law, I resolved to set out for that place, not through any desire I had to attend the lectures, for I had no heart for any such thing—but because I knew I should have chambers to myself in college, and thereby have an opportunity of being much alone, and of giving way to those thoughts with which my heart was big, as also of seeking the Lord with greater diligence, if perhaps I might find Him. Accordingly, when I arrived at the University, though to save appearances I dragged my body to several of the lectures, yet my poor heavy-laden soul engrossed all my attention; and so sharp was the spiritual anguish I labored under, that I scarcely saw a beggar in the streets—but I envied his happiness, and would most gladly have changed situations with him, had it been in my power. O, thought I, these happy souls have yet an offer of mercy, and a door of hope open to them—but it is not so with me; I have rejected God so long, that now God has rejected me as he did Saul; my day of grace is past, irrevocably past, and I have forever shut myself out of all the promises.

"All this while, one thing that greatly astonished me was to see the world about me so careless and unconcerned, especially many that were twice my age among the Doctors of Divinity, and Fellows of the College. Surely, thought I, these people must be infatuated indeed, thus to mind earthly things and to follow the lusts of the flesh, when an eternity of happiness or misery is before them, when they know not how short a time they have to live, and their everlasting state depends on the present moment.

"It was now the season of Lent, the first or second Sunday in which, the sacrament of the Lord's Supper is always administered in Magdalen College Chapel. I therefore besought the Lord with strong cryings, that He would vouchsafe me some token for good, some sense of His love towards me, and willingness to be reconciled to me, that I might wait upon Him at His table without distraction, and partake of those blessings which that ordinance is instituted to convey to the souls of true believers.

"And O, forever and forever blessed be His Holy Name, He did not reject the prayer of the poor destitute; He heard me at the time the storm fell upon me, and I make no doubt had heard, and in His purpose at least, answered me, from the first day He inclined my heart to understand and to seek after Him. But He knew better than I did myself, when it was fit to speak peace to my soul, and therefore waited that He might be gracious unto me.

First, in order to convince me the more deeply of the exceeding sinfulness of sin, and of the desert thereof.

Secondly, to show me more experimentally my own weakness and the insufficiency of any righteousness of my own to recommend me to His favor.

Thirdly, to make me prize more highly, and hunger and thirst more earnestly for Jesus Christ, and the salvation that is in Him.

These ends being in some measure answered, on Saturday, February 18, 1758, to the best of my remembrance, the night before the sacrament it pleased the Lord, after having given me for a few days before some taste of His love, first to bring me into a composed frame of spirit, and then to convey such a thorough sense of His pardoning grace and mercy to my poor soul, that I, who was but just before trembling upon the brink of despair, did now rejoice with joy unspeakable and full of glory! The love of God was shed abroad in my heart through the Holy Spirit who was given unto me, even that perfect love which casts out fear; and the Spirit itself bore witness with my spirit that I was a child of God.

"For some time after these sensible manifestations of God's love were withdrawn, my mind was composed and my hope lively; but I had still, at seasons, secret misgivings and many doubts as to the reality of my conversion, which put me seriously to examine my state, whether the Scripture marks of a work of grace were really to be found in me or not; and in these examinations I had great help from those excellent books, William Guthrie's Trial of a Saving Interest in Christ, and Anthony Palmer's Gospel New Creature. Add to this, that being now in London, I had there the opportunity of hearing that faithful minister of Christ, the Rev. William Romaine, whose discourses were so exactly descriptive of and adapted to my own experience, that they afforded me a good confirmation that I was indeed passed from death unto life, and from the power of Satan unto God.

"During my stay in London, it pleased God to make me acquainted with many of His people, to whom my heart was immediately knit with the closest affection; yes, so great was my love to all those in whom I discerned the divine image of the Lord Jesus, that the yearnings of Joseph's heart towards his brethren will but very faintly express it. Be they who or what they would, high or low, rich or poor, ignorant or learned, it mattered not; if I had reason to believe they were born of God and made partakers of a divine nature, they were equally dear to me; my heart was open to receive them without reserve, and I enjoyed the sweetest fellowship and communion with them, while all other company was insipid and irksome.

"For about two years after this, I was in a good measure relieved from those piercing terrors and that deep distress with which I was before overwhelmed. This, you will say, was living upon frames and experiences, more than upon the exceeding great and precious promises made to returning sinners in Christ Jesus. It is true it was so, and of this God soon convinced me; for I now began to doubt whether these great comforts I had set so high a value upon, might not be all delusion, or proceed from the workings of my own spirit; and if so, my case was just as bad as ever. My day of grace might still be past, and nothing yet remain for me but 'a fearful looking for of judgment and fiery indignation'. (Heb 10:27)

"This was in April, 1759, soon after my return from London into Shropshire, where I had not been long before I wrote to Mr. Fletcher, giving him an account of my state. After this it pleased the Lord to remove my burden, and to exchange these sharp terrors of the spirit of bondage for the sweet reviving comforts of the spirit of adoption, showing me the rich treasures of Gospel promises, and that they, and not my own frames, were to be the ground of my hope and my stay in every time of need. Since this time, I may say with Cowper, that my soul has never experienced the like extremity of terror; and though I have had many ups and downs, many grievous temptations and sharp conflicts, much aridity of soul, deadness, and strong corruptions to fight against—yet have I always found the Lord to be a very present help in trouble; His grace has been sufficient for me in every hour of need, and I doubt not but all His dealings with me, however thwarting to my own ideas of what was fit and necessary for me, have some way or other been subservient to my spiritual interest, since His most sure promise is that all things work together for good to those who love God and are called according to His purpose."

Chapter 10: Imperfect sanctification—the spiritual warfare

It may be difficult to account for the fact, that when the power of God was as sufficient to make the sinner perfect in the new creation—as to implant a principle of spiritual life—he should have left the work imperfect; and that this imperfection, according to the facts of both Scripture and experience, should continue through the whole period of human life, to whatever extent it may be protracted. Some, indeed, seem to suppose that the remainders of sin in believers are seated in the body, and therefore, as long as this sinful body continues, this inbred corruption will manifest itself more or less. This opinion seems to have been imbibed at a very early period of the history of the church, and was probably derived from the Platonic philosophy, which considers matter to be the origin of evil. From this view of the seat of indwelling sin, men in all ages who entertained it have been led to lay great stress on fasting and other bodily austerities—by which the body was enfeebled and emaciated. But the principle assumed being false, all that is built upon it must be false likewise.

The body, though infected with the pollution of sin, through its connection with the soul, is not and cannot be the source of iniquity. Mere matter, however curiously organized and animated, is, apart from the soul, no moral agent, and therefore not susceptible of moral qualities. Sin must have its origin and seat in the free rational soul. The appetites and passions which have their seat in the body, partake of the nature of sin by their excess and irregularity; and by their cravings often influence the will to choose that which is not good, or is not the best. Still, however, the body is a great clog to the soul, and the appetites and passions which are seated in the body, being very urgent in their cravings for gratification, greatly disturb the exercises of piety, and sometimes prevail against the higher principles which by grace have been implanted. As the body is also subject to various diseases, these, on account of the close connection between the soul and body, mightily affect the mind, and often create a great hindrance to devotion and the exercises of piety.

Where two opposite principles exist in the same soul, there must be a perpetual conflict between them, until "the weaker dies". But as the "old man", though crucified, never becomes extinct in this life, this warfare between the flesh and the spirit never ceases until death. As these opposite moral principles operate through the same natural faculties and affections, it is a matter of course, that as the one gains strength the other must be proportionately weakened; and experience teaches that the most effectual way to subdue the power of sin is to nourish and exercise the principle of holiness. But if love to God grows cold or declines in vigor, then the motions of sin become more lively, and the stirring of inbred corruption is sensibly experienced. Just then, in the same proportion, will the principle of evil be diminished as the principle of grace is strengthened. Every victory over any particular lust weakens its power; and by a steady growth in grace, such advantage is obtained over inbred sin, that the advanced Christian maintains the mastery over it, and is not subject to those violent struggles which were undergone when this warfare commenced. Young Christians, however, are often greatly deceived by the appearance of the death of sin, when it only sleeps or deceitfully hides itself, waiting for a more favorable opportunity to exert itself anew. When such a one experiences, in some favored moment, the love of God shed abroad in his heart, sin appears to be dead, and those lusts which warred against the soul, to be extinguished; but when these lively feelings have passed away, and carnal objects begin again to entice, the latent principle of iniquity shows itself; and often that Christian who had fondly hoped that the enemy was slain and the victory won, and in consequence, ceased to watch and pray, is suddenly assailed and overcome by the deceitfulness of sin! Christians are more injured in this warfare by the insidious and secret influence of their enemies lulling them into the sleep of carnal security, than by all their open and violent assaults. No duty is more necessary, in maintaining this conflict, than watchfulness. Unceasing vigilance is indispensable. "Watch and pray that you enter not into temptation!" (Matt 26:41) "And what I say unto you, I say unto all, Watch!" (Mark 13:37)

Lawful pursuits are more frequently a snare than those which are manifestly sinful. It is a duty "to provide things honest in the sight of all men", (Rom 12:17) but while this object is industriously pursued, the love of the world gradually gains ground. The possession of wealth is then viewed as important. Eternal things fade out of view, or viewed as at a great distance, and the impression from them is faint. Worldly entanglements are experienced; the spiritual life is weakened. A sickly state commences, and a sad declension ensues. Alas! What a forlorn state he is now in! Where is the burning zeal with which he commenced his course? Where now are the comforts of piety, with which he was so entirely satisfied that the world was viewed as an empty bauble? Where now is his spirit of prayer, which made this duty his delight? Where now is his love of the Bible, which drew him aside often from worldly business to peruse its sacred instructions? O! what a change! Reader, it is perhaps your own case. "You are the man!" (2 Sam 12:7) who has thus fallen, and left your first love. "Repent, therefore, and do the first works!", (Rev 2:5) lest some heavy judgment fall upon you.

God holds a rod for His own children, and when the warnings and exhortations of the Word, and the secret whispers of the Spirit are neglected, some painful providence is sent—some calamity, which has so much natural connection with the sin, as to indicate that it is intended as a chastisement for it. These strokes are often very cutting and severe—but they must be so to render them effectual. "God disciplines us for our good, that we may share in his holiness. No discipline seems pleasant at the time, but painful. Later on, however, it produces a harvest of righteousness and peace for those who have been trained by it." Hebrews 12:10-11 (NIV)

The followers of Dr. Robert Hawker, in England, who are ultra-Calvinists, entertain the opinion that "the law in our members" (Rom 7:23) is not in the least affected or weakened by our regeneration or sanctification—but that through life it remains the very same, in no way weakened in its strength by any progress in the divine life which the Christian may make. But this is contrary to the Word of God, which speaks of "dying daily unto sin" (Heb 3:13)—of "mortifying the deeds of the body" (Rom 8:13)—"crucifying the flesh", (Gal 5:24) etc. The same opinion, or one near akin to it, was held by Mr. William Walker of Dublin, which he brings to view in his able "Address to the Wesleyan Methodists". His opinion, however, I think, was that there is no such thing as a progressive work of sanctification, which word properly means a consecration to God.

In a former chapter I mentioned the different views of different denominations of Christians respecting the nature of the soul's exercises in conversion—but this difference is far more considerable as it relates to the spiritual conflict and sanctification. It is far from the wish of the writer to give offence to any body of Christians, much less to provoke controversy. This is no proper field for controversy. In the midst of this militant state, there ought to be one peaceful ground, where all true followers of Jesus might sit down together and compare their experiences of the loving kindness and faithful dealings of their Lord and Master. But surely it ought not to be offensive to any body of Christians simply to state what their views are in regard to experimental religion, and how far they agree or differ from those of other Christians. If there be mistakes or erroneous views on any side, they should be considered and corrected.

There has long been a difference of opinion respecting the true interpretation of the Rom 7, in regard to Paul's description of the spiritual conflict, whether he describes the exercises of a converted sinner, whom he personates; or whether he does not rather express honestly the feelings of his own heart, and describe the painful conflict between the powers of sin and holiness which was going on in his own bosom. The latter, undoubtedly, is the obvious meaning, for the apostle speaks in the first person, and gives no notice of introducing a person of another character; and some of the expressions here employed are as strongly descriptive of a regenerate heart as any in the Bible. Who but a regenerate man can say, "I delight in the law of God after the inward man"? (Rom 7:22) And the closing words show clearly enough that the apostle was detailing the exercises of his own soul, for he gives thanks to God for giving him the victory in this severe conflict—but still intimates that the two irreconcilable principles continued, according to their respective natures, to operate within him. "I thank God, through Jesus Christ our Lord. So then with the mind I myself serve the law of God—but with the flesh the law of sin." (Rom 7:25)

Arminius began his career of departure from the commonly received opinions of the Reformed churches by writing a book in exposition of Rom 7; and it is a remarkable coincidence that Faustus Socinus in Poland was engaged at the same time in writing a book on the same subject, and to support the same views. This subject is excellently treated in one of President Dickinson's Letters; and more largely by Fraser on Sanctification. The same subject is also treated accurately and judiciously by Charles Hodge in his Commentary on the Epistle to the Romans.

It is understood that the followers of John Wesley hold, in conformity with his recorded opinion, that sanctification is not a gradual and progressive work, which remains imperfect in the best in this life—but that, like regeneration, it is instantaneous, and that the result is a complete deliverance from indwelling sin; so that from that moment believers are perfectly holy, and sin no more—unless they fall from this high state of grace—in thought, word, or deed. Here then there can be no similarity between the religious experience of an Arminian, who has attained sanctification; and a Calvinist, who is seeking to grow in grace and in the knowledge of our Lord Jesus Christ. The one is conscious of no sin, inward or outward, of nature or of act, and must have perpetual joy—a heaven on earth; while the other is groaning under a deep sense of inherent depravity which works powerfully against his will, and continually interrupts and retards his progress. His frequent language is, "O wretched man that I am! who shall deliver me from the body of this death!" (Rom 7:24)

Here indeed we have a wide difference in the religious experience of professing Christians; and it must be acknowledged that if the experience of the Arminian is in accordance with the Word of God, he has greatly the advantage over the contrite, brokenhearted penitent, whose complaints are so great that they often cause him to wet his couch with tears. How to reconcile these widely different views of our condition as sanctified sinners, I know not. There must be a grand mistake somewhere; and I sincerely pray to God, that if my views on this subject are erroneous, they may be corrected!

The Christian is a soldier and must expect to encounter enemies, and to engage in many a severe conflict. The young convert may well be likened to a raw recruit just enlisted. He feels joyous and strong, full of hope and full of courage. When the veteran Christian warns him of coming dangers and formidable enemies, and endeavors to impress on his mind a sense of his weakness and helplessness without divine aid, the young convert does not understand what he says. He apprehends no dangers or enemies which he is not ready to face, and is ready to think that the aged disciples with whom he converses have been deficient in courage and skill, or have met with obstacles which are removed out of his way. He views the contests of which they speak as the young soldier does the field of battle at a distance, while he is enjoying his wages, and marches about with a conscious exultation on account of his military insignia, and animated with martial music.

The young Christian is commonly treated by his Lord with peculiar tenderness. He is like the babe dandled on the knee, and exposed to no hardships. His frames are lively and often joyous, and he lives too much upon them. His love to the Savior and to the saints is fresh and fervent—and his religious zeal, though not well regulated by knowledge—is ardent. He often puts older disciples to the blush by the warmth of his affections, and his alacrity in the service of his Redeemer. He often indulges a censorious spirit—in judging those who have been long exercised in the spiritual life. This is indeed the season of his "first love" which began to flow in the day of his espousals; and though occasionally dark clouds intercept his views, these are soon forgotten when the clear sunshine breaks forth to cheer him on his way. During this period he delights in social exercises, especially in communion with those of his own age; and in prayer and in praise and spiritual conversation, his heart is lifted up to heaven, and he longs for the time when he may join the songs of the upper temple.

But before long the scene changes. Gradually the glow of fervent affections subsides. Worldly pursuits, even the most lawful and necessary, steal away the heart; and various perplexing entanglements beset the inexperienced traveler. He begins to see that there were many things faulty in his early course. He blames his own weakness or enthusiasm; and in avoiding one extreme he easily falls into the opposite, to which human nature has a strong bias. He enters into more company with the world and, of course, imbibes insensibly some portion of its spirit. This has a deadening effect on his pious feelings; and his devotions become less fervent and less punctual; and far more interrupted with vain, wandering thoughts, than before. He is apt to fall into a hasty or formal attendance on the daily duties of the closet, and a little matter will sometimes lead him to neglect these precious seasons of grace. A strange forgetfulness of the presence of God, and of his accountableness for every thought, word, and action, seizes upon him. Close self-examination becomes painful and, when attempted, is unsuccessful. New evils begin to appear springing up in the heart. Before he is aware, the imagination is filled with sensual imagery, which affording carnal pleasure, the train of his thoughts is with difficulty changed. A lack of prompt resolution is often the occasion of much guilt and much unhappiness. Pride is sure to lift its head—when God is out of view; and it is astonishing how this and kindred evils will get possession and grow, so as to be visible to others, while the person himself is not aware of the disease. Anger, impatience, fretfulness, envy, undue indulgence of the appetites, love of riches, fondness for dress and show, the love of ease, aversion to spiritual duties, with numerous similar and nameless evils are now bred in the heart, and come forth to annoy and retard the Christian in his course. His pride makes him unwilling to open his ear to friendly and fraternal reproof; such words fall heavily on him and wound his morbid sensibility, so that a conflict takes place between a sense of duty and unmortified pride. He inwardly feels that the rebuke of a brother is just, and should be improved to the amendment of the evil pointed out; but pride cannot brook the thought of being exposed and humbled; and he tries to find something in the manner of the rebuke which can be censured; or suspicion will ascribe it to a bad motive.

If, in this spiritual conflict, pride should gain the victory, alas! how much sin follows in its train—resentment towards a kind brother, hypocrisy in concealing the real dictates of conscience, and approbation of the inner man; and a neglect of all efforts at improvement. The person thus circumstanced is instinctively led to endeavor to persuade himself that he has done right. Still, however, the language of his better part is that of self-condemnation. But he hushes it up, and assumes an air of innocence and boldness, and thus the Spirit is grieved. Who can describe the train of evils which ensue on one defeat of this kind? The mind becomes dark and desolate; communion with God is interrupted, and a course of backsliding commences, which sometimes goes on for years, and then the wanderer is not arrested and brought back without chastisement. In such cases the judgments of God against his own straying children are fearful. And if any who have thus declined does not experience them—it is because they are not God's children; "for what son is he whom the father chastens not?" (Heb 12:7)

Worldly prosperity has ever been found to be an unfavorable soil for the growth of piety. It blinds the mind to spiritual and eternal things, dries up the spirit of prayer, fosters pride and ambition, furnishes the appropriate food to covetousness, and leads to a sinful conformity to the spirit, maxims, and fashions of the world. Very few have been enabled to pass this ordeal without serious injury, and have come forth like the three children from Nebuchadnezzar's furnace, without the smell of fire on their garments; but this could not have been unless the Son of Man had been with them. Such people use all their health, influence, and wealth in promoting the kingdom of Christ; but generally, God in mercy refuses to give worldly prosperity to His children. He has "chosen the poor of this world, to be rich in faith"; (James 2:5) that is, He has commonly chosen poverty as the safest condition for His children. His are "an afflicted and poor people, and those who trust in the name of the Lord". (Zeph 3:12)

But the poor have their conflicts and temptations, as well as the rich. They are continually tempted to discontent; to envy at the prosperity of the rich; and sometimes to use unlawful means to satisfy their needs. On account of the dangers of both these conditions, Agur prayed, "Give me neither poverty nor wealth; feed me with the food I need. Otherwise, I might have too much and deny You, saying—Who is the Lord? or I might have nothing and steal, profaning the name of my God." (Prov 30:8-9) We should be content in whatever state Providence has placed us. Those who crave to be rich, are not governed by the wisdom which comes from above. No wonder that they pierce themselves through with many sorrows, and are often in danger of eternal perdition. If we sought wealth from no other motive but to use it for God's glory—it would do us no harm, for this principle would regulate the pursuit, so that it would not be detrimental to the kingdom of God within us.

The enemies of the Christian have been commonly divided into three classes—the world, the flesh, and the devil. But though these may be conceived of, and spoken of separately, they resist the Christian soldier by their combined powers. The devil is the agent; the world furnishes the bait or the object of temptation; and the flesh, or our own corrupt nature, is the subject on which the temptation operates. Sometimes, indeed, Satan injects his fiery darts, enkindled in hell, to frighten the timid soul and drive it to despair; but in this he often overshoots his mark, and drives the poor trembling soul nearer to his Captain, whose broad shield affords ample protection.

We are not to suppose that we are not often led astray by the enticements of sin within us, without the aid of Satan. We need not be afraid of charging too much evil upon this arch adversary. He is ever on the alert, and is exceedingly deceptive in his approaches. Long experience has doubtless greatly increased his power and subtlety, unless he should be more restrained than formerly. Some people make a mock of Satan's temptations, as though they were the dreams of superstitious souls. Not so Paul, and Peter, and John—not so Luther, and Calvin, and Zwingli. Not so any who understand the nature of the spiritual warfare. It is to the great injury of many professors, that they are not constantly on the watch against the wiles of the devil. If you wish to know where he will be likely to meet you, I would say, in your own room, in the church, on your bed, and in your daily company with others. A single thought which suddenly starts up in your mind will show that the enemy is near, and is suggesting such thoughts as without his agency never can be accounted for. "Watch, therefore!" (Matt 24:42; Matt 25:13) "Resist the devil—and he will flee from you!" (James 4:7)

Chapter 11: The spiritual conflict—Satan's temptations—Evil thoughts

We have spoken of the Christian's enemies, in the general; it is now intended to enter into a more particular view of the conflict which is experienced by the pilgrim to Zion.

Swarms of vain thoughts may be reckoned among the first and most constant enemies of the servant of God. The mind of man is like a fountain which is continually sending forth streams. There is not a moment of our waking time when the rational soul is entirely quiescent. How it may be in our sleeping hours, this is not the place to inquire—as we are not in that state engaged in this warfare. Perhaps this is saying too much. I believe that sin may be committed in sleep; for there is often a deliberate choice of evil, after a struggle between a sense of duty and an inclination to sin. And often the same vain and impure thoughts, which were too much indulged in waking hours, infest us when asleep, and may find much readier entertainment than when we have all our senses about us. It is difficult, indeed, to say when moral agency is suspended, so as to render the person inculpable for his volitions; and many know that they consent to temptations in sleep, when they abhor the evil as soon as they are awake. And, in other cases, inclination is indulged, where there is not the least sense of the moral turpitude of the act. But, in some cases, people in sleep consent to sin with a clear apprehension of the evil of the thing to which they consent. Here there must be some guilt, for if there was not an evil nature, prone to iniquity—

such volitions would not take place.

Two things are in our power, and these we should do: first, to avoid evil thoughts and such pampering of the body as has a tendency to pollute our dreams; and, secondly, to pray to God to preserve us from evil thoughts even in sleep. Particularly, we should pray to be delivered from the influence of Satan during our sleeping hours. Andrew Baxter, in his Enquiry into the Nature of the Human Soul, is of opinion that dreams can in no way be accounted for—but by the agency of other spirits acting on ours. While I do not adopt this theory of dreaming, I am inclined to believe that, somehow or other, both good and evil spirits have access to our minds in sleep. They actually seem to hold conversation with us, and suggest things of which we had never thought before.

To return from this digression—it may be safely asserted that no human mind in this world is free from the incursion of vain thoughts. The proportion of such thoughts depends on the circumstances of the individual and the degree of spirituality and self-government to which he has attained. The question very naturally arises here, Is the mere occurrence of vain or wicked thoughts sinful? This is a good question, and should not be answered inconsiderately. It is said in Scripture, "the thought of foolishness is sin"; (Prov 24:9) but by thought in this place we should probably understand "intention". The wise man would teach that sin may be committed in the mind without any external act, a doctrine abundantly taught in other parts of Holy Writ. Or we may understand it to mean that when thoughts of evil are entertained and cherished in the mind, there is sin. But as our thoughts are often entirely involuntary, arising from we know not what causes, it cannot be that every conception of a wrong thing, is itself sinful. If I conceive of another person stealing, or murdering, or committing adultery, if my mind abhors the deed, the mind is not thereby polluted. Thoughts may not in themselves be sinful, and yet they may become so, if they fill and occupy the mind to the exclusion of better thoughts. Ideas of present scenes and passing transactions are not in themselves sinful, because necessary, and often required by the duties which we have to perform; but if the current of these thoughts is so continuous that they leave no room for spiritual meditations, they become sinful by their excess.

Again, every Christian has set times for prayer and other devotional exercises; but if the mind on such occasions wanders off from the contemplation of those objects which should occupy it, such forgetfulness of God's presence, and vain wandering of the thoughts, are evidently sinful. And here is an arena on which many a severe conflict has been undergone, and where, alas! many overthrows have been experienced by the sincere worshiper of God. How our 'perfectionists' dispose of this matter, and what their professed experience is, I know not. I suppose, however, that they are at best no more exempt from wandering thoughts than other Christians; and if so, they must practice a double hypocrisy, first, in persuading themselves that there is no sin in all this; and, secondly, in denying, or concealing from others, their real experience on this subject. But is it not true, that from the very laws of association of ideas there will often be an involuntary wandering of the thoughts? This is admitted; and it is conceded also that it may be impossible in all cases to determine with precision which of our straying thoughts contracts guilt, and how much blame attaches to us, when our thoughts suddenly start aside from the mark, like a deceitful bow.

There are, however, some plain PRINCIPLES which sound reason can establish. If, when the thoughts thus start aside, they are not immediately recalled—then it is sinful. For the mind has this power over its thoughts, and when it is not exercised it argues negligence, or something worse. Again, if this deviation of our thoughts would have been prevented by a solemn sense of the divine presence and omniscience, then it is sinful; for such impressions should accompany us to the throne of grace. And, finally, if the true reason of these erratic trains of thought at such seasons is owing to a secret aversion to spiritual things, and a preference, at the moment, to some carnal or selfish indulgence—then, indeed, there is not only sin—but sin of enormous guilt. It is the direct acting of enmity against God.

There are many, it is to be feared, who take little or no account of their thoughts; and who, if they run through the external round of duties, feel satisfied. Multitudes are willing to be religious and even punctilious in duty, if no demand is made upon them for fixedness of attention, and fervency and elevation of affection. The carnal mind hates nothing so much as a spiritual approach to God, and the remainders of this enmity in the pious are the very "law in their members, which wars against the law of the mind". (Rom 7:23) This is the very core of their inbred sin, from which all evil thoughts proceed, on account of which they need to be humbled in the dust every day that they live.

There is much reason to fear, however, that many who appear to be serious Christians are not at all in the habit of watching their thoughts, and ascertaining the evil that is in them. I knew a person, nearly half a century ago, who, being greatly troubled with wandering thoughts in times of devotion, was solicitous to know whether any other person was troubled in the same way, and to the same degree, with such swarms of vain thoughts. He carefully wrote down what he experienced in this way, and then took it to two serious professors, of whose piety he had a good opinion, and, without intimating that it was his own experience, inquired whether they were acquainted with anything like this. They both acknowledged that they were often interrupted with wandering thoughts in prayer; but in the degree described in the paper, they were not, and could not believe that any real Christian was. There may be, and no doubt is, a constitutional difference among men in regard to this matter. In some minds the links of association are so strong that, when a particular idea is suggested, the whole train must come along, and thus the object previously before the mind is lost sight of, and will not be recovered without a resolute effort.

An old writer says, "What busy flies were to the sacrifices on the altar, such are vain thoughts to our holy services; their continued buzzing disturbs the mind and distracts its devotions". Bernard complained much of these crowds of vain thoughts. He said—"they pass and repass, come in and go out, and will not be controlled. I would fain remove them—but cannot." This is in perfect accordance with Paul's experience, "When I would do good, evil is present with me". (Rom 7:21) And Chrysostom says, "that nothing is more dreadful to the godly than sin. This is death—this is hell". Therefore, though nothing amiss be discerned by man, yet is he afflicted, deeply afflicted on account of his rebellious thoughts, which being in the secret closet of the heart, can only appear unto God.

The same old writer introduces a struggling soul, mourning on this account. "O the perplexing trouble of my distracting thoughts! How do they continually disturb the quiet of my mind, and make my holy duties become a weariness of my soul! They cool the heart, they dampen the vigor, they deaden the comfort of my devotions. Even when I pray God to forgive my sins, I then sin while I am praying for forgiveness; yes, whether it be in the church or in the secret place, so frequently and so violently do these thoughts withdraw my heart from God's service, that I cannot have confidence He hears my plea, because I know by experience I do not hear myself. Surely therefore God must needs be far off from my prayer while my heart is so far out of His presence, hurried away with a crowd of vain imaginations."

To this troubled soul he then applies the following consolations:

"1. These vain thoughts, being your burden, shall not be your ruin; and though they do take from the sweetness, they shall not take from the sincerity of your devotions.

2. It is no little glory which we give to God in the acknowledgment of His omnipresence and omniscience, that we acknowledge Him to be privy to the first risings of our most inward thoughts.

3. It is much the experience of God's children, even the devoutest saints, that their thoughts of God and of Christ, of heaven and holiness, are very unsteady and fleeting. Like the sight of a star through a telescope which is held by a palsied hand, such is our view of divine objects.

4. Know you have the gracious mediation of an all-sufficient Savior to supply your defects, and procure an acceptance of your sincere though imperfect devotions.

5. As you have the gracious mediation of an all-sufficient Savior to supply your defects, so have you the strengthening power of His Holy Spirit to help your infirmities; which strength is made perfect in weakness. (2 Cor 12:9) When you are emptied it shall fill you; when you are stumbled, it shall raise you. The experience of God's saints will tell you that they have long languished under this vexation of vain thoughts: yet, after long conflict, have obtained a joyful conquest, and from mourning doves have become mounting eagles."

The conflict with vain and wandering thoughts is common to all Christians and is the subject of their frequent and deep lamentations: but there are other conflicts which seem to be peculiar to some of God's children, or are experienced in a much greater degree by some than others. These arise from horribly wicked thoughts, blasphemous, atheistical, or abominably impure, which are injected with a power which the soul cannot resist, and sometimes continue to rise in such thick succession that the mind can scarcely be said to be ever entirely free from them. I have known people of consistent piety and sound intellect who have been infested with the continual incursion of such thoughts for weeks and months together: so that they had no rest during their waking hours; and even their sleep was disturbed with frightful dreams. While thus harassed, they had no composure to attend on religious duties. When they attempted to pray, Satan was present with his terrible suggestions, and when they presented themselves with God's people in His house, they found no comfort there, for the thought was continually introduced into their minds that there was no truth in the Bible, or in any of its doctrines.

And it is astonishing what new and unthought of forms of blasphemy and infidelity do, in such cases, arise; so that the ideas which occupy their minds are often inexpressible, and indeed not fit to be expressed in words. These may emphatically be called "the fiery darts of the wicked one". (Eph 6:16) They may be compared to balls or brands of fire cast into a house full of combustibles. The object of the enemy by such assaults is to perplex and harass the child of God, and to drive him to despair; and as many who are thus tempted are ignorant of Satan's devices, and of the "depths" of his subtlety, and charge upon themselves the fault of all these wicked thoughts, the effect aimed at does actually take place. The tempted, harassed soul is not only distressed above measure—but for a season is actually cast down to the borders of despair. We know of no affliction in this life which is more intolerable than such a state of temptation when continued long.

No doubt it is true, that there are certain states of the physical system which favor the effect of these temptations—but this does not prove that these thoughts do not proceed from Satan. This arch-fiend is deeply versed in the make-up of human nature, and wherever he discovers a weak point, there he makes his assault. The melancholic, and people wasted and weakened with excessive grief, are peculiarly susceptible of injury from such temptations; as is that class of doubting, mourning Christians who are forever disposed to look on the dark side of the picture, and who are accustomed "to write bitter things against themselves". (Job 13:26) On uninstructed minds, the effect often is to induce the belief that they have sinned the sin unto death by blaspheming the Holy Spirit; or that they have sinned beyond the reach of mercy, and that God has abandoned them to be a prey to sin and Satan. But it is not upon ignorant, weak, and diseased people only that these furious assaults are made. Such a man as Luther was in frequent conflicts of this kind; and he was so persuaded that these were the temptations of the devil, that he speaks of his presence with as much confidence as if he had seen him by his side.

A friend of the writer was for months so harassed by these fiery darts of the wicked one, that I never saw any human being in a more pitiable condition of extreme suffering; and although there was no intermission during his waking hours, there were seasons when these blasphemous suggestions were injected with peculiar and terrifying violence. Knowing this person to be discreet as well as pious, I requested, by letter, some account of this dreadful state of mind, if there was a freedom to make the communication. In answer I received recently a letter, from which the following is an extract: "I feel a singular reluctance to speak of my religious experience. I have felt that my case was a very remarkable one. I have thought at times that no one could recount a similar experience. It has appeared to me so uncommon, that I have refrained from disclosing the peculiar exercises of my mind to the most intimate friend. I know not that I ever opened to you my case, with the exception of that distressing point to which you refer, and even then I think I was not very particular. That was a season far more distressing than any I ever experienced—'I well remember my afflictions and my misery; the wormwood and the gall.' (Lam 3:19) My deliverance from it was an unspeakable mercy. I have no doubt that the state of my health had some connection with the mental sufferings I then endured. My constitution, which had always been feeble, had given to my disposition a proneness to melancholy; and in my bereaved and desolate state I was peculiarly susceptible of gloomy impressions. My nervous system was deeply affected. Sleep at one time forsook my pillow for successive nights. It was under these circumstances that I sunk into the darkness and distress which you witnessed. In all this there was nothing very remarkable. I think very many can record a similar experience.

"It was not the fact that in a feeble state of health I was dark and comfortless in spirit, that has so much tried me—but the peculiarity of my case seemed to consist in the nature of my spiritual conflicts. You may perhaps recollect that I stated to you that my chief distress arose from blasphemous suggestions—unnatural, monstrous, and horrid—which seemed to fill my mind, and hurry away my thoughts with a force as irresistible as a whirlwind. I strove against them—I prayed against them; but it was all in vain. The more I strove, the more they prevailed. The very effort to banish them appeared to detain them. My soul all this while was wrapped in midnight darkness, and tossed like the ocean in a storm. It seemed to me as if I was delivered over to the powers of darkness, and that to aggravate my wretchedness, some strange and awfully impious association would be suggested by almost every object that met my eye.

"You ask me to describe my deliverance. It was gradual. A return of domestic comforts, a restoration of health, and an occupation of the mind with duty, were the means which God was pleased to bless to the removal of this distressing experience. For twelve or thirteen years I have had no return of this state of mind, except to a partial extent. Yet I have at times been greatly harassed with these fiery darts of the wicked one, which I can truly say are my sorest affliction. I have always noticed that these painful exercises of mind have attended seasons of special examination and prayer. When I have thought most of my obligation to God, and endeavored to meditate most on divine things, then it has been that my mind has suffered most from the intrusion of thoughts at which my soul is filled with anguish, and from which I desire deliverance more than from death. This fact is mysterious to me. I cannot but think I love God. I am sure I do desire an entire consecration to Christ. It is my daily prayer to attain holiness. I esteem the way of salvation glorious, and justification through the alone righteousness of Christ is a precious doctrine. But did ever any Christian experience such trials, is a question which I am ready often to ask. I know of no uninspired writers that have come nearer a description of what I have experienced than John Bunyan and John Newton. The hymn of the latter, commencing with 'I asked the Lord that I might grow', contains many thoughts remarkably accordant with my experience.

"You see I have nothing to relate that is instructive or cheering—and yet I sometimes feel thankful for the terrible conflicts which I endure, for there is nothing which so constantly drives me to a throne of grace—nothing that strips me so entirely of self-dependence, and creates within me such longing after holiness. I am much inclined to think that Satan is far less dangerous when he comes as 'a roaring lion', (1 Pet 5:8) and frightens the soul with his horrid blasphemies, than when 'he transforms himself into an angel of light', (2 Cor 11:14) and seduces our affections gradually and secretly away from God, and attaches them sinfully to the world.

"P.S.—The most discouraging fact in all my experience has been, what I have already alluded to—the rushing in of a tide of unutterably impious thoughts or imaginations, at a time when I have sought the most elevated and glorious views of God, breaking up my peace and comfort when I have tried to fix my mind most intently on spiritual objects. Is the onset of the enemy to drive one from a close communion with God? or is it to be traced to a law of association recalling past experiences?

"If I had more confidence in my religious experience I think I could suggest many thoughts that might be useful to Christians under temptation, and especially when suffering under certain physical disorders. One thing I am free to say—useful occupation is essential to the restoration and peace of some minds."

Many other eminent servants of God have experienced in various forms the same conflicts with the great adversary: and when we describe these temptations as frequent in the experience of the children of God, we do not speak without authority. Paul says, "For we wrestle not against flesh and blood—but against principalities, against powers, against the rulers of the darkness of this world, against spiritual wickedness in high places." (Eph 6:12) From this passage it is evident that our spiritual foes are numerous and powerful, and that the believer's conflict with them is violent: it is a "wrestling", or a contention which requires them to put forth all their strength, and to exercise all their skill. Therefore it was, that the apostle, who was himself engaged in this conflict, urges it upon Christians to put on the armor of God. Against such enemies, armor, offensive and defensive, is requisite. And blessed be God, there is an armory from which such armor may be drawn. Hear Paul's enumeration of the several parts of this panoply: "The belt of truth, the breastplate of righteousness, sandals of gospel peace, the shield of faith (this he places highest, as being an indispensable defense against 'the fiery darts of the wicked'), the helmet of salvation, and the sword of the Spirit, which is the word of God." (Eph 6:14-17) To all which must be added prayer and watchfulness.

As one of God's methods of comforting and strengthening His mourning children is by good books, I embrace this opportunity of recommending to those engaged in the spiritual warfare, William Gurnall's Christian in Complete Armor. In such cases there is almost a necessity of referring to old authors; for somehow or other our modern sermons and tracts touch but seldom on these things, which filled so many of the pages of our fathers.

The soul struggling with the intrusion of wicked thoughts may be supposed to express its feelings in language like the following: "O my wretchedly wicked heart, which is the fountain from which proceed such streams of abominable thoughts! Surely, if I had ever been washed in the fountain of Christ's blood, or at all purified by His Spirit, so foul a corruption could never cleave unto my soul. Woe is me! for so far am I from being a holy temple of the Lord, that my heart rather seems to be the cage of every unclean bird, and even a den of devils. The flames of hell seem to flash in my face, and the amazing terrors of cursed blasphemies torture my soul and wound my conscience even unto death. I would rather choose to die ten thousand deaths than undergo the fears, and frights, and bitter pangs of my horrid thoughts and dreadful imaginations. In every place, in every action—in the church and in my own room—in my meditations and in my prayers, these abominable and tormenting thoughts follow and harass me, so that I loathe myself and am a burden to myself. O wretched man that I am, who shall deliver me from the body of this death! (Rom 7:24) Alas! I perish! While ashamed to speak what I abhor to think, I must needs despair of a cure, not knowing how to lay open my sore."

To a complaint of this kind, the pious Robert Mossom, once Bishop of Londonderry, addresses the following grounds of consolation:

I. "The horrid blasphemies which affright your soul, though they are your thoughts, yet are they Satan's suggestions; and not having the consent of your will, they bring no guilt upon your conscience. It is agreeable to the truth of God's Word, and the judgment of all divines, ancient and modern, that where the will yields no consent, there the soul may suffer temptation—but act no sin. The importunity and frequency of these suggestions which weary the soul, resisting, shall bring a greater crown of glory in its overcoming. True it is that 'We know that anyone born of God does not continue to sin; the one who was born of God keeps him safe, and the evil one cannot harm him'. (1 John 5:18) Is it meant of wicked temptations? No, surely—but of willful transgressions. He touches him not so as to leave the impress of sin and guilt upon the soul. It is no sin to be tempted; for Christ our Lord and Savior was tempted, 'but without sin'. (Heb 4:15) To admit the temptation with allowance or delight, that is sin.

2. "That these foul and frightful suggestions have not the consent of your will appears by this, that you have a loathing and abhorring of them; which speaks the greatest aversion, and so is far from a consenting of the will. What is forcibly cast into the mind cannot be said to be received with our consent. It is out of our power to prevent Satan from suggesting evil thoughts. These arise not from your own corrupt nature; they are brats laid at your door, not your own lawful children. There are the buffetings of Satan. Paul had 'a messenger of Satan to buffet him', (2 Cor 12:7) which was as a 'thorn in his flesh', constantly pricking and keeping him uneasy, and tempting him to impatience. He prayed earnestly and repeatedly to be delivered from this cross—but his request was not granted; yet he received an answer more gracious and beneficial than the removal of the thorn would have been, for the Lord said unto him, 'My grace is sufficient for you.'" (2 Cor 12:9)

The heart assailed by Satan is like a city besieged, within which there lie concealed many traitors who, as far as they dare, will give encouragement and aid to the enemy outside. And this creates the chief difficulty in the case of many temptations; for although there is not a full consent or a prevailing willingness, yet there is something which too much concurs with the temptation; except in shocking blasphemies which fill the soul with terror. The soul afflicted with these temptations is apt to think its case singular. It is ready to exclaim, "Never were any of God's children in this condition. It must be some strange corruption which induces the enemy thus to assault me, and some awful displeasure of God towards me, which makes Him permit such a temptation." To which it may be replied, "Afflictions of this kind are no new thing, and that with the real children of God. Such cases are not uncommon in every age, and occur in the pastoral experience of every faithful minister. Some people have for years been so afflicted with these temptations, that they have pined away and have been brought near the gates of death; and these, too, people of no ordinary piety."

Take then the following directions:

1. Learn to discriminate between the temptations and the sin.

2. Examine with care what transgressions may have occasioned this sore affliction.

3. Humble yourself before God with fasting and prayer, and supplicate the throne of grace to obtain the mercy of God through the merits of your Savior, for the full and free pardon of whatever sin has occasioned these temptations. Beseech God to rebuke Satan, and then make an unreserved resignation of yourself into the hands of Jesus, the Great Shepherd of the flock, that He may keep you as a tender lamb from the paw and teeth of the roaring lion.

4. If still these thoughts intrude, turn your mind quickly away from them; they are most effectually subdued by neglect.

5. "O you afflicted, tossed with tempest and not comforted", (Isa 54:11) act as children do with their parents when they see anything frightful: they cling closer and hold faster. So do you with your God and Savior. Satan's aim is to drive you from God into some desperate conclusions, or into some ruinous act. But you may disappoint this subtle adversary by running to Christ as your refuge, and cleaving to Him with humble, believing confidence; and when Satan sees this, he will soon cease from the violence of his temptations. And when the devil has left you, angels will come and minister unto you; especially the angel of the covenant—Christ Jesus. He shall rejoice your soul with the quickening graces and cheering comforts of His Spirit.

Chapter 12: Growth in grace—Signs of it—Practical directions how to grow in grace—Hindrances to it

"But grow in the grace and knowledge of our Lord and Savior Jesus Christ. To him be glory both now and forever! Amen." 2 Peter 3:18 (NIV)

When there is no growth, there is no life. We have taken it for granted that among the regenerate, at the moment of their conversion, there is a difference in the vigor of the principle of spiritual life, analogous to what we observe in the natural world; and no doubt the analogy holds as it relates to growth. As some children who were weak and sickly in the first days of their existence become healthy and strong, and greatly outgrow others who commenced life with far greater advantages, so it is with the "new man". Some who enter on the spiritual life with a weak and wavering faith, by the blessing of God on a diligent use of means, far outstrip others who in the beginning were greatly before them.

It is often observed that there are professors who never appear to grow—but rather decline perpetually, until they become in spirit and conduct entirely conformed to the world, from whence they professed to come out. The result in regard to them is one of two things; they either retain their standing in the Church and become dead formalists, "having a name to live while they are dead" (Rev 3:1)—they have "a form of godliness, while they deny the power thereof" (2 Tim 3:5). Or they renounce their profession and abandon their connection with the Church, and openly take their stand with the enemies of Christ, and not infrequently go beyond them all in daring impiety. Of all such we may confidently say, "They were not of us, or undoubtedly they would have continued with us." (1 John 2:19) But of such I mean not now to speak further, as the case of backsliders will be considered hereafter.

That growth in grace is gradual and progressive is very evident from Scripture; as in all those passages where believers are exhorted to mortify sin and crucify the flesh, and to increase and abound in all the exercises of piety and good works. One text on this subject will be sufficient: "Grow in grace and in the knowledge of our Lord and Savior Jesus Christ." (2 Pet 3:18) And this passage furnishes us with information as to the origin and nature of this growth. It is knowledge, even the knowledge of our Lord and Savior Jesus Christ. Just so far as any soul increases in spiritual knowledge, in the same degree it grows in grace. People may advance rapidly in other kinds of knowledge, and yet make no advances in piety—but the contrary. They may even have their minds filled with correct theoretical knowledge of divine truth, and yet its effect may not be to humble—but to "puff up". (1 Cor 8:1) Many an accurate and profound theologian has lived and died without a ray of saving light. The natural man, however gifted with talent or enriched with speculative knowledge, has no spiritual discernment. After all his acquisitions, he is destitute of the knowledge of Jesus Christ. But it should not be forgotten that divine illumination is not independent of the Word—but accompanies it. Those Christians, therefore, who are most diligent in attending upon the Word in public and private, will be most likely to make progress in piety.

Young converts are prone to depend too much on joyful frames, and love high excitement in their devotional exercises; but their heavenly Father cures them of this folly, by leaving them for a season to walk in darkness and struggle with their own corruptions. When most sorely pressed and discouraged, however, He strengthens them with might in the inner man. He enables them to stand firmly against temptation; or, if they slide, he quickly restores them, and by such exercises they become much more sensible of their entire dependence than they were at first. They learn to be in the fear of the Lord all the day long, and to distrust entirely their own wisdom and strength, and to rely for all needed aid on the grace of Jesus Christ. Such a soul will not readily believe that it is growing in grace. But to be emptied of self-dependence, and to know that we need aid for every duty, and even for every good thought—is an important step in our progress in piety. The flowers may have disappeared from the plant of grace, and even the leaves may have fallen off, and wintry blasts may have shaken it—but now it is striking its roots deeper, and becoming every day stronger to endure the rugged storm.

One circumstance attends the growth in grace of a real Christian which renders it exceedingly difficult for him to know the fact, upon a superficial view of his case, and that is—the clearer and deeper insight which he obtains into the evils of his own heart. Now this is one of the best evidences of growth; but the first conclusion is apt to be, "I am growing worse every day! I see innumerable evils springing up within me which I never saw before!" This person may be compared to one shut up in a dark room where he is surrounded by many loathsome objects. If a single ray of light is let into the room, he sees the more prominent objects; but if the light gradually increases, he sees more and more of the filth by which he has been surrounded. It was there before—but he did not perceive it. His increased knowledge of the fact is a sure evidence of increasing light.

Hypocrites often learn to talk by rote of the wickedness of their hearts; but go to them and seriously accuse them of indulging secret pride or envy or covetousness or any other heart sins—and they will be offended! Their confessions of sin are only intended to raise them in the opinion of others, as truly humble people; and not that any should believe that corruption abounds within them.

Growth in grace is evidenced by a more habitual vigilance against besetting sins and temptations, and by greater self-denial in regard to personal indulgence. A growing conscientiousness in regard to what may be called minor duties is also a good sign. The counterfeit of this is an over-scrupulous conscience, which sometimes haggles at the most innocent gratifications, and has led some to hesitate about taking their daily food.

Increasing spiritual mindedness is a sure evidence of progress in piety; and this will always be accompanied by deadness to the world. Continued aspirations to God, in the house and by the way, in lying down and rising up, in company and in solitude, indicate the indwelling of the Holy Spirit, by whose agency all progress in sanctification is made. A victory over besetting sins by which the person was frequently led away, shows an increased vigor in grace. Increasing solicitude for the salvation of men, sorrow on account of their sinful and miserable condition, and a disposition tenderly to warn sinners of their danger, evince a growing state of piety. It is also a strong evidence of growth in grace when you can bear injuries and provocations with meekness, and when you can from the heart desire the temporal and eternal welfare of your bitterest enemies. An entire and confident reliance on the promises and providence of God, however dark may be your horizon, or however many difficulties environ you, is a sign that you have learned to live by faith. And humble contentment with your condition, though it be one of poverty and obscurity, shows that you have profited by sitting at the feet of Jesus.

Diligence in the duties of our calling, with a view to the glory of God, is an evidence not to be despised. Indeed there is no surer standard of spiritual growth than a habit of aiming at the glory of God in everything. That mind which is steady to the main end gives as good evidence of being touched by divine grace as the tendency of the needle to the pole proves that it has been touched by the magnet. Increasing love to the brethren is a sure sign of growth; for as brotherly love is a proof of the existence of grace, so is the exercise of such love a proof of vigor in the divine life. This love, when pure, is not confined within those limits which party spirit circumscribes—but overleaping all the barriers of sects and denominations, it embraces the disciples of Christ wherever it finds them. A healthy state of piety is always a growing state; that child which grows not at all, must be sickly. If we would enjoy spiritual comfort, we must be in a thriving condition. None enjoy the pleasures of bodily health—but they who are in health. If we would be useful to the Church and the world we must be growing Christians. If we would live in daily preparation for our eternal change, we must endeavor to grow in grace daily.

The aged saint, laden with the fruits of righteousness, is like a shock of corn fully ripe, which is ready for the garner; or like a mature fruit which gradually loosens its hold of the tree until at last it gently falls off. Thus the aged, mature Christian departs in peace.

As growth in grace is gradual, and the progress from day to day imperceptible, we should aim to do something in this work every day. We should die daily unto sin and live unto righteousness. Sometimes the children of God grow faster when in the fiery furnace than elsewhere. As metals are purified by being cast into the fire, so saints have their dross consumed and their evidences brightened, by being cast into the furnace of affliction. "Beloved, think it not strange concerning the fiery trial which shall try you, as though some strange thing happened unto you", (1 Pet 4:12) but rejoice, because "the trial of your faith, being much more precious than of gold that perishes, though it be tried with fire, shall be found unto praise, and honor, and glory". (1 Pet 1:7)

We shall here present some practical directions how to grow in grace and make progress in piety.

1. Set it down as a certainty that this object will never be attained without vigorous continued effort; and it must not only be desired and sought—but must be considered more important than all other pursuits, and be pursued in preference to everything else which claims your attention.

2. While you determine to be assiduous in the use of the appointed means of sanctification, you must have it deeply fixed in your mind that nothing can be effected in this work without the aid of the Divine Spirit. "Paul may plant and Apollos water—but it is God who gives the increase." (1 Cor 3:6-7) The direction of the old divines is good: "use the means as vigorously as if you were to be saved by your own efforts, and yet trust as entirely to the grace of God as if you made use of no means whatever".

3. Be much in the perusal of the Holy Scriptures, and strive to obtain clear and consistent views of the plan of redemption. Learn to contemplate the truth in its true nature, simply, devoutly, and long at a time, that you may receive on your soul the impression which it is calculated to make. Avoid curious and abstruse speculations respecting things unrevealed, and do not indulge a spirit of controversy. Many lose the benefit of the good impression which the truth is calculated to make, because they do not view it simply in its own nature—but as related to some dispute, or as bearing on some other point. As when a man would receive the genuine impression which a beautiful landscape is adapted to make, he must not be turned aside by minute inquiries respecting the botanical character of the plants, the value of the timber, or the fertility of the soil; but he must place his mind in the attitude of receiving the impression which the combined view of the objects before him will naturally produce on the taste.

In such cases the effect is not produced by any exertion of the intellect; all such active striving is unfavorable, except in bringing the mind to its proper state. When the impression is most perfect, we feel as if we were mere passive recipients of the effect. To this there is a striking analogy in the way in which the mind is impressed with divine truth. It is not the critic, the speculative or polemic theologian, who is most likely to receive the right impression—but the humble, simple-hearted, contemplative Christian. It is necessary to study the Scriptures critically, and to defend the truth against opposers; but the most learned critic and the most profound theologian must learn to sit at the feet of Jesus in the spirit of a child, or they are not likely to be edified by their studies.

4. Pray constantly and fervently for the influences of the Holy Spirit. No blessing is so particularly and emphatically promised in answer to prayer as this; and if you would receive this divine gift, to be in you as a well of water springing up to everlasting life, you must not only pray—but you must watch against everything in your heart or life which has a tendency to grieve the Spirit of God. Of what use is it to pray, if you indulge evil thoughts and imaginations almost without control? or if you give way to the evil passions of anger, pride and avarice, or bridle not your tongue from evil speaking? Learn to be conscientious; that is, obey the dictates of your conscience uniformly. Many are conscientious in some things and not in others; they listen to the monitor within when it directs to important duties; but in smaller matters they often disregard the voice of conscience, and follow present inclination. Such people cannot grow in grace.

5. Take more time for praying to "the Father who sees in secret", (Matt 6:6,18) and for looking into the state of your soul. Redeem an hour daily from sleep if you cannot obtain it otherwise. As the soul's concerns are apt to get out of order, and more time is needed for thorough self-examination than an hour a day, set apart, not periodically but as your necessities require, days of fasting and humiliation before God. On these occasions, deal faithfully with yourself. Be in

earnest to search out all your secret sins and to repent of them. Renew your covenant with God, and form holy resolutions of amendment in the strength of divine grace. If you find, upon examination, that you have been living in any sinful indulgence, probe the corrupting wound to the core; confess your fault before God, and do not rest until you have had an application of the blood of sprinkling. You need not ask why you do not grow, while there is such an ulcer festering within you. Here, it is to be feared, is the root of the evil. Sins indulged are not thoroughly repented of and forsaken; or the conscience has not been purged effectually, and the wound still festers. Come to "the fountain opened for the washing away of sin and uncleanness". (Zech 13:1) Bring your case to the great Physician.

6. Cultivate and exercise brotherly love more than you have been accustomed to do. Christ is displeased with many of His professed followers, because they are so cold and indifferent to His members on earth, and because they do so little to comfort and encourage them; and with some, because they are a stumbling block to the weak of the flock, their conversation and conduct not being edifying—but the contrary. Perhaps these disciples are poor and in the lower walks of life, and therefore you overlook them as beneath you. And thus would you have treated Christ Himself, had you lived in His time; for He took His station among the poor and afflicted; and He will resent a neglect of His poor saints with more displeasure than He would of the rich. Perhaps they do not belong to your party or sect, and you are only concerned to build up your own denomination. Remember how Christ condescended to treat the sinful woman of Samaria, and the poor woman of Canaan, and remember what account He has given of the last judgment, when He will assume to Himself all that has been done, or neglected to be done, to His humble followers. There should be more Christian conversation and friendly fellowship between the followers of Christ. In former days, "those who feared the Lord spoke often one to another, and the Lord hearkened and heard it, and a book of remembrance was written for those who feared the Lord and thought upon his name." (Mal 3:16)

7. If you are in good earnest to make greater progress in piety, you must do more than you have done for the promotion of God's glory and of Christ's kingdom on earth. You must enter with livelier, deeper feeling into all the plans which the Church has adopted to advance these objects. You must give more than you have done. It is a shame to think how small a portion of their gains some professors devote to the Lord. Instead of being a tithe, it is hardly equal to the single sheaf of first fruits. If you have nothing to give, labor to get something. Sit up at night and try to make something, for Christ has need of it. Sell a corner of your land and throw the money into the treasury of the Lord. In primitive times many sold houses and lands and laid the whole at the apostles' feet. Do not be afraid of making yourself poor by giving to the Lord or to His poor. His word is better than any bond, and He says, "I will repay it." (Philem 19) Cast your bread on the waters, and after many days you will find it again. Send the Bible—send missionaries—send tracts to the perishing heathen.

8. Practice self-denial every day. Lay a wholesome restraint upon your appetites. Be not conformed to this world. Let your dress, your house, your furniture, be plain and simple, as becomes a Christian. Avoid vain parade and show in everything. Govern your family with discretion. Forgive and pray for your enemies. Have little to do with party politics. Carry on your business on sober, judicious principles. Keep clear of speculation and suretyships. Live peaceably with all men as much as in you lies. Be much in spontaneous prayer. Keep your heart

with all diligence. Try to turn to spiritual profit every event which occurs, and be fervently thankful for all mercies.

9. For your more rapid growth in grace, some of you will be cast into the furnace of affliction. Sickness, bereavement, bad conduct of children and relatives, loss of property or of reputation, may come upon you unexpectedly and press heavily on you. In these trying circumstances, exercise patience and fortitude. Be more solicitous to have the affliction sanctified, than removed. Glorify God while in the fire of adversity. That faith which is most tried is commonly most pure and precious. Learn from Christ how you ought to suffer. Let perfect submission to the will of God be aimed at. Never indulge a murmuring or discontented spirit. Repose with confidence on the promises. Commit all your cares to God. Make known your requests to Him by prayer and supplication. Let go your too eager grasp of the world. Become familiar with death and the grave. Wait patiently until your eternal change comes; but desire not to live a day longer than may be for the glory of God.

If we are on the watch we may often find good things when they were least expected. It is seldom that I consult an almanac for any purpose—but wishing the other day to see when the moon would change, I opened the calendar at the current month, and the first thing which struck my eye was the heading of a paragraph in the very words which I had selected as the subject of this essay—"Hindrances to Growth in Grace". Of course I perused the short paragraph, and I was so well pleased with what I read that I resolved to take it for my text—and here it is, word for word: "The influence of worldly relatives and companions—embarking too deeply in business—approximations to fraud for the sake of gain—devoting too much time to amusements—immoderate attachment to worldly objects—attendance on an unbelieving or unfaithful ministry—languid and formal observance of pious duties—shunning the society and pious converse of Christian friends—relapse into known sin—non-improvement of graces already attained."

Now all this is very good and very true. The only objection is that several of the particulars mentioned should rather be considered as the effects of a real declension in religion than merely as hindrances to growth; although it is true that nothing so effectually hinders our progress as an actual state of backsliding. It seems desirable to ascertain, as precisely as we can, the reasons why Christians commonly are of so diminutive a stature and of such feeble strength in their religion. When people are truly converted they always are sincerely desirous to make rapid progress in piety; and there are not lacking exceeding great and gracious promises of aid to encourage them to go forward with alacrity. Why then is so little advancement made? Are there not some practical MISTAKES very commonly entertained, which are the cause of this slowness of growth? I think there are, and will endeavor to specify some of them.

1. First, there is a defect in our belief in the freeness of divine grace. To exercise unshaken confidence in the doctrine of gratuitous pardon is one of the most difficult things in the world; and to preach this doctrine fully without verging towards antinomianism is no easy task, and is therefore seldom done. But Christians cannot but be lean and feeble when deprived of their proper nutriment. It is by faith that the spiritual life is made to grow; and the doctrine of free grace, without any mixture of human merit, is the only true object of faith. Christians are too much inclined to depend on themselves, and not to derive their life entirely from Christ. There is

a spurious legal religion, which may flourish without the practical belief in the absolute freeness of divine grace—but it possesses none of the characteristics of the Christian's life. It is found to exist in the greatest growth, in systems of religion which are utterly false. But even when the true doctrine is acknowledged in theory, often it is not practically felt and acted on.

The new convert lives upon his spiritual frames rather than on Christ, while the older Christian is still found struggling in his own strength and, failing in his expectations of success, he becomes discouraged first, and then he sinks into a gloomy despondency, or becomes in a measure careless. At that point the spirit of the world comes in with resistless force. Here, I am persuaded, is the root of the evil; and until Christian teachers inculcate clearly, fully, and practically, the grace of God as manifested in the Gospel, we shall have no vigorous growth of piety among professing Christians. We must be, as it were, identified with Christ—crucified with Him, and living by Him, and in Him by faith, or rather, have Christ living in us. The covenant of grace must be more clearly and repeatedly expounded in all its rich plenitude of mercy, and in all its absolute freeness.

2. Another thing which prevents growth in grace is that Christians do not make their obedience to Christ include every other object of pursuit. Their religion is too much a separate thing, and they pursue their worldly business in another spirit. They try to unite the service of God and Mammon. Their minds are divided, and often distracted with earthly cares and desires which interfere with the service of God. Whereas they should have but one object of pursuit, and all that they do and seek should be in subordination to this. Everything should be done for God and to God. Whether they eat or drink—they should do all to His glory. As the ploughing and sowing of the wicked is sin, because done without regard to God and His glory; in like manner, the secular employments and pursuits of the godly should all be consecrated to God, and become a part of their piety. Thus they would serve God in the field and in the shop, in buying and selling and getting gain—all would be for God. Thus their earthly labors would prove no hindrance to their progress in piety; and possessing an undivided mind, having a single object of pursuit, they could not but grow in grace daily. He whose eye is single shall have his whole body full of light.

3. Another powerful cause of hindrance in the growth of the life of God in the soul, is that we make general resolutions of improvement—but neglect to extend our efforts to particulars. We promise ourselves that in the 'indefinite future' we will do much in the way of reformation—but are found doing nothing each day in cultivating piety. We begin and end a day without aiming or expecting to make any particular advance on that day. Thus our best resolutions evaporate without effect. We merely run the round of prescribed duty, satisfied if we do nothing amiss and neglect no external service which we feel to be obligatory. We resemble the man who purposes to go to a certain place, and often resolves with earnestness that he will some day perform the journey—but never takes a step towards the place. Is it at all strange that that person who on no day makes it his distinct object to advance in the divine life, at the end of months and years is found stationary?

The natural body will grow without our thinking about it, even when we are asleep—but not the life of piety, which only increases by and through the exercises of the mind, aiming at higher measures of grace. And as every day we should do something in this good work, so we should direct our attention to the growth of particular graces, especially of those in which we know ourselves to be defective. Are we weak in faith? let us give attention to the proper means of strengthening our faith and, above all, apply to the Lord to increase our faith. Is our love to God cold and hardly perceptible, and greatly interrupted by long intervals in which God and Christ are not in all our thoughts? let us have this for a daily lamentation at the throne of grace—let us resolve to meditate more on the excellency of the divine attributes, and especially on the love of God to us—let us be much in reading the account of Christ's sufferings and death, and be importunate in prayer, until we receive more copious effusions of the Holy Spirit; for the fruit of the Spirit is love, and the love of God is shed abroad in our hearts by the Holy Spirit who is given unto us. And so we should directly aim at cultivating and increasing every grace; for the divine life, or "new man", consists of these graces, and the whole cannot be in health and vigor while the constituent parts are feeble and in a state of decay.

4. The same remarks are applicable to the mortification of sin. We are prone to view our depravity too much in the general, and under this view to repent of it, and humble ourselves on account of it; whereas, in order to make any considerable growth in grace, we must deal with our sins in detail. We must have it as a special object to eradicate pride and vain glory, covetousness, indolence, envy, discontent, anger, etc. There should be appropriate means used, suited to the extirpation of each particular vice of the mind. It is true, indeed, that if we water the root we may expect the branches to flourish; if we invigorate the principle of piety, the several Christian virtues will flourish. But a skillful gardener will pay due attention both to the root and the branches; and, in fact, these graces of the heart are parts of the root, and it is by strengthening these that we invigorate the root. The same is true as it relates to the remaining principle of sin. We must strike our blows chiefly at the root of the evil tree. And those inherent vices which were mentioned, and others, should be considered as belonging to the root, and when we aim at their destruction particularly and in detail, our strokes will be most effectual.

5. I shall mention at present but one other cause of the slow growth of believers in piety; and that is the neglect of improving in the knowledge of divine things. As spiritual knowledge is the foundation of all genuine exercises of religion, so growth in religion is intimately connected with divine knowledge. Men may possess unsanctified knowledge and be nothing the better for it; but they cannot grow in grace without increasing in the knowledge of our Lord Jesus Christ. "Being," says Paul, "fruitful in every good work, and increasing in the knowledge of God." (Col 1:10) "Grow in grace," says Peter, "and in the knowledge of our Lord Jesus Christ." (2 Pet 3:18) Jonathan Edwards remarks that the more faithful he was in studying the Bible, the more he prospered in spiritual things. The reason is plain—and other Christians will find the same to be true.

Chapter 13: There is a perpetual, and there is a temporary backsliding.

1. The first is the case of those who, being partially awakened and enlightened by the Word accompanied by the common operations of the Spirit, make a profession of religion, and for a while seem to run well, and to outstrip the humble believer in zeal and activity; but having no root in themselves, in the time of temptation fall totally away, and not only relinquish their profession—but frequently renounce Christianity itself, and become the bitterest enemies of religion. Or, seduced by the pride of their own hearts, they forsake the true doctrines of the Gospel, fall in love with some flattering, flesh-pleasing form of heresy, and spend their time in

zealous efforts to overthrow that very truth which they once professed to prize. Or, thirdly, they are overcome by some insidious lust or passion, and fall into the habitual practice of some sin, which at first they secretly indulge—but after a while cast off all disguise, and show to all that they are enslaved by some hurtful and hateful iniquity.

People who thus apostatize from the profession and belief of Christianity, or who fall into a habitual course of sinning, are commonly in the most hopeless condition of all who live in the midst of the means of grace. When they openly reject Christianity, their infidelity is commonly accompanied by contempt and a malign temper, which often prompts them to blasphemy; and they are, according to our apprehension, in great danger of committing the unpardonable sin; and some who in these circumstances are actuated by inveterate hatred to the truth, and who make use of their tongues to express the feelings of enmity which rankle in them, do often fall into this unpardonable sin.

The case of such seems to be described by Paul in Heb 6:6: "For it is impossible for those who were once enlightened, and have tasted of the heavenly gift, and were made partakers of the Holy Spirit, and have tasted the good word of God and the powers of the world to come, if they shall fall away, to renew them again to repentance, seeing they crucify to themselves the Son of God afresh and put him to an open shame." Some suppose that the apostle here describes the character of the true Christian, and that he merely supposes the case, if such should fall away, what would be the fearful consequence; but this seems to us a forced construction. It seems more reasonable to believe that he is describing a case which may, and often does occur, and that the description applies to such professors as had received the miraculous endowments of the Holy Spirit, and yet apostatized: and by crucifying the Son of God afresh he probably alludes to the manner in which those who went back to the Jews were required to execrate the name of Christ in the synagogues, and to profess that He deserved to be crucified as He had been, and thus put Him to an open shame.

But whether such apostates do actually commit the unpardonable sin or not seems in most cases to be of little consequence, for they commonly die in their sins, and all sin unrepented of is unpardonable. In some cases, however, apostates stop short of infidelity and blasphemy, and while they stand aloof from religion, content themselves with decency, and do not treat religion with disrespect; yet it will be found on examination, that the hearts of such are extremely callous, and their consciences are seared as with a hot iron. The Spirit of God evidently has left them, and strives no more with them; and they often die as they have lived—fearfully insensible, having "no bands in their death". (Psalm 73:4) But sometimes conscience is let loose upon them in their last hours, and they are left to die in the horrors of despair. In the days of the apostles they seem to have had some way of knowing when a man had committed "the sin unto death", (1 John 5:16) and for such, Christians were not to pray, as their destiny was irretrievably fixed; but such knowledge cannot be possessed now, and we may therefore pray for all, as long as they are in the place of repentance.

2. But when we speak of backsliding, we commonly mean those sad departures of real Christians from God which are so common, and often so injurious to the cause of religion. These cases are so common, that some have thought that all Christians have their seasons of backsliding, when they leave their first love, and lose the sweet relish of divine things, and are excluded from

intimate communion with God. But, however common backsliding may have been among Christians, there is no foundation for the opinion that it is common to all. We find no such declension in the experience of Paul or John, and in the biographies of some modern saints we find no such sad declension. We could refer to many recorded accounts of personal experience—but it will be sufficient to mention Richard Baxter, Gardiner, George Whitefield, and David Brainerd. No doubt all experience short seasons of comparative coldness and insensibility, and they who live near to God have not always equal light and life and comfort in the divine life. Those fluctuations of feeling which are so common are not included in the idea of a state of backsliding.

Backsliding occurs when the Christian is gradually led off from close walking with God, loses the lively sense of divine things, becomes too much attached to the world and too much occupied with secular concerns; until at length the keeping of the heart is neglected, prayer and the seeking of the Lord in private are omitted or slightly performed, zeal for the advancement of religion is quenched, and many things once rejected by a sensitive conscience are now indulged and defended.

All this may take place and continue long before the person is aware of his danger, or acknowledges that there has been any serious departure from God. The forms of religion may still be kept up, and open sin avoided. But more commonly backsliders fall into some evil habits; they are evidently too much conformed to the world, and often go too far in participating in the pleasures and amusements of the world; and too often there is an indulgence in known sin into which they are gradually led, and on account of which they experience frequent compunction, and make solemn resolutions to avoid it in future. But when the hour of temptation comes, they are overcome again and again, and thus they live a miserable life, enslaved by some sin, over which, though they sometimes struggle hard, they cannot get the victory.

There is in nature no more inconsistent thing than a backsliding Christian. Look at one side of his character and he seems to have sincere, penitential feelings, and his heart to be right in its purposes and aims; but look at the other side, and he seems to be "carnal, sold under sin". (Rom 7:14) O wretched man! how he writhes often in anguish, and groans for deliverance—but he is like Samson shorn of his locks—his strength is departed, and he is not able to rise and go forth at liberty as in former times.

All backsliders are not alike. Some are asleep—but the one now described is in a state of almost perpetual conflict which keeps him wide awake.

Sometimes when his pious feelings are lively, he cannot but hope that he loves God and hates sin, and is encouraged; but oh, when sin prevails against him, and he is led away captive, he cannot think that he is a true Christian. Is it possible that one who is thus overcome can have in him any principle of piety? Sometimes he gives up all hope, and concludes that he was deceived in ever thinking himself converted; but then again, when he feels a broken and contrite heart, and an ardent breathing and groaning after deliverance, he cannot but conclude that there is some principle above mere nature operating in him.

The sleeping backslider is one who, being surrounded with earthly comforts and engaged in secular pursuits, and mingling much with the decent and respectable people of the world, by degrees loses the deep impression of divine and eternal things. His spiritual senses become obtuse, and he has no longer the views and feelings of one awake to the reality of spiritual things. His case nearly resembles that of a man gradually sinking into sleep. Still he sees dimly and hears indistinctly—but he is fast losing the impression of the objects of the spiritual world, and is sinking under the impression of the things of time and sense.

There may be no remarkable change in the external conduct of such a person, except that he has no longer any relish for pious conversation, and rather is disposed to waive it. And the difference between such an one and the rest of the world becomes less and less distinguishable. From anything you see or hear, you would not suspect him to be a Christian, until you see him taking his seat at church. Such backsliders are commonly awakened by some severe judgments; the earthly objects on which they had too much fixed their affections are snatched away; and they are made bitterly to feel that it is an evil thing to forget and depart from the living God.

There is still another species of backsliding, in which by a sudden temptation, one who appeared to stand firm is cast down. Such was the fall of Peter. Many others have given full evidence that a man's standing is not in himself; for frequently men are overcome in those very things in which they were least afraid, and had most confidence in their own strength. These cases are usually more disgraceful than other instances of backsliding—but they are less dangerous; for commonly, where there is grace they produce such an overwhelming conviction of sin, and shame for having acted so unworthily, that repentance soon follows the lapse, and the person, when restored, is more watchful than ever against all kinds of sin, and more distrustful of himself. Such falls may be compared to a sudden accident by which a bone is broken or put out of joint; they are very painful, and cause the person to go limping all the remainder of his life—but do not so much affect the vitals as more secret and insidious diseases, which prey inwardly, without being perceived.

There are many people who never make a public profession of religion, who for a while are the subjects of serious impressions, whose consciences are much awake, and whose feelings are tender. They seem to love to hear the truth, and in a considerable degree fall under its influence, so as to be almost persuaded to be Christians; and for a season give to the pious, lively hopes of their speedy conversion. They are such as the person to whom Christ said, "You are not far from the kingdom of God." (Mark 12:34) But through the blinding influence of avarice or ambition, or some other carnal motive, they are led away and lose all their serious thoughts and good resolutions. Such people usually lose their day of grace. I have seen an amiable young man weeping under the faithful preaching of the Gospel, and my hopes were expectant that I would soon see him at the table of the Lord; but alas! I believe that on that very day he quenched the Spirit, and has been going further and further from the Lord ever since!

The backsliding believer can only be distinguished from the final apostate, by the fact of his recovery. At least, when Christians have slidden far back, no satisfactory evidence of the genuineness of their piety can be exhibited, nor can they have any which ought to satisfy their own minds. In the course of pastoral visitation I once called upon an habitual drunkard who had been a flaming professor. I asked him what he thought of his former exercises of religion. He said that he was confident that they were genuine, and expressed a strong confidence that the

Lord would recover him from his backsliding state. Now here was the very spirit of Antinomianism. Whether he was ever recovered from his besetting sin I cannot tell—but I rather think that he continued his decadent habits to the very last.

I have often noticed how tenaciously the most profane and obstinate sinners will cleave to the hope of having been once converted, if they have ever been the subjects of religious impressions. One of the profanest men I ever heard speak, and one of the most outrageous drunkards, when asked on his deathbed, to which he was brought by alcohol, respecting his prospects beyond the grave, said, that when a very young man he had been among the Methodists, and thought that he was converted; and though he had lived in the most open and daring wickedness for more than twenty years since that time, yet he seemed to depend on those early exercises. Miserable delusion! But a drowning man will catch at a straw. An old sea-captain whom I visited on his deathbed seemed to be trusting to a similar delusion. He related to me certain religious exercises which he had when he first went to sea—but of which he had no return ever since, though half a century had elapsed. I have met with only a few people who had neglected to cherish and improve early impressions, who were ever afterwards hopefully converted. They are generally given up to blindness of mind and hardness of heart. But some of these are sometimes brought in, in times of revival; or, at a late period, driven to the Gospel refuge by severe affliction.

The conviction of a Christian backslider is often more severe and overwhelming than when first awakened. When his eyes are opened to see the ingratitude and wicked rebellion of his conduct, he is ready to despair, and to give up all hopes of being pardoned. He sinks into deep waters where the billows of divine displeasure roll over him; or he is like a prisoner in a horrible pit and in the miry clay. All around him is dark and desolate, and he feels himself to be in a deplorably helpless condition. His own strivings seem to sink him deeper in the mire; but as his last and only resource, he cries out of the depths unto God. As his case is urgent he cries with unceasing importunity, and the Lord hears the voice of his supplications. He brings him up out of the horrible pit, and places his feet upon a rock, and establishes his goings, and puts a new song into his mouth, even of praise to the Redeemer. The freeness of pardon to the returning backslider is a thing which is hard to be believed until it is experienced.

No sooner is the proud heart humbled, and the hard heart broken into contrition, than Jehovah is near with His healing balm. To heal the broken in heart, and to revive the spirit of the contrite ones—is the delight of Immanuel. And he receives the returning penitent without reproaches. He pardons him freely, sheds abroad His love in his heart, and fills him with the joy of the Holy Spirit. It is in fact, somewhat of a new conversion; though there is but one regeneration. We never hear of a sinner being born a third time—but we remember that Christ said unto Peter, "When you are converted, strengthen your brethren." (Luke 22:32) Indeed, the exercises of the soul on these occasions may be so much more clear and comfortable than on its first conversion, that the person is disposed to think that this is the real commencement of spiritual life, and to set down all his former experience as spurious, or at least essentially defective.

Christians, when recovered from backsliding, are commonly more watchful, and walk more circumspectly than they ever did before. They cannot but be more humble. The remembrance of their base departure from God fills them with self-loathing. Whenever spiritual pride would lift up its head, one thought of a disgraceful fall will often lay the soul in the dust. And whether the backslider's sins have been open or secret, the recollection of his traitorous behavior fills him with shame and self-abhorrence. When such people have so conducted themselves as to bring upon them the censures of the church, so as to be separated from the communion of the Lord's people, at first, it is probable, resentment will be felt towards the officers of the church who perform the painful duty. But after reflection, these resentments are turned against themselves, and they pass much heavier censures on themselves than the church ever did.

Judicious, seasonable discipline is a powerful means of grace, and often would be the effectual means of recovering the backslider, if exercised as it should be. Indeed, this may be said to be one main design of its appointment. If whenever there is an appearance of declension in a church member, the pastor, or some other officer of the church, should go to the person, and in the spirit and by the authority of Christ should address a serious admonition to him, and then a second and a third; and if these were unheeded, then bring him before the church—backsliding, in most cases, would be arrested before it proceeded far.

But all Christians have a duty to perform towards erring brethren. When they see them going astray, they should not act towards them as if they hated them—but should rebuke them in the spirit of meekness. Christian reproof from one Christian to another seems to be almost banished from our churches. There is a quick eye to discern a brother's faults, and a ready tongue to speak of them to others; but where do we now find the faithful reprover of sin, who goes to the man himself, without saying a word to anyone, and between themselves, faithfully warns, exhorts, and entreats a straying brother to return. The serious discipline of formal accusations, and witnesses, etc., by such a course would be in a great measure rendered unnecessary. But the common practice is to let the evil grow until it has become inveterate, and breaks out into overt acts—and then there is a necessity to pay attention to the matter, and to put in force the discipline of the church. But even this often proves beneficial, and is a powerful means of reclaiming the offender; or, if he persists in his evil courses, it serves to separate an unworthy member from the communion of saints.

But when church officers and private Christians utterly fail in their duty towards backsliding brethren, God Himself often makes use of means of His own, which do not require the intervention of men. He smites the offender with His rod, and causes him to smart in some tender part. He sends such afflictions as bring his sins forcibly before his conscience. He deprives him of the objects for the sake of which he forsook the Lord—it may be of the wife of his youth, or of a beloved child, on which his affections were too fondly fixed so as to become idolatrous. Or if it was the love of the world which was the seductive cause of his backsliding, riches are caused to "make to themselves wings and fly away like the eagle to heaven". (Prov 23:5) Or was the love of ease and indulgence of the sensual appetites the cause of his delinquency, the stroke falls on his own body. He is brought low by sickness, and is tried upon his bed with excruciating pains, until he cries out in his distress and humbly confesses his sins. Or if he was carried away by an undue love of the honor from men, it is not unlikely that his reputation, which he cherished with a fondness which caused him to neglect the honor of his God, will be permitted to be tarnished by the tongue of slander, and things may be so situated that, although innocent, he may not have it in his power to make the truth appear. Children, too much indulged, become by their misconduct, heavy causes of affliction to parents; and thus they are made to suffer in the very point where they had sinned. Look at the case of Eli and of David.

All afflictions are not for chastisement--but sometimes for trial; and those whom God loves best are the most afflicted in this world. They are kept in the furnace, which is heated seven times hotter--until their dross is consumed, and their piety shines forth as pure gold which has been tried in the fire. "I will put this third through the fire; I will refine them as silver is refined, and test them as gold is tested. They will call on My name, and I will answer them. I will say: They are My people, and they will say: The Lord is our God." Zechariah 13:9. "You have tested us, O God; you have purified us like silver melted in a crucible." (Psalm 66:10) "I have refined you in the furnace of suffering." (Isaiah 48:10)

But we are now concerned only with those afflictions which are most effective to bring back the backslider, the virtue of which the psalmist acknowledges when he says, "Before I was afflicted I went astray, but now I keep Your word. It was good for me to be afflicted so that I could learn Your statutes. I know, Lord, that Your judgments are just and that You have afflicted me fairly. (Psalm 119:67, 71, 75) It may be truly said that many who had backslidden never would have returned had it not been for the rod; other means seemed to have lost their power—but this comes home to the feelings of everyone. Whether a believer is ever permitted to die in a backslidden state is a question of no practical importance; but it seems probable that Christians die in all conditions, including spiritual declension. No one has any right to presume that if he backslides, death may not overtake him in that unprepared condition. Backsliding then is a fearful evil; may we all be enabled to avoid it; or if fallen into it, to be recovered speedily from so dangerous a state!

Chapter 14: The rich and the poor—The various trials of believers

They are not 'the happy' whom the blinded world think to be such. The man of successful enterprise and increasing wealth had some enjoyment while busily occupied in making a fortune—but now when he has arrived at a higher pitch of wealth than his most expectant hopes had anticipated—he is far from being happy, or even contented. The desire of acquisition has grown into an inveterate habit, and he cannot stop in his career; he must find out some new enterprise; he must engage in some new speculation; and before all is over, it is well if he loses not all he had gained. Being accustomed to live high, he is unprepared to meet poverty; and to preserve his family from such a mortifying change of circumstances, he contrives ways and means to defraud his creditors. This man is not happy in his prosperity, and under a reverse of fortune he is truly miserable. He has put away a good conscience, which is the most essential ingredient in that peace which Christ gives to His disciples. His reputation too, if not tarnished, remains under a dark cloud of suspicion which never can be removed. In the world around he meets with neglect and sometimes contempt from those on whom he once looked down; at home he has before him the sad spectacle of a family degraded from their former rank and under all the feelings of mortified pride, struggling to conceal their poverty from the gaze and contempt of an unpitying world.

But even if no reverse is experienced and the man continues to be successful in all his enterprises, and if at the close of his career he can calculate millions in the bank or in real estate, his only remaining difficulty is how to dispose of such a mass of wealth. He has a son, it is true—but he is a base profligate, and in a single year would, by reckless speculation or at the gaming table, dissipate the whole which has been so carefully hoarded up. And yet this man could scarcely be induced to give a dollar to any benevolent object, lest he should lessen the amount which he was by every means raking together for this unworthy son. He has daughters, too, whose husbands in selecting them had more respect to their fortunes than to any personal qualifications, and these are impatient that the old man should live so long, and hold the purse-strings with so close a grip. Though they will go through all the ceremonial of deep grief, and mourn as decently and as long as fashion requires, yet no event is heard with more heart-felt pleasure than that their aged relative is at last obliged to give up all his possessions!

Are the rich happy? Not such as have been described. But there are a favored few who seem to have learned the secret of using wealth so as to do much good, and to derive from it much enjoyment. They are desirous of making increase too—but it is all for the Lord; not to be hoarded until they are obliged to leave it, and then to be distributed among benevolent societies. No! They are continually contriving methods of making it produce good—now. They are frugal to themselves, that they may be liberal to the poor, and may be able to enrich the treasury of the Lord. Such men are blessed in their deed; and though unostentatious in their charities, their light cannot be hidden. A few rich men of this description have lived in England, and even our new country records with gratitude the names of a few benefactors of the public; and we trust in God that the number will be multiplied. Reader, go and do likewise.

But, more commonly, the elect of God are not called to glorify Him in this way. Wealth is a dangerous talent, and is very apt so to block up the way to heaven, that those who do press in, have, as it were, to squeeze through a gate as difficult of entrance as the eye of a needle to a camel. Alas! many professors who bid fair for heaven when in moderate circumstances, after becoming rich are found "drowned in perdition"—"pierced through with many sorrows". (1 Tim 6:9-10)

Poverty and suffering are by infinite wisdom judged best for the traveler to Zion. Let the Lord's people be contented with their condition, and thankful that they are preserved from snares and temptations which they would have found it difficult to withstand. God will not allow them to be tempted above what they are able to bear—but with the temptation provides a way for their escape.

The rich are exposed to suffering as well as the poor, though their sufferings may be of a different kind. The poor man may be forced by necessity to live on coarse bread; the rich man also, while tantalized with the daily sight of the finest of the wheat, is obliged for the sake of his health to live upon bran. The poor man lies on a hard bed because he can afford to get no better; the rich man lies as hard to preserve himself from the aches and pains which are the natural fruit of luxury. The poor man has little of the honors of the world—but then he is envied by none, and passes along in obscurity, without being set up as a mark to be shot at by envy and malignity, which is often the lot of the rich. When sickness comes, the rich man has some advantages—but when oppressed with painful sickness, neither a bed of down, nor rich hangings and carpets, contribute anything to his relief; and in such a time of distress the privations of the poor, though the imagination readily magnifies them, add not much to the pain produced by disease.

But we have dwelt too long on this comparison between the real sufferings of the rich and the poor. Happiness after all, depends upon the submission and patient temper of the mind, than upon external circumstances. And indeed, so short is the time of man's continuance upon earth, and so infinite the joys or miseries of the future world, that to make much of these little differences would be like estimating the weight of a feather, when engaged in weighing mountains. Who thinks it a matter of any concern, whether the circumstances of people who lived a thousand years ago were affluent or destitute, except so far as these external enjoyments and privations contributed to their spiritual improvement, or the contrary? If we could be duly impressed with the truths which respect our eternal condition, we would consider our afflictions here on earth, as scarcely worthy of being named. Thus the apostle Paul seemed to view his own sufferings, and those of his fellow Christians, when he said, "For I reckon that the sufferings of this present time, are not worthy to be compared with the glory which shall be revealed in us." (Rom 8:18) Compared with the sufferings of others, those of the apostle were neither few nor small; but in the view of eternity by faith, he calls them "these light afflictions which are but for a moment"; (2 Cor 4:17) and he had learned the happy are, not only of being contented in whatever state he was—but of rejoicing in all his tribulations. Not that tribulation, considered in itself, could be a matter of rejoicing, for who ever found pain and reproach to be pleasant? But he rejoiced in these things on account of their beneficial effects, "but we also rejoice in our afflictions, because we know that affliction produces endurance, endurance produces proven character, and proven character produces hope." (Rom 5:3-4) The primitive Christians were encouraged to bear patiently and joyfully their present sufferings, on account of the rich and gracious reward which awaited them in the world to come. Upon the mere principle of contrast, our earthly sorrows will render our heavenly joys the sweeter.

But this is not all: hear the words of Jesus Himself, "Blessed are those who are persecuted for righteousness' sake, for theirs is the kingdom of heaven. Blessed are you when men shall revile you, and persecute you, and say all manner of evil against you falsely, for my sake: rejoice and be exceeding glad, for great is your reward in heaven." (Matt 5:10-12) Peter also testifies, "and if you suffer for righteousness' sake, happy are you" (1 Pet 3:14)—"for it is better, if the will of God be so, that you suffer for well doing than for evil doing. For Christ once suffered, the just for the unjust." (1 Pet 3:17-18) He was also of the same opinion with his brother Paul, that Christians ought to rejoice in all their sufferings for righteousness' sake. "Beloved," says he, "do not be surprised at the painful trial you are suffering, as though something strange were happening to you. But rejoice that you participate in the sufferings of Christ, so that you may be overjoyed when his glory is revealed. If you are insulted because of the name of Christ, you are blessed, for the Spirit of glory and of God rests on you." (1 Pet 4:12-14) "However, if you suffer as a Christian, do not be ashamed, but praise God that you bear that name." (1 Pet 4:16)

Let Zion's mourners lift up their heads and rejoice, for though weeping may endure for a night, joy comes in the morning! Let all Christians manifest to others the sweetness and excellency of piety by rejoicing continually in the Lord. The perennial sources of their spiritual joy can never fail—for while God lives and reigns they ought to rejoice. Since Christ has died, and ever lives to make intercession for them, they have ground of unceasing joy. While the throne of grace is accessible, let the saints rejoice; let them rejoice in all the promises of God, which are exceeding great and precious, and are all yes and amen in Christ Jesus to the glory of God.

In one sense all our sufferings are the fruits of sin—for if we had never sinned we would never have suffered. But in another sense, the sufferings of believers are produced by love: "whom the Lord loves he chastens, and scourges every son whom he receives". (Heb 12:6) As in the economy of salvation, God leaves His chosen people to struggle with the remainders of sin in their own hearts, so He has ordained, that their pilgrimage to the heavenly Canaan shall be through much tribulation. From the beginning, the saints have generally been a poor and afflicted people, often oppressed and persecuted; and when exempt from sufferings from the hands of men, they are often visited with sickness, or have their hearts sorely lacerated by the bereavement of dear friends, are punished with poverty, or loaded with calumny and reproach. There seems to be an incongruity in believers enjoying ease and prosperity in this world, when their Lord was "a man of sorrows and acquainted with grief". (Isa 53:3) It seems, indeed, to be a condition of our reigning with Him, that we should suffer with Him. When James and John, under the influence of ambition, asked for the highest places in His kingdom, He said to them, "Can you drink of the cup which I drink of, and be baptized with the baptism that I am baptized with?" (Mark 10:38) They seem not to have understood His meaning, for with self-confidence they answered, "We are able." (Matt 20:22) He replied, "You shall indeed drink of the cup that I drink of, and be baptized with the baptism that I am baptized with." (Mark 10:39)

For the Christian to seek great things for himself here in this world, does not befit the character of a disciple of the meek and lowly Jesus. The early Christians were called to endure much persecution—but they did not count their lives dear unto them. When the apostles, after our Lord's ascension, were publicly beaten for preaching that the Savior was risen, they rejoiced together that they were counted worthy to suffer such things for His name's sake.

It is a striking peculiarity in the religion of Christ, that in the conditions of discipleship, "taking up the cross" (Matt 16:24; Mark 8:34; Luke 9:23) is the first thing. He never enticed any to follow Him with the promise of earthly prosperity, or exemption from suffering. On the contrary, He assures them that in the world they shall have tribulation. (John 16:33) He does, indeed, promise to those who forsake father and mother, wife and children, brothers and sisters, houses and lands—a compensation of a hundredfold more than they had left; but He permits them not to fall into the delusion that this hundredfold was to consist in earthly good things, for He immediately adds, "with persecutions". (Mark 10:30) Whoever will not take Christ with His cross shall never sit with Him on His throne. "No cross, no crown", holds out an important truth in few words. In his intercessory prayer, Christ does request for His disciples that they may be kept from the evil which is in the world, (John 17:15) but He means from the "evil one"—from the evil of sin, and from temptations above their strength to endure.

The reasons why Christ has chosen that His people should be afflicted, and often sorely persecuted, are not difficult to ascertain. We have already shown that the rod is one of God's means for recovering backsliders from their wanderings; but afflictions are also employed to prevent Christians from backsliding. In prosperity, pride is apt to rise and swell; carnal security blinds their eyes; the love of riches increases; spiritual affections are feeble; and eternal things are viewed as far off, and concealed by a thick mist. These circumstances are, indeed, the common precursors of backsliding; but to prevent this evil, and to stir up the benumbed feelings of piety, the believer is put into the furnace. At first he finds it hard to submit, and is like a wild bull in a net. His pride and his love of carnal ease resist the hand that smites him; but severe pain awakes him from his spiritual sleep. He finds himself in the hands of his heavenly Father, and sees that nothing can be gained by murmuring or rebelling. His sins rise up to view, and he is convinced of the justice of the divine dispensations. His hard heart begins to yield, and he is stirred up to cry mightily to God for helping grace. Although he wishes and prays for deliverance from the pressure of affliction, yet he is more solicitous that it should be rendered effectual to subdue his pride, wean him from the love of the world, and give perfect exercise to patience and resignation, than that it should be removed. He knows that the furnace is the place for purification. He hopes and prays that his dross may be consumed, and that he may come forth as gold which has passed seven times through the refiner's fire.

Paul attributes a powerful efficacy to afflictions, so as to place them among the most efficacious means of grace. "For," says he, "our light affliction, which is but for a moment, works out for us a far more exceeding and eternal weight of glory." (2 Cor 4:17) "Furthermore, we had natural fathers discipline us, and we respected them. Shouldn't we submit even more to the Father of spirits and live? For they disciplined us for a short time based on what seemed good to them, but He does it for our benefit, so that we can share His holiness. No discipline seems enjoyable at the time, but painful. Later on, however, it yields the fruit of peace and righteousness to those who have been trained by it." (Heb 12:9-11) When faith is in very lively exercise, believers can rejoice even in tribulation. Not that they cease to feel the pain of the rod—for then it would cease to be an affliction—but while they experience the smart they are convinced that it is operating as a beneficial, though bitter medicine; and they rejoice in the prospect or feeling of returning spiritual health.

But again, God does not pour the rich consolations of His grace into a heart that is not broken. "He sends the rich empty away." (Luke 1:53) "The whole need not a physician." (Matt 9:12; Luke 5:31) But when by affliction He has broken the hard heart and emptied it of self-confidence, He delights to pour in the joy of the Holy Spirit. Therefore it often occurs that the believer's most joyful seasons are his suffering seasons. He has, it is true, more pungent pain than when in prosperity and ease—but he has also richer, deeper draughts of consolation. Though sorrow and joy are opposite, there is a mysterious connection between them. Sorrow, as it were, softens and prepares the heart for the reception of the joy of the Lord.

As the dispensations of God towards His children are exceedingly diverse in different ages; likewise His dealings with individual believers who live at the same time are very different. Why it is so we cannot tell; but we are sure that He has wise reasons for all that He does. In some cases pious people appear to pass through life with scarcely a touch from His rod; while others, who to us do not appear to need more chastisement than those, are held the greater part of their life under the heavy pressure of affliction, with scarcely any intermission. Here is a Christian man who has nearly reached the usual termination of human life, and has hardly known what external affliction is in his own experience. Prosperity has attended him through his whole course. But there is a desolate widow who has been bereaved of her husband and children, and has neither brother nor sister, nephew nor niece, and for eight years has been confined to her bed by wasting and painful disease, and has no hope of relief on this side of the grave.

Such a disparity is striking; but we see only the outside of things. There are sore afflictions of the mind, while the body is in health. That man may have had severer chastisement of the mind—than this afflicted, desolate widow. I have heard an aged Christian declare that though he had experienced much sickness, lost many dear friends, and met with many sore disappointments in life, his sufferings on these accounts were not to be compared with the internal anguish which he often endured, and of which no creature had the least conception. This shows that we are not competent to form an accurate judgment of the sufferings of different people. Besides, when affliction has been long continued, we become in a measure accustomed to it and, as it were, hardened against it; but when we judge of such cases, we transfer our own acute feelings to the condition, which are no correct standard of the sufferings, of the patient under a lingering disease.

The widow to whom I referred was not a fictitious person—but a real person. I once visited her and conversed with her and found her serene and happy, desiring nothing but a speedy departure, that she might be absent from the body, and present with the Lord. But she was not impatient; she was willing to remain and suffer just as long as God pleased. Her heart was truly subdued to the obedience of Christ. There was only one earthly object for which she seemed to feel solicitude, and that was the little forsaken and almost desolate church of which she was a member. For a series of years disaster after disaster had fallen upon this little flock. Their house of worship had been accidentally burned, and was in need of repair; and they had been so long without a pastor that they dwindled down to a few disheartened and scattered members, and only one aged elder remained. Seldom was there a sermon, as they had no convenient house of meeting. Now although this poor widow could not have attended if there had been preaching every Lord's day, yet that little church lay as a burden on her mind; and I heard a minister who knew the circumstances say, that as once a poor wise man saved a city, so this poor, pious widow by her prayers saved a church from extinction. For before her death, a neat, new church was erected, and a pastor settled, and a number of souls hopefully converted and gathered into the church.

I was once on a visit with a friend who requested me to accompany her to see a sick woman, supposed to be near her end. The house was a mere wreck of a once comfortable dwelling. Every appearance of comfort was absent. The partitions appeared to have been taken down, and the whole house was turned into one large room. There was no glass in the windows. Upon entering this desolate place, I saw the sick woman lying on a miserable bed, unable to raise her head from the pillow, and attended only by an aged mother over eighty years of age, and a little daughter about seven or eight. I was told that her brutal husband generally came home drunk, and never gave her a kind or soothing word. Here, indeed, seemed to be the very picture of wretchedness. Hear the conclusion. I truly thought before I left the house--that this was the happiest woman I ever saw! Her devout and tender eye was sweetly fixed on heaven. Her countenance was serene, and illumined with a heavenly smile. "Let me die the death of the righteous—and may my end be like theirs!" Numbers 23:10

Chapter 15: Deathbed of the believer

We have arrived now at a very solemn part of our subject. The writer feels that it is so to himself, as he knows that he must soon be called to travel the road which leads to the narrow house appointed for all living. If after having gone through this scene, he were permitted to return and finish these papers on Religious Experience, by narrating what the soul suffers in passing the gate of death, and more especially what are its views and feelings the moment after death—he would be able to give information which at present no mortal can communicate.

The thought has often occurred, when thinking on this subject, that the surprise of such a transition as that from time to eternity—from the state of imprisonment in this clay tenement to an unknown state of existence—would be overwhelming even to the pious. But these are shortsighted reflections. We undertake to judge of eternal things by rules only suited to our present state of being and our present feelings. That the scene will be new and sublime, beyond all conception, cannot be doubted; but what our susceptibilities and feelings will be, when separated from the body, we cannot tell.

Is it not possible that our entrance on the unseen world may be preceded by a course of gradual preparation for the wonderful objects which it contains, analogous to our progress through infancy in the present world? That knowledge of future things will be acquired gradually and not instantaneously, we are led to believe from the constitution of the human mind, and from all the analogies of nature. The soul may therefore have to go to school again, to learn the first elements of celestial knowledge; and who will be the instructors, or how long this training may continue, it would be vain to conjecture.

Whether in this gradual progress in the knowledge of heavenly things our reminiscence of the transactions in which we were engaged upon earth will be from the first vivid and perfect, or whether these things will at first be buried in a sort of oblivion, and be brought up to view gradually and successively, who can tell us? But I must withdraw my imagination from a subject to which her powers are entirely inadequate. Though I have been fond of those writings of Thomas Dick, Isaac Taylor, and Isaac Watts, which give free scope to reasonings from analogy in regard to the future condition of the believer; yet I am persuaded that they add nothing to our real knowledge. Their lucubrations resemble the vain efforts of a man born blind to describe to his fellow-sufferers the brilliance of the stars, the splendors of the sun, or the milder beauties of a lovely landscape. While he seems to himself to approach nearest to the object, he is in fact most remote from any just conceptions of it.

This brings to recollection, what has often appeared highly probable in regard to the development of our mental powers, that as in infancy some of our most important faculties, as for example, reason, conscience, and taste, are entirely dormant, and gradually and slowly make their appearance afterwards; so, probably, this whole earthly life is a state of infancy in relation to that which is to come, and there may exist now, in these incomprehensible souls of ours, germs of faculties never in the least developed in this world—but which will spring into activity as soon as the soul feels the penetrating beams of celestial light, and which will be brought to maturity just at the time when they are needed. The capacity of the beatific vision may now be possessed by the soul, deeply enveloped in that darkness which conceals the internal powers of the mind even from itself, except so far as they are manifested by their actual exercise. How shallow then is all our mental philosophy, by which we attempt to explore the depths of the human mind!

But are these conjectural speculations for edification? Do they bring us any nearer to God and to our beloved Redeemer? I cannot say that they do. At the best they are no more than an innocent amusement. In indulging them, we are in great danger of becoming presumptuous, and even foolish, by supposing that we possess knowledge, when in fact our brightest light is but darkness. Vain man would be wise. Let us then cease from man. Let us cease from our own unsubstantial dreams, and lay fast hold of the sure word of prophecy as of a light shining in a dark place. "To the law and to the testimony; if they speak not according to these, there is no light in them", (Isa 8:20) or as some render the passage, "light shall never rise to them".

One simple declaration of the Word of God is worth more to a soul descending into the valley and shadow of death, than all the ingenious and vivid imaginings of the brightest human minds.

In view of the absolute and undoubted certainty of our departure out of life, it seems very strange that we should be so unconcerned. If even one of a million escaped death, this might afford some shadow of a reason for our carelessness; but we know that "it is appointed unto men once to die". (Heb 9:27) In this warfare there is no discharge, and yet most men live as if they were immortal. I remember the foolish thought which entered my childish mind when my mother informed me that we all must die. I entertained the hope that before my time came, some great change would take place, I knew not how—by which I would escape this dreaded event.

I will not address the death of the wicked at present. The dying experience of the believer is our proper subject, and we read that one object of Christ's coming into the world was "to deliver such as were all their life time subject to bondage through fear of death".

Death, in itself considered, is a most formidable evil, and can be desirable to none. The fear of death is not altogether the consequence of sin; the thing is abhorrent to the constitution of man. Death was held up in terror to our first parents when innocent, to prevent their transgression, and having entered the world by their sin in whom we all sinned, this event has been ever since a terror to mortals—"The King of Terrors!"

Man instinctively cleaves to life; so does every sentient being. There are only two things which can possibly have the effect of reconciling any man to death. The first is the hope of escaping from misery which is felt to be intolerable: the other an assurance of a better, that is, a heavenly country. The Captain of our salvation conquered death and him who had the power of death, that is the Devil—by dying Himself. By this means he plucked from this monster his deadly sting—by satisfying the demands of God's holy law. "For the sting of death is sin, and the strength of sin is the law." (1 Cor 15:56) All those, therefore, who are united to Christ meet death as a conquered and disarmed enemy. Against them he is powerless. Still, however, he wears a threatening aspect, and although he cannot kill, he can frown and threaten—and this often frightens the timid sheep. They often do not know that they are delivered from his tyranny, and that now he can do nothing but falsely accuse, and roar like a hungry lion disappointed of his prey. There are still some who all their lifetime are subject to bondage "through fear of death". (Heb 2:15) Their confidence is shaken by so many distressing doubts, that though sincerely engaged in the service of God, they can never think of death without sensible dread; and often they are afraid that when the last conflict shall come, they will be so overwhelmed with terror and despair, that they shall prove a dishonor to their Christian profession.

I recollect a sickly but pious lady who, with a profusion of tears, expressed her anxiety and fear in the view of her approaching end. There seemed to be ground for her foreboding apprehensions because, from the beginning of her profession, she had enjoyed no comfortable assurance—but was of the number of those who, though they "fear God, and obey the voice of his servant, yet walk in darkness and have no light" (Isa 50:10) of comfort. But mark the goodness of God and the fidelity of the Great Shepherd. Some months afterwards I saw this lady on her deathbed—and was astonished to find that Christ had delivered her entirely from her bondage. She was now near to her end and knew it—but she shed no tears now but those of joy and gratitude. All her darkness and sorrow were gone. Her heart glowed with love to the Redeemer, and all her anxiety now was to depart and be with Jesus. There was, as it were, a beaming of heaven in her countenance. I had before tried to comfort her—but now I sat down by her bedside to listen to the gracious words which proceeded from her mouth, and could not but send up the fervent aspiration, "O let me die the death of the righteous, and let my last end be like hers!" (Num 23:10) Then I knew that there was one who had conquered death, and him who has the power of death; for Satan, to the last moment, was not permitted to molest her.

No arguments have ever so powerfully operated on my mind, to convince me of the reality and power of experimental religion, as witnessing the last exercises of some of God's children. Some of these scenes, though long past, have left an indelible impression on my memory; and I hope a beneficial impression on my heart.

Another lady I had often observed passing along her way—humble, gentle, silent—evidently not seeking to be conspicuous, but rather to remain unnoticed and unknown. She had a few chosen female friends with whom she freely communicated, for her heart was affectionate and her disposition sociable. To these she poured out her inmost soul and received from them a similar return. She was crushed under an habitual feeling of domestic affliction—but not of that kind which freely utters its complaints and engages the sympathy of many. Her sorrows were such as her delicacy of feeling did not permit her even to allude to. The conduct of an imprudent father weighed heavily on her spirits—but towards him—and her mother being dead, she kept his house—she was assiduously respectful; and while he made himself the laughing stock of his acquaintances, she endeavored to make his home comfortable. But often I thought that her lively sensibility to the ridicule and reproaches which fell upon him would be an injury to her delicate constitution; and the more so, because this was a subject on which she would not converse—not even with the intimate, confidential friends before mentioned. It was evident that her health was slowly giving way, and that the disease which carries off nearly one half of the adults in this land was secretly consuming her vitals. But she never complained, and seemed rather to become more cheerful as her eye became more brilliant and her cheeks more ashen. She was, for a long time after this, seen occupying her humble retired place in the house of God, and still went her accustomed rounds among her poor and sick neighbors, while doing everything to render home comfortable to her restless, unhappy parent. At length, however, her strength failed, and she was obliged to confine herself to the house, and before long to her bed. Being informed of this, as her pastor, I visited her.

Hitherto her extreme modesty and retired habits had prevented me from having much personal acquaintance with this excellent woman. I was accompanied to the house by one of her intimate friends. The house was a cottage, and all its furniture of home manufacture; but upon the whole there was impressed a neatness and order, which indicated a superior taste in her who had long had the sole management. I did not know but that from her habitual reserve and silence she would be embarrassed in her feelings and reserved in her communications—but I was happily disappointed. She received me with an affectionate smile and a cordial shake of the hand, and said that she was pleased that I had thought it worth my while to come and see a poor dying woman. Not many minutes were spent in compliments or general remarks; she entered freely and most intelligently into a narrative of her religious exercises which had commenced at an early period of her life, and expatiated in the sweetest manner on the divine excellencies of the Savior, not as one who was speaking what she had learned from others, or from the mere exertion of her own intellect—but as one who felt in the heart every word which she uttered. There was a gentleness, a suavity, and a meek humility expressed in every tone of her voice, and the same was depicted on every lineament of her countenance. Though, when in health, she was never reckoned beautiful, yet there was now in her countenance, animated with hope and love and pious joy—or rather peace—a beauty of countenance which I never saw equaled. It was what may without impropriety be called spiritual beauty. I found what I had not known before, that her mind had been highly cultivated by reading. This was manifest in the propriety, and indeed I may say, elegance of her language. Not that she aimed at saying fine things. Such an idea never entered her humble mind; but possessing, naturally, a good understanding which she had carefully improved by reading, especially the best Christian authors, and being now animated with a flow of pious affection which seemed never to ebb, all these things gave her language a fluency, a glow, and a vividness, which was truly remarkable. I have often regretted that I did not put down at the time her most striking expressions—but the mere words could convey no more than the shadow of such a scene.

It has often been remarked that the speeches of great orators, when written and read, have scarcely a resemblance to the same speeches delivered with all the pathos, the grace, and the varied intonations and gestures of the orator. The same may more truly be said of the sayings of the dying Christian; we may catch the very words—but the spirit, the sacred and solemn tones, free from all affectation, the heavenly serenity of countenance, and the countless methods of manifesting the pious affections of the heart, never can be preserved, nor distinctly conveyed by words to others. The mind of this young lady possessed a uniform serenity, undisturbed with fears, doubts, or cares. Everything seemed right to her submissive temper. It was enough that her heavenly Father appointed it to be so. For many weeks she lay in this state of perfect tranquility, as it were in the suburbs of heaven, and I believe no one ever heard a complaint from her lips. Even that grief which had preyed on her health, when she was able to go about, had now ceased to cause her pain. Hers was, in my apprehension, the nearest approximation to complete happiness which I ever saw upon earth; yet there was no violence of feeling, no agitation, no rapture. It was that kind of happiness which, from its gentleness and calmness, is capable of continuance.

As it was her request that I should visit her often, I did so as frequently as the distance of my residence and my other avocations would permit; not, as I often said, with any expectation of communicating any good to her—but of receiving spiritual benefit from her heavenly conversation. O! how often did I wish that the boldest infidels—and they were rampant at that time—could have been introduced into the chamber of this dying saint. Often, especially after witnessing this scene, I endeavored to describe to such as attended preaching, the power of true religion to sustain the soul in the last earthly conflict; but they were incredulous as to the facts, or ascribed them to some strange enthusiasm which buoyed up the soul in an unusual manner. But here there was no enthusiasm—nothing approaching to what may be called a heated imagination. All was sober—all was serene—all was gentle—all was rational. And, although forty-five years have passed since this scene was witnessed, the impression on my mind is distinct and vivid. The indescribable countenance, calm but animated, pale with disease but lighted up with an unearthly smile; the sweet and affectionate tones of voice; the patient, submissive, cheerful, grateful temper—are all remembered with a vividness and permanence with which I remember nothing of recent occurrence. When I think of such scenes, I have often thought and said, "If this be delusion, then let my soul forever remain under such delusion!"

If the foregoing was a sample of the deathbed exercises of all Christians, then would I say that their last days are their best days, and the day of death happier than the day of birth. This, however, is far from being a true view of the general fact. It is a select case—one of a thousand—upon the whole the happiest death I ever witnessed.

I have, indeed, seen dying people agitated with a kind of delirious rapture, in which the imagination has been so excited, that the person looked and spoke as if the objects of another world were actually present to the view. In such case the nervous system loses its tone, and when the general feelings are pious and the thoughts directed heavenward, the whole system is thrilled with an indescribable emotion. We have a number of recorded death-scenes which partake of this character, and are greatly admired and extolled by the injudicious and fanatical. Scenes of this kind are frequently the effect of disease, and sometimes of medicine operating on the idiosyncrasy of particular people. Such people may be pious—but the extraordinary exhilaration and ecstasy of which they are the subjects ought not to be ascribed to supernatural influence—but to physical causes. Between such experiences and the case described above, there is no more resemblance than between a blazing meteor which soon burns itself out, and the steady, warming beams of the spring sun.

I once witnessed an extraordinary scene of this kind in a sceptic, who neglected religion and scoffed at its professors until very near the close of life. He then seemed to be agitated and exhilarated with religious ideas and feelings, leading him to profess his faith in Christ, and to rejoice and exult in the assurance of salvation—and all this without any previous conviction of sin, and unmingled at the time with deep penitential feelings. Well, why might it not have been an instance of sovereign grace, like that of the thief on the cross? It is possible.

As in life, that piety which is founded on knowledge, and in which the faculties of the mind continue to be well balanced and the judgment sound, is by far the least suspicious; so those deathbed exercises, which are of a similar character, are much to be preferred to those which are flighty, and in which reason seems to regulate the helm no longer; but an excited and irregular imagination assumes the government of the man. According to this rule, some glowing narratives of death-scenes will be set aside, as, if not spurious—yet not deserving to be admired and celebrated as they often are.

Chapter 16: Remarks on Deathbed Exercises

The cases of religious experience, at the close of life, furnish much reason for encouragement and hope to the real Christian. We learn from them, that death, however terrible to nature, may be completely divested of its terrors; that the Christian religion, when it has been cordially embraced, has power to sustain the soul in the last conflict; that the supplies of grace may be so rich and abundant, that the bed of death may be the happiest situation which the child of God ever occupied, and his last hours the most comfortable of his whole life; that it is possible for such a flood of divine consolation to be poured into the soul, that the pains of the body are scarcely felt; by which we may understand how it was that the martyrs could rejoice in the midst of flames, and on the rack. We learn, also, that these blessed communications of the joy of the Holy Spirit are conveyed to the soul through the promises of God; and that all that is necessary to fill it with these divine consolations is a firm and lively faith.

There is, in all these ecstatic and triumphant feelings, nothing miraculous; nothing different from the common mode of God's dealing with His people, except in the degree. The things of eternity are more clearly apprehended; confidence in the promises is more unshaken; submission to the will of God is more unreserved, and gratitude for His goodness more fervent.

Another thing suggested by such happy deathbed exercises is that the dying saint never entertained a more humble sense of his own unworthiness than during this season of the anticipation of the joys of heaven. These experiences, therefore, furnish strong evidence of the truth of the doctrines of grace; indeed, free grace is the predominant theme in the minds of these highly favored servants of God. It is also highly worthy of our marked attention, that the Lord Jesus Christ is precious to the dying believer in proportion as His consolations abound. He attributes all that he enjoys, or hopes for, to this blessed Redeemer. And He who loved him, and died for him, is most faithful to His gracious promises at this trying moment. Now, when heart and flesh fail, He will be the strength of their hearts. Now, He enables them to say with confidence, "Though I walk through the valley of the shadow of death, I will fear no evil, for you are with me; your rod and staff comfort me." (Psalm 23:4) Death is, indeed, a formidable enemy when armed with his envenomed sting; but when this sting is extracted, death is harmless; death comes as a friend to release us from a body of sin and misery. "The sting of death is sin, and the strength of sin is the law"; (1 Cor 15:56) but when the law has received a full satisfaction, and all sin is pardoned through the blood of Christ, the sting exists no longer. There is no condemnation to those who are in Christ Jesus. "It is God who justifies, who is he that condemns? It is Christ who died; yes, rather who is risen again." (Rom 8:33-34) "Precious in the sight of God is the death of his saints." (Psalm 116:15) The meek shall sing even on a dying bed. Here, often, the timid grow bold; the feeble strong. Here doubts and fears which harassed the weary pilgrim all the journey through are dismissed forever; and that joyful assurance is realized, which had long been ardently desired and hoped for.

Where else—but among real Christians, do we witness such happy scenes at the near approach of death? Can the infidel point to any of his associates who could thus exult in the prospect of death? Can the man of the world exhibit anything like this? Alas! they are driven away from all they love: they may die stupidly; they may be under an awful, blinding delusion; but the positive joys of the believer, they cannot experience. Now, as we must all die, and that soon—ought we not to take all pains, and use all possible diligence, to be ready to die the death of the righteous? When that solemn hour shall arrive, worldly honors and worldly possessions will be nothing to us. Royal scepters and crowns and treasures will be utterly unavailing. But the humble believer, however racked with pain of body, is safe in the hands of a kind Redeemer, who having Himself experienced the pangs of death, knows how to sympathize with and support His beloved disciples when they are called to this last trial. He will not then forsake those whom He has supported through their whole pilgrimage. His everlasting arms of love and faithfulness will be placed underneath them, and He will bear them as on eagles' wings. Truly, then, for them to die is gain! They rest from their labors and exchange darkness, sin and sorrow, for perfect light, perfect purity, and perfect felicity. Lift up your heads, then, you servants of God, for the day of your redemption draws near. The night is far spent, the day is at hand. With some of us, it must be near the dawn. The darkness will soon be past forever. Let us then rejoice in the hope of the glory of God, and wait until our salvation comes. Now is our salvation nearer than when we believed.

But, it may be asked, do all real Christians die in such joy and triumph as those whose experience has been related? No; this is not pretended. Some, no doubt, die under a cloud, and go out of the world in distressing doubt respecting their eternal destiny. It is to guard against such an event, that we would exhort all professors of religion, and include ourselves in the number, to begin in time to make preparation for death. Dear brethren, let us look well to the foundation of our hope; we cannot bestow too much pains and diligence in making our calling and election sure. We shall never regret, on a deathbed, that we were too much concerned to secure the salvation of our souls; or, that we were too careful in making preparation for another world. Let us remember that our time on earth is short, and that whatever is done must be done quickly. There will be no opportunity of coming back to rectify what has been done amiss, or to supply what is lacking. "Now is the accepted time, now is the day of salvation." (2 Cor 6:2) Let us work while it is day, knowing that the dark night comes when no man can work. Let us then awake to righteousness. Let us watch and be sober. Let us put on the armor of light, and especially let us see to it, that we have on the wedding garment; else we shall never find admittance to the marriage-supper of the Lamb. The only robe which can bear the scrutinizing inspection of the King, is the perfect and spotless robe of Christ's imputed righteousness. This will render us acceptable in the Beloved. With this, we must put on the robe of inherent righteousness; for "without holiness, no man shall see the Lord"; (Heb 12:14) and these two, though distinct, are never separated. Only, the latter is never perfect until we come to the end of the course.

This single consideration should reconcile us to the thoughts of death—that then we shall be freed from all sin. O how blessed is that state, where we shall see no more darkly through a glass—but face to face; where we shall know no more in part—but as we are known! (1 Cor 13:12) O bright and delightful vision of the glory of God in the face of Jesus Christ! Surely this is worth dying for.

But it may be asked, Is there not evidence of too much excitement in the experiences which have been narrated? May not a part at least of the elevated and exhilarated feelings be the effect of delirium? In answer I would say, that this may be admitted to have some effect in increasing the degree of excitement; but it never can account for the bright views and unspeakable joys which some experience. And the truth is, we are poor judges of the degree of elevated excitement which the sense of God's love will produce.

It must be confessed, that while we may admire and breathe after such an elevated and triumphant state of mind, yet we cannot so readily sympathize with such high emotions, as with a more calm and deliberate frame of spirit. Indeed, it is here as in health; when we see people much excited in regard to religion, or anything else, we do not place such entire confidence in what they utter, as when the same people calmly and soberly express their sentiments. The reason is, that in all great excitements, the imagination and feelings predominate over the judgment. Experience teaches that in all such cases there is a tendency to exaggeration, and to the use of strong expressions; and it cannot be doubted that, in some cases, the religious exultation experienced is somewhat delirious. The nervous system loses its control, and although its agitations are violent, they are somewhat irregular and excessive, so as to produce an irrepressible thrilling through the soul.

It is not wonderful, that while the mysterious connection between soul and body is coming to an end, there should be in the emotions something new, and in the looks, tones, and gestures, something out of the common way. This does not alter or vitiate the nature of the pious exercises of the soul, though it may modify them, and give them a peculiar aspect and expression. If any person chooses to suppose that, in some of the cases specified, while faith was triumphant and hope full of assurance, there might be superadded an exhilaration arising out of the peculiar state of the body, he will not have me objecting. The last exercises of that useful and devoted man, Jeremiah Evarts, were very remarkable for the degree of powerful excitement manifested; and the more remarkable, because his mind was highly intellectual, and very little subject to excitement, in common. Still it was well known to those intimate with him, that when he was aroused, his feelings were very strong.

Often, officious friends and physicians are extremely averse to have anything said on the subject of religion to the sick, lest it should disturb their minds, and so increase the violence of the disease. I would not, it is true, admit every loquacious old man or woman into the chamber of a friend dangerously ill—but a discreet and pious counselor is of great value at such a time. If the patient is hopefully pious, none can doubt the propriety and comfort of aiding such by holding forth to their view, the rich promises of a faithful God. But even when the character of the sick is different, it often gives relief to have an opportunity of conversation with a pious friend or minister. Anxious feelings, pent up in the soul and finding no vent, are far more injurious than a free expression of them; and if the person is in danger of death, will you, can you, be guilty of the cruelty of debarring him from the only opportunity of salvation which he may ever have? If you do, his blood will be found on your hands. To show how erroneous the opinion is, that religious conversation tends to injure the sick person by increasing his disease, I will relate a fact which fell under my own observation.

A young gentleman of fortune and liberal education had been for some months thinking seriously about his soul's salvation; but the work had not come to any maturity, when by making too great an exertion of his bodily strength, he ruptured a large blood vessel in the lungs, and was brought to death's door; not being able to speak above a low whisper. As he had been a pupil of mine, I was permitted to see him. When I inquired as to the state of his mind, he whispered in my ear that he was overwhelmed with the most awful darkness and terror—not one ray of light dawned upon his miserable soul. I prayed with him and presented to him a few Gospel invitations and promises, and left him, never again expecting to see him alive. Next day when I called, the physician, coming out of his room, informed me that while they were waiting for his last breath, a favorable change seemed unexpectedly to have taken place, and that he had revived a little.

When I approached his bed, he looked joyfully in my face, pressed my hand, and said, "All is well—I have found peace. This morning, about the dawn, I had the most delightful view of Christ, and of His ability and willingness to save me." And upon inquiry, I found that that was the moment when the favorable change took place in his symptoms. Faith and joy accomplished what no medicine could, and acted as a reviving cordial to his dying body. He so far recovered as to live a number of years afterwards, though his lungs were never sound, and his consistent walk and piety attested the reality of his change. He soon joined himself to the communion of the church, and died in her communion.

While spending a summer in Germantown, near Philadelphia, I was sent for to visit a young man whom I had often seen. He did not belong to my charge—but two pious ladies who did, were his friends, and had come out of the city to nurse him. He had a hemorrhage of the lungs, which left little room to hope for recovery. As he was a mild and moral man, I did not know but that he might be a professor of religion; but upon asking him a question respecting his hope, he frankly told me that he had been skeptical for many years, and had no belief that the Gospel was divine. I never felt more at a loss. The man was too weak to attend to argument, and if I could by reasoning convince him of his error, it would not be a saving faith, and he must die before this process could be gone through. I found that his infidelity afforded him no comfort in a dying hour, and that he wished he could believe in Christ. It occurred to me that the Word of God contained light and energy in itself, and that if he could not attend to the external evidences, the beams of truth might shine in upon his soul, and thus generate a saving faith by the efficient aid of the Spirit. After pointing out the probable sources of his scepticism, I requested the ladies who were attending on him to read certain portions of the Gospel to him, as he could bear it—for he was very sick. This was done; and next day, when I came to see him, he declared that his doubts were all scattered, and that he had hope in Christ. Afterwards, he was never able to converse; but as far as is known he died in hope.

I never saw anyone approach death so deliberately and composedly, as the late Robert Ray, pastor of the church of Freehold, in New Jersey. He had spent a winter at St. Augustine, with the hope of restoring his health—but came home more diseased than before he went. His lungs were deeply affected, and he foresaw that his end was approaching. But as long as he was able to speak, he caused himself to be carried to the church and to be assisted into the pulpit, where he would preach and exhort until his breath failed, when he would pant as if about to die, and then be conveyed home as he came. This was done not once or twice—but for many weeks; for he said, as he must die, he might as well die preaching. He felt a strong desire to be the means of saving the people committed to his charge, and he hoped that a voice of affectionate warning from the grave might have the effect of awakening some of them. As he suffered but little acute pain, he appeared, until his dying day, as calm and cheerful as a man long absent from home would, when the time came to return to his friends. He conversed as familiarly and composedly about his approaching change, as if there was nothing formidable in it. Indeed, it had no terrors for him. Even when death was upon him, having observed some of his neighbors coming in, he said, "Well, you have come to see your pastor die." He then remarked that his feelings were very peculiar, such as he had never experienced before; and without any perturbation of mind or bodily agony, he gently fell asleep.

I wish to remark, that in all my life I have known few people who lived like Christians when in health, who did not, in their approach to death, manifest as much hope and fortitude in that trying hour, as could reasonably have been expected from the character of their piety. In many cases, as I have before stated, the comfort and assurance of some timid and desponding believers have risen far above what any of their friends dared to hope. In general the result of my observation is, that the pious find death less terrible on their near approach to the event, than when it was viewed at a distance. Some people have naturally a much greater dread of death than others, though their piety may be more lively.

The difference between the comforts of dying saints may be attributed, first, to divine sovereignty, which distributes grace and consolation as seems good unto Him; secondly, to bodily temperament, some people being more fearful than others, and more prone to suspect their own sincerity; and thirdly, to the nature of the disease by which the body is brought down to the grave. It is the tendency of some diseases, while they do not disturb the intellect, to exhilarate the spirits and enliven the imagination; while a distressing depression or perturbation is the effect of others; to say nothing of the different degrees of pain experienced by different people; and we know that some diseases have a deplorable stupefying effect. A fourth and frequent cause of difference in the exercises of dying people is produced by the medicine which is administered. When physicians can do nothing to cure, they think it right to lull their patients by opiates, or excite them by alcohol. I have, when sick, been more afraid of nothing than these intoxicating and stupefying, or even exhilarating drugs. O let no artificial means be ever used with me, in that dread hour, to interrupt sober and deliberate reflection!

Mr. Wilson with great propriety remarks, "It is the tenor of the life, not that of the few suffering and morbid scenes which precede dissolution, which fixes the character. We are not authorized from Scripture to place any dependence on the last periods of sinking nature, through which the Christian may be called to pass to his eternal reward. But though no importance is to be attached to these hours of fainting mortality, with reference to the acceptance and final triumph of the dying Christian, yet, where it pleases God to afford one of His departing servants, such a measure of faith and self-possession, as to close a holy and most consistent life with a testimony which sealed, amidst the pains of acute disease and in the most impressive manner, all his doctrines and instructions during his preceding years, we are called on, as I think, to record with gratitude the divine benefit, and to use it with humility, for the confirmation of our own faith and joy."

Chapter 17: Preparation for death—The state of the soul after death

Since all men are appointed to die, there is no subject in the world which ought to be more interesting to all men. Whatever other evils we may escape, "in this war there is no discharge". Death is a scene of which we can have no previous experience, and therefore, it is prudent to learn what we can from the experience of those who have gone before us.

Death is an important and an solemn scene, and should therefore occupy many of our thoughts. If due preparation has been neglected in life and health—there is small probability that it will be made on a dying bed. If I had set down all that I have witnessed and read of the dying exercises of unconverted sinners, it would have presented an appalling object for our contemplation. Such scenes have often been exhibited in print, and are not without their use—but such narratives did not fall in with the scope of these essays. But however insipid, or even disgusting these accounts of the dying exercises of believers may be to some readers, there is a class, and a large one too, who will take a deep interest in these things, because they are now waiting until their change comes, and are looking forward with intense interest to that inevitable event of which we have been writing so much. These are the people whom the author has had principally in view, in selecting these experiences of departing saints; and as the hopes and comforts of the children of God in life are very various, so he has endeavored to show that a like variety is found in their views and exercises at the time of their departure out of the world.

The writer confesses also that, in dwelling so long on this subject, he had some regard to his own edification and preparation for death. As he knows from infallible evidence that he will soon be required to put off this tabernacle, and to emigrate from this lower world, he was solicitous to acquire as much information as he was able from those who have gone before, what were the difficulties, sufferings, and encouragements of pilgrims in this last stage of their journey. And, however it may be with others, he has derived instruction and encouragement from the contemplation of such scenes as are here described. It appears to him supremely reasonable, that during the short time which remains of his life, he should be chiefly concerned in the meditation of the things of another world, and in making actual preparation for his own departure. He once supposed that the near approach of death would of itself be sufficient to arouse the mind, and impress upon it the reality and solemn importance of eternal things; but he finds by sad experience, that however his judgment is convinced of the certainty of death and its consequences, nothing will bring these things to bear on the heart but the illumination of the Holy Spirit. He wishes, therefore, to engage in such reading, meditation, and writing, as may have a tendency to fix his thoughts on the solemn scene before him, when he must close his eyes on the light of this world, and bid adieu to all his friends and objects with which he has been conversant here.

He is not of opinion, however, that the best way to make preparation for death is to sit down and pore over the condition of our own souls, or to confine our exertions to those things which are directly connected with our own salvation. We are kept here to do our Master's work, and that relates to others as well as ourselves. We have a stewardship of which we must give an account; and the faithful and wise steward is careful and diligent in dispensing to others the blessings committed to him. This is especially the case in regard to ministers of the Gospel. We have a responsible office, and our account before the tribunal of Jesus Christ must be solemn and sincere; and it will not do to relinquish the proper work of our calling, upon the pretext of seeking our own salvation. Our own seeking will be entirely unavailing without the aid and blessing of God, and this we may expect most confidently when we are diligently engaged in doing His work, which is always the duties of our station and calling. Active duty must be performed as long as we have strength for the work; and like the Levites, we must attend around the tabernacle and altar, when we are too old for more laborious services. Many of the faithful servants of God have expressed a strong desire not to outlive their usefulness; and some have wished that their departure might occur in the very act of preaching. These things we may better leave to the wisdom of God, who directs all the circumstances of the death of His people, as well as of their lives. Even when, by reason of bodily infirmities, the servants of God are obliged to desist from public labors, they do not cease from serving their Master; their lives are not useless. God is as much honored by patient submission and cheerful resignation—as by zealous public exertion; and the greatest and most effectual work which can be performed by any on earth, they can perform—I mean the offering of prayers and intercessions, day and night, at the throne of grace.

Let not the infirm and aged say that they can now do nothing for God. They can do much; and for anything they can tell, more than they ever did in the days of their vigor. It is a beautiful sight to see men laden with gospel fruit, even in old age. Such fruits are generally more mature than those of earlier days; and the aged saint often enjoys a tranquility and repose of spirit, which is almost peculiar to that age. David, or whoever is the author of Psalm 71, prays most earnestly a prayer which should be daily on the lips of the aged: "Cast me not off in the time of old age; forsake me not when my strength fails." (Psalm 71:9) And again: "Now also when I am old and grey-headed, forsake me not, until I have showed your strength to this generation, and your power to all that are to come." (Psalm 71:18) Let the aged then tell to those that come after them, the works of divine grace which they have witnessed or which their fathers have told them. Let them be active as long as they can, and when bodily strength fails, let them wield the pen; or if unable to write for the edification of the church, let them exhibit consistent and shining example of the Christian temper—in kindness and good will to all—in uncomplaining patience—in contented poverty—in cheerful submission to painful providences—and in mute resignation to the loss of their dearest friends. And when death comes, let them not be afraid or dismayed; then will be the time to honor God by implicitly and confidently trusting in His promises. Let them "against hope believe in hope". (Rom 4:18) It is by faith that the last enemy must be conquered.

He who believes shall not be confounded, in this trying hour. The great Shepherd will not forsake His redeemed flock, for whom He has shed His blood; and though the adversary may rage and violently assault dying saints, he shall not overcome them. Each one of them may say with humble confidence: "Though I walk through the valley of the shadow of death, I will fear no evil, for you are with me, your rod and your staff they comfort me." (Psalm 23:4)

Let us not desire to make a parade and ostentatious display on a dying bed. Death has been called the honest hour—but hypocrisy may be practiced even on a dying bed. Although this event often reveals secrets, and brings deceived souls to a conviction of the sandy foundation on which they have built their hopes—yet some keep on the mask to the last moment. More, however, suppress the expression of their fears and distress of mind. So much is said often about the manner in which people meet death, that some good men have wished and requested to be left very much alone: they have feared lest they should be tempted to vainglory, even on a dying bed; or they have feared lest their courage should fail them in the last struggle, and they should, through pain and imbecility of mind, be left to bring dishonor on their profession. The excellent and evangelical Simeon of Cambridge seems to have been under the influence of a feeling of this kind. But the best and safest way is submissively to commit all the circumstances of our death unto God.

We have no conception of the soul—but as a thinking, active being. The body is merely an organ, or instrument by which the soul acts while connected with it; indeed, it cannot be demonstrated that the soul performs all its acts here by the use of this organ. But whether or not is of little consequence. We know that activity belongs to the soul, not to the body; and it would be a strange conclusion, that that which is essentially active should cease to act, because it had been deprived of one set of organs. The only legitimate inference is that, when separated from the body, the mode of action is different from what it was before. As we learn the various operations of the soul only by experience, it is plain that we cannot fully understand or explain the precise mode of its action after it is separated from the body. Paul teaches us that the soul may exist and have conscious exercises of a very exalted kind; for he says, speaking of his rapture into heaven, "Whether in the body or out of the body, I cannot tell." (2 Cor 12:2-3) Now, if the soul could not act without the body, he could have told certainly that he was in the body, when he witnessed in the third heaven things which it is not lawful for a man to utter. But this truth is taught more clearly and directly by Christ Himself, when He said to the penitent thief on the cross, "This day shall you be with me in paradise." (Luke 23:43) This testimony is of itself abundantly sufficient, and there is no evasion of its force—but by an interpretation so frigid and farfetched, that it only serves to betray the weakness of the cause which it is brought to support.

Paul in another passage, speaks clearly and explicitly on this point: "Therefore we are always confident and know that as long as we are at home in the body we are away from the Lord. We are confident, I say, and would prefer to be away from the body and at home with the Lord." (2 Cor 5:6,8) In the previous context the apostle intimates that when the clay tabernacle is dissolved, the soul will not be found naked—but that there will be another house ready to receive it; so that it will not be unclothed—but clothed. "Now we know that if the earthly tent we live in is destroyed, we have a building from God, an eternal house in heaven, not built by human hands. Meanwhile we groan, longing to be clothed with our heavenly dwelling, because when we are clothed, we will not be found naked. For while we are in this tent, we groan and are burdened, because we do not wish to be unclothed but to be clothed with our heavenly dwelling, so that what is mortal may be swallowed up by life." (2 Cor 5:1-4)

It would seem, then, that the soul is never without a suitable dwelling; it will not be unclothed; it only passes from one house to another—from an earthly to a heavenly habitation. But what this celestial clothing will be, of course, we cannot now tell. When Stephen was dying, he cried, "Lord Jesus, receive my spirit." (Acts 7:59) The Lord Jesus is everywhere near to His saints; and as He watches over His sheep during their whole passage through the wilderness, so He is especially near to them when they come to the "valley of the shadow of death" (Psalm 23:4), so that they may then sing with the sweet psalmist of Israel, "Though I walk through the valley of the shadow of death, I will fear no evil; for you are with me; your rod and your staff, they comfort me." But as Jesus the Lord has His residence in heaven, where He occupies a place on the throne of God, at the right hand of the Father, and is surrounded by an innumerable army of angels ready to execute all His commandments; so He commissions messengers to attend at the dying bed of believers, and receive the spirits of the just and conduct them to His presence.

It is evident that the departing soul will need a guide and convoy, for utterly ignorant of the glorious world into which it has entered, it would not know which way to direct its course, or where to find its allotted mansion. For heaven is a wide domain. The house of the Father of our Lord Jesus Christ has many dwelling places, and every redeemed soul has provided for it an appropriate residence, for Christ says, "I go to prepare a place for you." (John 14:2) And that guardian angels are sent to perform these kind offices for departed saints, we are not left to conjecture, for we read that as soon as Lazarus died, he "was carried by the angels into Abraham's bosom". (Luke 16:22) There is no reason for supposing that the privilege now conferred on the beggar was peculiar to him; every saint needs the guidance and guardianship of angels as well as Lazarus; and we may conclude, therefore, that angels will attend on every departing saint.

Although we cannot now understand how the soul will act in the future world, when divested of the body of clay, we cannot doubt that its consciousness of its identity will go with it. The memory of the past, instead of being obliterated, will in all probability be much more perfect than while the person lived upon earth. It is by no means incredible, that memory, in the future world, will present to men everything which they have ever known, and every transaction in which they were ever engaged. The susceptibility of joyful emotions will also accompany the soul into the invisible world; and one of the first feelings of the departed saint will be a lively sense of complete deliverance from all evil, natural and moral. The pains of death will be the last pangs ever experienced. When these are over, the soul will enjoy the feelings of complete salvation from every distress. What a new and delightful sensation will it be, to feel safe from every future danger, as well as saved from all past trouble.

But the most important change experienced at this time will be the perfect purification of the soul from sin. The soul, heretofore struggling with inbred corruption which damped its ardor, darkened its views, and stupefied its feelings, now can act without any moral obstruction. Who that has often complained, like Paul, "O wretched man that I am, who shall deliver me from the body of this death?" (Rom 7:24)—but will feel this to be indeed heaven begun, when there will no more be felt any secret working of pride, or envy, or selfishness; but when it shall be pure and sweetly conscious of its own purity?

As perfection in holiness supposes a clear knowledge of spiritual objects, so we know that we shall no more see the divine glory, as it were, by reflection from a glass—but directly, or "face to face". (1 Cor 13:12) The soul of man probably greatly enlarged in its powers, may have new faculties developed, for which there was no use here, and of which it had no consciousness; yet the field of knowledge being boundless, and our minds being capable of attending only to one thing at a time, our knowledge of celestial things will be gradually acquired, and not perfected at once. Indeed, there can be no limit set to the progression in knowledge; it will be endless. And no doubt the unalloyed pleasures of the future state will be intimately connected with this continual increase of divine knowledge. And as here, knowledge is acquired by the aid of instructors, why may not the same be the fact in heaven? What a delightful employment to the saints who have been drinking in the knowledge of God and His works for thousands of years to communicate instruction to the saint just arrived! How delightful to conduct the pilgrim who has just finished his race, through the ever blooming bowers of paradise, and to introduce him to this and the other ancient believer, and to assist him to find out and recognize, among so great a multitude, old friends and earthly relatives.

There need be no dispute about our knowing, in heaven, those whom we knew and loved here; for if there should be no faculty by which they could at once be recognized, yet by extended and familiar fellowship with the celestial inhabitants, it cannot be otherwise but that interesting discoveries will be made continually; and the unexpected recognition of old friends may be one of the sources of pleasure which will render heaven so pleasant.

But as the fleshly bond of relationship is dissolved at death, it seems reasonable to think that the only bond of union and kindred in heaven will be the spiritual bond, which unites all believers in one body, and to Christ their living Head. Therefore, we may presume that there will be felt an ardent desire to form an acquaintance with the most remarkable personages who have lived from Adam downward. Who, if admitted into paradise, could repress his curiosity to see, and if possible, to converse with the progenitor of our race? Doubtless, he could tell us some things which we do not fully understand. And who would not wish to see the first person who ever entered those blessed abodes from our earth? Yes, and Enoch too, who never tasted death, and who still possesses his original body, changed and glorified, it is true—but still substantially the same. We might expect to find him in the company of Elijah, who is similarly circumstanced; and some think that the body of Moses, though it was dead and buried, was raised again, as he seems to have appeared in his own proper body on the mount of Transfiguration. And where is Abraham, that venerable saint, who in faith and obedience exceeded all other men, and obtained from God the honorable appellation of "the father of the faithful", (Rom 4:11) and "the friend of God". (James 2:23) And who would be in heaven ever so short a time, without desiring to see Paul, the apostle of the Gentiles; and not him only—but Peter, and John, and all the college of the apostles?

But methinks we are in danger of indulging our imaginations too far, and of transferring to a heavenly state too many of the feelings and associations of our earthly condition. And I am reminded also, that as the twinkling stars are lost in the blaze of the rising sun, so there is one Person in the highest heavens, visible to all who enter that place, whose glory irradiates all the celestial mansions; whose love and smiles diffuse ineffable joy through all the heavenly multitudes, and in whom every believer has an absorbing interest with which no other can be compared. On His head He wears many crowns, and in His hand He holds a scepter by which He governs the universe; but yet He exhibits, visibly, the marks of the violent death which, for us, He once endured. His name is the Word of God, King of Kings, and Lord of Lords; the Alpha and Omega; the Almighty! And behold, all the angels of God worship Him. And the army of the redeemed, which no man can number, sing a song of praise to the Lamb, which no man can learn except those that are redeemed from among men; for the theme of their song is, "To him who loved us, and washed us from our sins in his own blood! (Rev 1:5) These are those who have washed their robes, and made them white in the blood of the Lamb!" (Rev 7:14) Every redeemed soul, upon being admitted into heaven, will for a while be so completely absorbed in the contemplation of that Divine Person, that he will be incapable of paying much attention to any others!

Like that Armenian princess, of whom Xenophon gives an account, who, after all the rest of the company had been expressing their admiration of Cyrus, one praising one thing and one another, upon being asked what about this royal personage she admired most, answered, that she did not even look at them, because her whole attention had been absorbed in admiring him (her young husband) who had offered to die for her. But the saved sinner may say, that his attention was completely absorbed in gazing upon Him, who not only said that He would die for him—but who actually did die in his place, and by this sacrifice redeemed him from the curse of the law, and from all iniquity!

The sweet and intimate fellowship which the redeemed soul will have with his Savior cannot now be conceived. It will far transcend all the ideas which we now can form, and will be a perfection of bliss so great that nothing can be added to it in any other way, than by an increase of the capacity of the soul. But still, all that is enjoyed in this intermediate state between death and judgment is but a part of that felicity to which the redeemed of the Lord are destined hereafter. It is only the enjoyment of a separate soul. But "the exceeding great and eternal weight of glory" (2 Cor 4:17) laid up in heaven for the children of God is for the whole man, made up of soul and body! And as even in this world many pleasures are enjoyed by means of bodily organs, who can tell what new and ever varying delights may be let into the soul by means of bodies of a celestial mold, bodies fashioned after the model of the glorious body of Jesus Christ! If our senses now bring to our view so many glorious objects both in the heavens and the earth, how rich and delightful will be the vision of the upper heavens by the eyes of the resurrection body? Then shall we see Jesus with our bodily eyes—then shall we behold what now no tongue can describe, nor even heart conceive!

The departed saints, therefore, though blessed to the full amount of their present capacity, yet are living in joyful expectation of a more glorious state. We should not think that the redemption and resurrection of the body is a small matter. The body is an essential part of human nature, and the glorified body will add to the felicity of the redeemed in a degree which we have no means of calculating. The inspired writers, therefore, when they speak of the blessedness of heaven, speak sparingly of the state of the separate soul; but when they describe the resurrection, they seem to be enraptured. Hear Paul, drawing a comparison between this mortal, corrupt, and earthly body, and that immortal, pure, and spiritual body, which will be possessed by every saint. "So will it be with the resurrection of the dead. The body that is sown is perishable, it is raised imperishable; it is sown in dishonor, it is raised in glory; it is sown in weakness, it is raised in power; it is sown a natural body, it is raised a spiritual body. If there is a natural body, there is also a spiritual body." (1 Cor 15:42-44) "Just as we are now like Adam, the man of the earth—so we will someday be like Christ, the man from heaven." (1 Cor 15:49) "For our perishable earthly bodies must be transformed into heavenly bodies that will never die!" (1 Cor 15:53)

No sooner shall these resurrected bodies open their immortal eyes, than they shall behold the Son of Man coming in the clouds of heaven. And no sooner is the judgment set, than all these shall be caught up to meet the Lord in the air, and shall be so highly honored as to have a place, as judges, on the judgment seat with Him. And when the solemn transactions of that day are ended, the redeemed shall accompany their Lord and Savior to heaven, where they shall be put in full and eternal possession of that felicity and glory which Christ has purchased for them by His precious blood. In this sublime temple, their songs shall mingle with those of the holy angels forever and ever.

It need not be supposed that saints in heaven will be continually employed in nothing but praise. This, indeed, will be their noblest employment; and the anthems of praise to God and the Lamb will never cease. But may we not reasonably suppose that the exercises and pursuits of the saints will be various? The wonderful works of God will open to their contemplation. They may be employed, as angels are now, as messengers to distant worlds, either as instruments of justice or mercy: for we find that the angels are employed in both these ways. While, then, one choir surrounds the throne, and elevates the celestial song of praise for redemption, others may be employed in executing the commands of their Lord; and then, in their turn, these last ones may keep up the unceasing praise, while the first ones go forth on errands of mercy or wrath.

Some have divided the angels into worshiping and serving: the first are supposed to be always engaged in acts of worship, while the last are always employed in other services. But it would be much more reasonable to suppose that they all, in turn, take their part in both these services. Here, however, it becomes us to pause, and in deep humility, on account of our ignorance and unworthiness, to put our hands on our mouths, and our mouths in the dust. We are slow to learn earthly things; how then can we comprehend those which are heavenly? But if we are the children of God, we shall have experience of these celestial employments and never-ending joys! Soon, very soon, these things which are now dimly discerned by means of faith, will be realized, when every humble saint shall appear with Christ in glory—and shall never be exposed any more to danger of suffering! Let us, then, now begin the song which shall never cease to Him who loved us and washed us from our sins in His own precious blood!

Chapter 18: A prayer for one who feels that he is approaching the borders of another world

Most merciful God, I rejoice that You reign over the universe with a sovereign sway, so that You do according to Your will, in the armies of heaven and among the inhabitants of the earth. You are the Maker of my body, and Father of my spirit, and You have a perfect right to dispose of me in that manner which will most effectually promote Your glory: and I know that whatever You do is right and wise and just and good. And whatever may be my eternal destiny, I rejoice in the assurance that Your great name will be glorified in me. But as You have been pleased to reveal Your mercy and Your grace to our fallen miserable world; and as the word of this salvation has been preached unto me, inviting me to accept of eternal life upon the gracious terms of the Gospel, I do cordially receive the Lord Jesus Christ as my Savior and only Redeemer, believing sincerely the whole testimony which You have given respecting His divine character, His real incarnation, His unspotted and holy life, His numerous and beneficent miracles, His expiatory and meritorious death, and His glorious resurrection and ascension. I believe, also, in His supreme exaltation, in His prevalent intercession for His chosen people, in His affectionate care and aid afforded to His suffering members here below, and in His second coming to receive His humble followers to dwell with Himself in heaven; and to take vengeance on His obstinate enemies.

My only hope and confidence of being saved rests simply on the mediatorial work and prevailing intercession of the Lord Jesus Christ; in consequence of which the Holy Spirit is graciously sent to make application of Christ's redemption, by working faith in us, and repentance unto life; and rendering us fit for the heavenly inheritance, by sanctifying us in the whole man, soul, body, and spirit.

Grant, gracious God, that the rich blessings of the new covenant may be freely bestowed on Your unworthy servant. I acknowledge that I have no claim to Your favor on account of any goodness in me by nature; for alas! there dwells in me, that is, in my flesh, no good thing! nor on account of any works of righteousness done by me; for all our righteousnesses are as filthy rags. Neither am I able to make atonement for any one of my innumerable transgressions which, I confess before You, are not only many in number—but heinous in their nature, justly deserving Your displeasure and wrath; so that if I were immediately sent to hell, You would be altogether just in my condemnation. Although I trust that I have endeavored to serve You with some degree of sincerity; yet whatever good thing I have ever done, or even thought, I ascribe entirely to Your grace, without which I can do nothing acceptable in Your sight. And I am deeply convinced that my best duties have fallen far short of the perfection of Your law, and have been so mingled with sin in the performance, that I might justly be condemned for the most fervent prayer I ever made. And I would confess with shame and contrition, that I am not only chargeable with sin in the act—but that there is a law in my members, warring against the law of my mind, aiming to bring me into captivity to the law of sin and death. This corrupt nature is the source of innumerable evil thoughts and desires, and damps the exercise of faith and love, and stands in the way of well-doing, so that when I would do good, evil is present with me. And so deep and powerful is this remaining depravity, that all efforts to eradicate or subdue it are vain, without the aid of Your grace. And when at any time I obtain a glimpse of the depth and turpitude of the sin of my nature, I am overwhelmed, and constrained to exclaim with Job, "I abhor myself and repent in dust and ashes." (Job 42:6)

And now, Righteous Lord God Almighty, I would not attempt to conceal any of my actual transgressions, however vile and shameful they are—but would penitently confess them before You; and would plead in my defense, nothing but the perfect righteousness of the Lord Jesus Christ, who died, the just for the unjust, to bring us near to God. For His sake alone do I ask or expect the rich blessings necessary to my salvation. For although I am unworthy, He is most worthy; though I have no righteousness, He has provided by His expiatory death, and by His holy life, a complete justifying righteousness, in which spotless robe I pray that I may be clothed; so that You my righteous Judge, will see no sin in me—but will acquit me from every accusation, and justify me freely by Your grace, through the righteousness of my Lord and Savior, with whom You are ever well pleased.

My earnest prayer is, that Jesus may save me from my sins, as well as from their punishment; that I may be redeemed from all iniquity, as well as from the condemnation of the law; that the work of sanctification may be carried on in my soul by Your Word and Spirit, until it be perfected at Your appointed time. And grant, O Lord, that as long as I am in the body, I may make it my constant study and chief aim to glorify Your name, both with soul and body, which are no longer mine—but Yours; for I am "bought with a price" (1 Cor 6:20; 1 Cor 7:23)—not with silver and gold—but with the precious blood of Christ, as of a lamb without blemish and without spot. Enable me to let my light so shine, that others, seeing my good works, may be led to glorify Your name. Make use of me as an humble instrument of advancing Your kingdom on earth, and promoting the salvation of immortal souls. If You have appointed sufferings for me here below, I beseech You to consider my weakness, and let Your chastisements be those of a loving father, that I may be made partaker of Your holiness. And let me not be tempted above what I am able to bear—but with the temptation make a way of escape.

O most merciful God, cast me not off in the time of old age; forsake me not when my strength declines. Now, when I am old and grey-headed, forsake me not; but let Your grace be sufficient for me; and enable me to bring forth fruit, even in old age. May my hoary head be found in the ways of righteousness! Preserve my mind from senility and imbecility, and my body from protracted disease and excruciating pain. Deliver me from despondency and discouragement in my declining years, and enable me to bear affliction with patience, fortitude, and perfect submission to Your holy will. Lift upon me perpetually the light of Your reconciled countenance, and cause me to rejoice in Your salvation, and in the hope of Your glory. May the peace that passes all understanding be constantly diffused through my soul, so that my mind may remain calm through all the storms and vicissitudes of life.

As, in the course of nature, I must be drawing near to my end, and as I know I must soon put off this tabernacle, I do humbly and earnestly beseech You, O Father of mercies, to prepare me for this inevitable and solemn event. Fortify my mind against the terrors of death. Give me, if it pleases You, an easy passage through the gate of death. Dissipate the dark clouds and mists which naturally hang over the grave, and lead me gently down into the gloomy valley. O my kind Shepherd, who has tasted the bitterness of death for me, and who knows how to sympathize with and support the sheep of Your pasture, be present to guide, to support, and to comfort me. Illumine with beams of heavenly light the valley and shadow of death, so that I may fear no evil. When heart and flesh fail, be the strength of my heart and my portion forever. Let not my courage fail in the trying hour. Permit not the great adversary to harass my soul in the last struggle—but make me a conqueror and more than a conqueror in this fearful conflict. I humbly ask that my reason may be continued to the last, and if it be Your will, that I may be so comforted and supported, that I may leave a testimony in favor of the reality of religion, and Your faithfulness in fulfilling Your gracious promises; and that others of Your servants who may follow after may be encouraged by my example to commit themselves boldly to the guidance and keeping of the Shepherd of Israel.

And when my spirit leaves this clay tenement, Lord Jesus, receive it. Send some of the blessed angels to convoy my inexperienced soul to the mansion which Your love has prepared. And O! let me be so situated, though in the lowest rank, that I may behold Your glory. May I have an abundant entrance administered unto me into the kingdom of our Lord and Savior Jesus Christ— for whose sake, and in whose name, I ask all these things. Amen.

Printed in Great Britain
by Amazon